"*Reasons We Believe* is a wholesome, faith-affirming volume. It will appeal mostly to Christians who recognize many of the convictions they hold regarding the Christian faith, but who have not seen this many reasons, all organized carefully under one cover. It is well known that evidences are person-relative, in that particular arguments appeal to certain people, while other presentations may reach a different audience. As Nathan Busenitz points out, listing five different categories and fifty topics allows readers to skip around and find those subjects that appeal especially to them."

—Gary R. Habermas, Distinguished Research Professor and
Chair, Department of Philosophy and Theology,
Liberty University

"Nathan Busenitz's *Reasons We Believe* stands out among apologetic texts in several respects. First, it is both comprehensive and concise, qualities one rarely finds in the same volume. Further, and more important, the book maintains a remarkable focus on Scripture itself. Though it does not neglect references to extra-biblical literature when appropriate, it might actually be described as the Bible's own apologetic for itself. Therefore, the book shows how Christians can make use of traditional evidences and arguments within the Bible's own framework of thought. Thus it brings presuppositions and evidences together, rather than placing them in competition."

—John Frame, Professor of Systematic Theology and Philosophy,
Reformed Theological Seminary; author of *Apologetics to
the Glory of God*, *Cornelius Van Til: An Analysis*, and
The Doctrine of God

"We live in a day when the new atheism tells us that 'religion poisons everything' and that 'God is not good' and when authors prostitute their scholarship to become rich on sensationalist books about so-called 'lost Christianities' and 'lost Scriptures.' In the midst of this stench, Nate Busenitz's sane and sound treatment of Christian evidences comes as a breath of fresh air. The author has done his homework and conveys the results in a very clear and convincing manner. In my student days, there was a classic book along these lines titled *Reasons to Believe*. Now we have a worthy successor to this classic in *Reasons We Believe*. May it have a wide circulation and strengthen the hands of those who live and labor in the shadow of John Bunyan's 'Doubting Castle.'"

—William Varner, Professor of Biblical Studies,
The Master's College; author of *The Messiah: Revealed,
Rejected, Received*

"Tremendous! Nathan Busenitz's *Reasons We Believe* is one of the most helpful apologetic guides to appear in a long time—one that you can really sink your teeth into. Hugely helpful and highly recommended!"
—RON RHODES, President, Reasoning from the
Scriptures Ministries

"Life is fully lived only when lived in conformity to reality. In this work Nathan Busenitz masterfully demonstrates that Christianity is that reality. With numerous references to Scripture, and an amazingly rich source of documented evidence from history, science, and existential human experience, Busenitz shows how all of these coalesce to demonstrate the reality of God, the absolute truthfulness of the Bible, and the historical reality of Jesus' life, death, and resurrection. The work is thoroughly researched, providing an excellent source for further study, well-reasoned, contemporary, and interestingly written. Aptly arranged so that it can be read straight through or used as a resource for specific issues, *Reasons We Believe* is an excellent resource for strengthening any believer's faith or helping someone come to faith."
—ROBERT SAUCY, Distinguished Professor, Systematic Theology,
Talbot School of Theology

"That the Christian faith clearly stands head and shoulders above all other religions of all time is laid out by the author in a compelling fashion. A seemingly endless stream of Scripture references as well as a wide array of quotations from the literature of the world of academia back up the author's claims and contentions on God, Jesus Christ, and the Bible. Explanations from the reasons given will prove to be richly nourishing for the heart and mind of the believer, yet will also serve to challenge forthrightly the unbeliever."
—TREVOR CRAIGEN, Professor of Theology, The Master's Seminary

REASONS WE BELIEVE

REASONS WE
BELIEVE

*50 lines of evidence
that confirm the Christian faith*

Foreword by John MacArthur
NATHAN BUSENITZ

CROSSWAY BOOKS
WHEATON, ILLINOIS

PDF ISBN: 978-1-4335-0470-9

Mobipocket ISBN: 978-1-4335-0471-6

Library of Congress Cataloging-in-Publication Data
Busenitz, Nathan.
   Reasons we believe : 50 lines of evidence that confirm the
Christian faith / Nathan Busenitz.
     p. cm.
  Includes bibliographical references and index.
  ISBN 978-1-4335-0146-3 (tpb)
  1. Apologetics. I. Title.
BT1103.B87   2008
239—dc22   2008001187

VP												
	17	16	15	14	13	12	11	10	09	08		
15	14	13	12	11	10	9	8	7	6	5	4	3	2	1

To my four wonderful children:

ASHLEY, ISAAC, AUSTIN, and ABIGAIL

May you grow in the love and knowledge
of our Savior, Jesus Christ

CONTENTS

Section 3:
Reasons We Believe in the Bible (Part 1)

Section 4:
Reasons We Believe in the Bible (Part 2)

Section 5:
Reasons We Believe in Jesus (Part 1)

We Believe in Jesus Christ:

Section 6:
Reasons We Believe in Jesus (Part 2)

FOREWORD

If there is one word that best describes the Christian worldview, it is *truth*. In an age of changing opinions, multiple perspectives, and varying viewpoints, biblical Christianity stands by itself as objective, absolute, and abiding truth. Scripture alone teaches us how to perceive the world in a way that accurately corresponds to reality. As such, its message of salvation is as timely as it is timeless. And its truth is as reliable as it is unchanging.

In contrast to the enduring character of the gospel, the theories and philosophies of men are constantly in flux. Worldviews that dominate popular thinking, whether for decades or for centuries, are eventually discarded as outmoded and passé. New discoveries, developments, or insights render previous frameworks of thought no longer tenable. In a very real sense, when it comes to human wisdom the only constant is change.

But not so with God.

Unlike men, God is not in flux. He never changes but is the same yesterday, today, and forever. Unlike men, God is neither finite nor fallible. He has never been mistaken about anything because He knows all and controls all. God is always consistent with Himself. He cannot contradict Himself, and He cannot lie. He is not the author of confusion. Moreover, His Word is true not simply because it accords with reality but because it comes from the very One who *established* reality—and who did so by the word of His power.

As God's written Word, the Bible reflects the perfection and consistency of its Author. The facts it sets forth are reliable because God is reliable. The assertions it makes—whether in areas of faith and practice or in areas of science and history—can be trusted because God is inherently trustworthy. In the same way that God is eternally true, His written Word is also true. As the psalmist exclaimed, speaking to

God, "The sum of Your word is truth, and every one of Your righteous ordinances is everlasting" (Psalm 119:160, NASB).

Because the Bible is perfect and free from error, having been revealed by God Himself, it follows that it is the most authoritative document in the world—the final word on truth. It is the place from which our understanding of truth must start; and it is the final test by which we are to measure every other truth claim. Confronting the errors of the unbelieving world with biblical truth, through the power of the Holy Spirit, is what evangelism and apologetics are all about. After all, it is the truth that sets men free. The lost cannot be saved unless they hear and, by God's grace, embrace the truth of the gospel.

When Christians share the good news with others, giving a defense for the hope that is in them, they are right to anchor that defense firmly in the Bible. As the supreme standard of truth, it is the believer's most powerful weapon against doubt and falsehood. As the sword of the Spirit, its message is accompanied by the convicting power of the Holy Spirit. As the Word of God, it is able to penetrate to the deepest parts of the human soul. No other evangelistic approach—from philosophy, science, or human reason—is more effective than starting with (and staying with) the Bible, because no other approach is supernaturally empowered.

That kind of Scripture-saturated approach is what makes *Reasons We Believe* such an outstanding resource. Instead of starting elsewhere, Nathan Busenitz begins with the Bible, showing how God's Word convincingly defends its own truth claims and then subsequently demonstrating how those claims are also confirmed by extra-biblical sources. Thoroughly biblical and meticulously researched, yet readily accessible and straightforward, *Reasons We Believe* belongs on every Christian's bookshelf, whether you are looking to be equipped for evangelism or simply encouraged in the faith.

In a doubting age, believers must not buy into the postmodern tolerance so rampant in our society. God has given us the truth. He has given us His Word. We therefore have an unassailable defense, because we have the only defense that is absolutely true. Having been armed with that truth, and accompanied by the power of the Spirit, we are ready to do battle against the false speculations, ideologies, and philosophies of the present age.

If you are a Christian, you must be ready to make a defense for the hope that is in you (1 Peter 3:15)—and the best way to do that is to go to the Spirit-empowered Word of God. The pages that follow will show you where to begin.

John MacArthur

PREFACE

Reasons We Believe is a survey of fifty lines of evidence that support the biblical understanding of God, the Bible, and Jesus Christ. Though many excellent books have been written on the subject of Christian apologetics, this book is unique in several respects.

First, its format is intended to allow readers the option of either reading the book from start to finish or skipping around from place to place depending on their own questions or interests. Though many readers will only use the material for personal study, it is also hoped that the structure of each section will prove useful for small-group discussions or larger teaching venues.

Second, the book deliberately includes a substantial number of Scripture references—the aim being to bring the full force of God's Word to bear on the discussion. Our conviction is that any defense of biblical Christianity must begin with the Bible, and we have attempted to model that approach here. These references are intended to equip readers both in their own study of these issues and as they explain the truth to others.

Finally, in making the case for biblical Christianity, *Reasons We Believe* cites several hundred other works, which is admittedly more than most popular books of its size. This too is purposeful, stemming from a desire on our part to present a credible argument—one that is not only well-documented but is also generally representative of evangelical Christianity. We trust that those wanting to do further research will find the footnotes helpful, though they should be aware that a number of the works we reference are non-evangelical. Thus, just because a work is cited does not necessarily imply that we endorse its full contents.

A REASONABLE FAITH

The Christian Faith Is Unseen, but It Is Not Blind

Truth is Christianity's most enduring asset.

CARL F. H. HENRY[1]

---

[1]Carl F. H. Henry, *Carl Henry at His Best* (Sisters, OR: Multnomah, 1989), 203.

INTRODUCTION

Faith, no matter how sincere, is only a fantasy if it is based on bad information.

Consider the misguided ventures of Juan Ponce de León, a sixteenth-century Spanish explorer. Ponce de León was appointed governor of Puerto Rico (then called Boriquien) in 1509. Having been a crew member on the second voyage of Christopher Columbus, he had decided to stay in the New World when Columbus returned to Spain. While serving as governor, Ponce de León began hearing rumors about an alleged "fountain of youth," a spring that reversed the effects of aging and gave eternal life. His imagination was immediately captivated, and he became determined to find the magical source of immortality.[2]

On March 3, 1513, Ponce de León set out from Puerto Rico with several ships to locate the island of Bimini, where the fountain of youth was supposedly situated. He was convinced that the island existed, and he planned on doing everything in his power to find it. But, although he did discover Florida, he never found the legendary Bimini or its life-giving spring. His search ended in 1521 when he was fatally wounded during one of his exploits.

Despite good intentions and repeated attempts, this treasure-hunter was doomed to fail from the outset because he was chasing something that didn't exist. He *believed* that it existed, but his faith was ultimately disappointed because it was based on faulty data. The unverifiable reports he had received about the fountain of youth were false, meaning that Ponce de León was trusting in sources that had given him bad information. Though his faith was surely sincere, it was ultimately worthless because it was founded on error.

---

[2]Some historians assert that the fountain of youth was only a secondary motivation behind Ponce de León's exploits (cf. Robert H. Fuson, *Juan Ponce de Leon and the Spanish Discovery of Puerto Rico and Florida* [Blacksburg, VA: McDonald & Woodward, 2001], 118). However, most sources suggest it was primary in his thinking (cf. Laurence Bergreen, *Over the Edge of the World* [New York: Harper-Collins, 2004], 75–76; Beatrize Pastor Bodmer, *The Armature of Conquest: Spanish Accounts of the Discovery of America* [Palo Alto, CA: Stanford University Press, 1992], 105; Peter O. Koch, *To the Ends of the Earth: The Age of European Explorers* [Jefferson, NC: McFarland, 2003], 222; and Diane Sansevere-Dreher, *Explorers Who Got Lost* [New York: Macmillan, 1992], 78). Our recounting of Ponce de León's story follows this majority perspective.

Ponce de León's negative example can be contrasted with one of his contemporaries, another Spanish explorer named Hernán Cortés. While Ponce de León was searching for the mythical fountain, Cortés was learning about a city so magnificent, it too sounded legendary. But there was something different about the information Cortés received. Unlike Ponce de León, Cortés had good reason to believe that the city actually existed. He had received specific details about the city's king, Montezuma. He had also been met by one of the city's ambassadors, Teudile. He had even been given precious stones and featherware from the city as a token of Montezuma's goodwill. Although he had not yet visited the city, Cortés found the evidence for its existence impossible to ignore.[3]

The name of the city was Tenochtitlán; it was the capital of the Aztec Empire and one of the largest cities in the world at that time. The city was known as "the Venice of the New World," and Cortés and his men thought they were dreaming when they finally saw it for the first time (on November 8, 1519). But Cortés was not dreaming. His quest for Tenochtitlán had not been in vain, because it had been based on credible information. His faith in the city's existence was not founded on legends or myth; it was founded on trustworthy evidence. His faith was vindicated because his sources were reliable.

So how do the exploits of Juan Ponce de León and Hernán Cortés compare? Both men were Spanish explorers and conquerors. Both made expeditions for the purpose of discovery in the New World. Both believed that what they were searching for truly existed. Both had faith in their respective pursuits. But only one of the two men was right about what he believed. Only Cortés believed in something that actually corresponded to reality.

IS CHRISTIANITY BASED ON GOOD INFORMATION?

When it comes to contemporary religious beliefs, people exercise faith in many different belief systems. Certainly every religion can boast of ardent followers—morally good people, humanly speaking, who strongly believe that their respective religion is correct. Like Ponce de

---

[3]For more on Cortés, see Michael Wood, *Conquistadors* (Berkeley, CA: University of California Press, 2001), 15–78.

León they spend their lives pursuing what they believe to be true. But unless their faith is based on an accurate source of information (a correct authority), they are pursuing nothing more than a fantasy.

In this book, we will survey the case for the reliability of the two-fold authority on which Christianity rests—namely, the Bible and the person of Jesus Christ (cf. Hebrews 1:1–2). In order to do this we will go to the Bible itself, which is "the word of Christ" (Colossians 3:16), to see what reasons it gives for why we should accept its claims about God, about itself, and about Jesus. Rather than starting with philosophy, history, science, or even human reason, it is only right that an examination and defense of biblical Christianity begin with the Bible. The renowned evangelist D. L. Moody reportedly noted, "There's no better book with which to defend the Bible than the Bible itself." He was absolutely right. As we will see in the upcoming pages, Scripture not only invites scrutiny, it also consistently demonstrates itself to be a trustworthy source of information.[4]

Once we have developed each reason from Scripture, we can then show how extra-biblical evidence corresponds with, and thereby attests to, what the Bible claims. To be clear, this external evidence does not *establish* the truthfulness of the Christian faith. If Christianity is true, it is because there really is a God, and He has revealed Himself to us through His Son and in His Word. Nonetheless, external evidence does *corroborate* the claims of Christianity. Because the God of the Bible is also the God of creation, time, and truth (cf. Psalm 19:1–6; Acts 17:26–28; John 17:17), the facts of science, history, and logic will necessarily correspond to what the Bible reveals.[5] Such evidence therefore provides wonderful confirmation for believers, because it bears witness to both the reliability of Scripture and the authenticity of Jesus Christ.

The empirical, forensic, and philosophical evidence that backs up Christianity sets it apart from other worldviews and belief systems. In the words of Christian author Morris Inch, "There is a case to be made

---

[4]We would add that, for Christians, there can be no higher court of authority than the book we believe to be from God Himself. Insofar as our reasons are derived from Scripture, we believe they come with God's inherent authority.

[5]This is not to say that science, history, or human reason should be considered of greater or equal authority to the Scriptures. Rather, we are noting that when the Bible is rightly interpreted, and when the facts of science, history, or logic are fully known, the two will not be in contradiction to each other. Rather, the general revelation of the world around us testifies to the truthfulness of the special revelation found in Scripture (cf. Psalm 19:1–11).

for Christianity. It passes the philosophic criteria with highest honors; it focuses on the incomparable figure of Jesus; it draws credibility from accumulative evidence; and it satisfies the conditions of trust. We need not, and ought not, settle for less."[6] In fact, the Christian faith is unique in the amount of evidence that supports it. As Christian apologist and scientist Henry Morris observes:

> The entire subject of evidences is almost exclusively the domain of *Christian* evidences. Other religions depend on subjective experience and blind faith, tradition and opinion. Christianity stands or falls upon the objective reality of gigantic supernatural events in history and the evidences therefore. This fact in itself is an evidence of its truth.[7]

Other scholars agree, noting that "only Christianity stakes its claim to truthfulness on historical events open to critical investigation."[8] Irwin H. Linton, in his book *A Lawyer Examines the Bible*, contends that the evidence for Christianity confirms it to be true beyond any reasonable doubt. After all, it "rests on definite, historical facts and events" that, due to the overwhelming evidence that supports them, must "be regarded as proved under the strictest rules of evidence used in the highest American and English courts."[9]

But what about other religious beliefs? How do they fare? Like Christianity, they too have "authorities" on which they base their beliefs.[10] For the Muslim, authority is found in the Qur'an, the *Hadith* (Muslim traditions), and the *Sunnah* (customs of Muslim life). For the Hindu, the authority is the *Scruti* (the revealed canon, which includes the *Bhagavad Gita*) and the *Smitri* (semi-canonical literature). Buddhist teachings center on "four basic truths" and the "eightfold path." Atheists too are people of faith. Though they cannot disprove that God exists, they choose to *believe* it nonetheless. For them, the naturalistic theories of evolution or the musings of contemporary philosophers are often appealed to as sources of

[6]Morris Inch, *A Case for Christianity* (Wheaton, IL: Tyndale House, 1997), 132.
[7]Henry Morris, *Many Infallible Proofs* (San Diego: Creation-Life Publishers, 1974), 1.
[8]John Ankerberg and John Weldon, *Fast Facts on Defending Your Faith* (Eugene, OR: Harvest House, 2002), 41.
[9]Irwin H. Linton: *A Lawyer Examines the Bible* (Grand Rapids, MI: Baker, 1943; reprint, San Diego: Creation-Life Publishers, 1978), 16.
[10]The information here on comparative religions is taken from Robert P. Lightner, *The God of the Bible and Other Gods* (Grand Rapids, MI: Kregel, 1998), 171–195.

authority. But what happens when these supposed authorities are put to the test?[11]

Christian apologists John Ankerberg and John Weldon give us the answer: "Other religions . . . can also be tested by examining their claims and looking critically at the facts—but again, one finds that they are invalidated by such a procedure." In fact, "no genuinely historical or objective evidence exists for the foundational claims of Hinduism, Buddhism, Islam, or any other world religion [besides Christianity]."[12] Author Robert Morey concurs, noting that "the faith of the non-Christian is externally and internally groundless." On the other hand, "there is more than enough evidence on every hand from every department of human experience and knowledge to demonstrate that Christianity is true."[13]

Though a thorough examination of other religions is outside the scope of this book, we will consider them briefly at the end of Section 2 (in considering pantheistic and polytheistic religions) and also in Section 3 (where we will specifically address the Qur'an). Many excellent books have been written that compare Christianity with other religions.[14] Our purpose here is to show that Christianity does not shy away from critical investigation and that its twofold authority stands when put to the test.

EVIDENCE MADE CERTAIN

As we will see in the upcoming pages, there are many excellent reasons to believe in God, the Bible, and Jesus Christ. These reasons and the corresponding pieces of evidence that confirm them do much to bolster the confidence of Christians in the veracity of their faith. They also serve as powerful tools in witnessing to non-Christians.[15]

---

[11]According to the law of non-contradiction, opposing truth claims cannot both be simultaneously correct. Thus, in spite of the pluralistic attitude of our postmodern society, the claims of Christianity cannot be construed as compatible with any other religious perspective (cf. John 14:6). If Christianity is true, all other religions are necessarily false. For a lay-level discussion of the law of non-contradiction see Norman Geisler and Peter Bocchino, *Unshakable Foundations* (Minneapolis: Bethany House, 2001), 22–24.

[12]John Ankerberg and John Weldon, *Fast Facts*, 44.

[13]Robert A. Morey, *Introduction to Defending the Faith* (Southbridge, MA: Crowne Publications, 1989), 38.

[14]Readers are encouraged to visit their local Christian bookstore for helpful resources on comparative religions. A few suggested titles would include: *So What's the Difference? How World Faiths Compare to Christianity* by Fritz Ridenour (Ventura, CA: Gospel Light, 2001); *Handbook of Today's Religions* by Josh McDowell and Don Stewart (Nashville: Thomas Nelson, 1993); *The Compact Guide to World Religions* by Dean C. Halverson (Minneapolis: Bethany House, 1996); *But Don't All Religions Lead to God?* by Michael Green (Grand Rapids, MI: Baker, 2002); and *Answering Islam* by Norman L. Geisler (Grand Rapids, MI: Baker, 2002).

[15]As James W. Sire, "On Being a Fool for Christ and an Idiot for Nobody," *Christian Apologetics in the Postmodern World*, 101–127, ed. Timothy R. Phillips and Dennis L. Okholm (Downers

Nonetheless, it is the Holy Spirit who ultimately makes the truth of Christianity certain in the hearts of believers (1 Corinthians 2:12–13). He gives us absolute confidence in both God's Word and God's Son, assuring us of our salvation and our heavenly hope (Romans 8:14–17). As Josh McDowell and Don Stewart explain, "To those outside the Christian faith, Christianity can be shown to rest on strong evidence and have a high degree of probability for its truth claims. But when a person becomes a Christian, the 'assurance' or 'certainty' becomes a reality. Christianity from a 'morally certain' standpoint becomes as undeniable as one's own existence."[16] For Christians, then, the reasons surveyed in this book only confirm what they already know to be true.

By the same token, it is the Holy Spirit who finally convinces the non-Christian of his need for a Savior (cf. John 16:8; 1 Thessalonians 1:5). Evidence alone is not enough; only God can bring spiritual life where there was no life (Ephesians 2:1–10). To be sure, the case for Christianity is a substantial one. But without the Holy Spirit's power, the most that the evidence can do is win a debate. True belief is only possible through the Spirit's working.

If you are already a believer in Jesus Christ, I trust you will be strengthened and encouraged by the reasons given in this book—to know that, although our faith is unseen (Hebrews 11:1), it is not blind. And if you are not yet a believer in Jesus Christ, my prayer for you is that the Holy Spirit would open your eyes to see the truth as you honestly consider the case presented here. I sincerely hope that, by His grace, God will use the reasons included in this book to draw you to Himself.

WHAT IS CHRISTIANITY ALL ABOUT?

Before we survey the many evidences for Christianity, we must first take a brief look at what it teaches. After all, what are we defending? What is the message that all of the reasons support?

The essence of the Christian message is called the gospel, which

---

Grove, IL: InterVarsity Press, 1995), 110–111 notes: "The task of apologetics is to demonstrate that Christianity is reasonable and thus (a) to assure Christians that their faith is not idiotic and (b) to clear away the obstacles and objections that keep nonbelievers from considering the arguments and evidence for the truth of Christianity."
[16]Josh McDowell and Don Stewart, *Answers to Tough Questions* (Nashville: Thomas Nelson, 1993), 154.

means "good news." It is the message of how men and women can have peace with God. The gospel explains how we can be forgiven of sin and how we can have eternal life in heaven. It tells us about God's righteous expectations, man's hopeless condition, Jesus' perfect sacrifice, and our necessary response.

God's Righteous Expectations

The Bible begins by telling us that God is the creator and sustainer of the universe (Genesis 1:1; Acts 17:24–27). He is therefore the rightful ruler of all things (1 Timothy 6:15), meaning that He alone deserves the heartfelt worship and obedience of every person (Exodus 20:3). In fact, the reason God created human beings was so they would lovingly serve Him and bring Him glory as the caretakers of this earth (Genesis 1:28; Isaiah 43:7), and so that as a result they might find perfect fulfillment and joy in their loving fellowship with Him (cf. Revelation 21:2–3; 22:3–4).

The Scriptures go on to teach that God is completely righteous and holy (Deuteronomy 32:4). Both His character and His Word are absolutely perfect (Psalm 19:7–11). As the just Judge of the universe, He knows and evaluates the thoughts and actions of every person (Psalm 139:1–4; Proverbs 15:3). Each man and woman will one day stand before Him to give an account for how he or she lived (Ecclesiastes 11:9).

Man's Hopeless Condition

The universe was originally created perfect, until Adam and Eve (the first man and woman) directly disobeyed their Creator (Genesis 1:1–3:6). Their disobedience or "sin" introduced evil, suffering, and death into the world (Genesis 3:7–19). It also permanently stained the moral fiber of mankind, not only for Adam and Eve but also for their descendants (Romans 5:12). As a result, every person who has ever lived (with the exception of Jesus Christ) is a sinner—both by nature and by choice (Romans 3:23). Because no one perfectly worships God or follows His commands (Mark 12:30; James 2:10), we are all sinners who deserve to be punished.

The Bible teaches that the consequence for our sin is twofold: physical death in this life and spiritual death in the next (Romans 6:23).

Spiritual death is described in Scripture as eternal separation from God in a place called hell (Revelation 20:11–15). The Bible also explains that, like convicted criminals on death row, there is nothing we can do in our own efforts to erase our guilt (Romans 3:10–18). Though we might consider ourselves to be "good" people, God's standard is perfection—and there are no perfect people. We all therefore stand hopelessly condemned before the divine Judge, God Himself.

Jesus' Perfect Sacrifice

Thankfully, in His infinite mercy and love, God has offered us a pardon for our sin. He knew that we could not save ourselves, so He sent us His Son Jesus Christ (John 3:16). Jesus, who as God took on human flesh (John 1:1, 14), was born in Israel some two thousand years ago. He lived a perfect life and then paid the penalty for sin by dying on a cross (Philippians 2:8; 1 Peter 3:18). He did not deserve to die because He never sinned. Yet He chose to die so that He could take the place of those He came to save. He endured the penalty that they rightfully deserved, meaning that He was their substitute (2 Corinthians 5:21; 1 John 4:9–10).

Jesus was buried after the Roman soldiers confirmed that He was dead. But, miraculously, He didn't stay in the tomb. Three days later He conquered death and rose from the grave, demonstrating that His sacrifice had satisfied God's justice (Romans 1:4). He then ascended into heaven, where He remains to this day (Acts 1:9–11).

As the Savior of the world, Jesus offers forgiveness from sin and salvation to all those who place their faith in Him (John 6:40; Romans 5:8–10). The Bible makes it clear that He is the only way to be made right with God (John 14:6). Pardon for sin comes by no other means. Acts 4:12 clearly says, "There is salvation in no one else, for there is no other name under heaven given among men by which we must be saved." Jesus Christ alone is God's solution for our sin.

Our Necessary Response

Since salvation is found only in Christ, it cannot be found in our own righteous efforts (Ephesians 2:8–10). It is based on His work, not ours. The Bible is very clear that there is nothing we can do to earn God's saving grace (Titus 3:5–7). Nonetheless, Jesus' free offer of salvation demands a response on our part.

Recognizing that we are sinners in desperate need of a Savior, we must cry out to God for mercy and wholly embrace in faith the pardon He has provided for us through His Son (cf. Luke 18:13–14; Acts 16:30–31). We must believe that Jesus is who He claimed to be (see Section 5 of this book) and trust in His death as the payment for our sin (John 11:25–26; Colossians 2:13–14). As Romans 10:9 promises, "If you confess with your mouth that Jesus is Lord and believe in your heart that God raised him from the dead, you will be saved."

In turning to God, we must also repent and turn away from our sin (Luke 24:47; Acts 17:30; 1 Thessalonians 1:9). With our hearts regenerated by the Holy Spirit (Titus 3:5), our greatest aim will be to follow and serve the Lord wholeheartedly (John 10:27; 12:26). After all, those who are genuine children of God will embrace His Son in love (John 8:42) and demonstrate that love through a life of obedience (John 14:15; cf. Romans 6:17–18).

Those who truly believe in Christ are given the promise of heaven, where they will spend eternity worshiping their Lord and Savior (Revelation 21–22). But those who do not trust in Christ will one day stand before God and face the devastating consequences of their sin (Hebrews 9:27). Because they have no substitute, they will pay for their sins themselves.

Coming Full Circle

The message that wicked people can find everlasting peace with God through Jesus Christ is what Christianity is all about. The Bible even says that God freely extends His forgiveness and salvation to any and all who are willing to receive it (John 6:37; Matthew 11:28). The promise of heaven, the freedom of forgiveness, a saving relationship with God Himself—that is what the Bible offers.

But is it reasonable to believe this message? In the pages that follow, we will look to the Bible itself for the answer to that question.

REASONS WE BELIEVE IN GOD

He Exists and We Can Know Him

I want to know how God created this world. I am not interested in this or that phenomenon, in the spectrum of this or that element. I want to know His thoughts; the rest are details.

ALBERT EINSTEIN[1]

If there were not God, there would be no atheists.

G. K. CHESTERTON[2]

---

[1]Cited from Ronald William Clark, *Einstein: The Life and Times* (New York: Avon Books, 1972), 37.
[2]G. K. Chesterton, *The Collected Works of G. K. Chesterton* (San Francisco: Ignatius Press, 1990), 3:38.

INTRODUCTION

The story is told of a raving madman who on a bright morning lit a lantern and ran to the marketplace calling out unceasingly, "I seek God! I seek God!" As there were many people standing nearby who did not believe in God, he caused a great deal of amusement. "Why? Is God lost?" said one. "Has he strayed away like a child?" said another. "Or does he keep himself hidden? Is he afraid of us? Has he taken a sea voyage? Has he emigrated?" the people cried out laughingly, making a great commotion.

The insane man jumped into their midst and transfixed them with his glances. "Where has God gone?" he called out. "I mean to tell you! *We have killed him*, you and I! We are all his murderers! But how have we done it? How were we able to drink up the sea? Who gave us the sponge to wipe away the whole horizon? Is there still an above and below? Do we not wander through infinite nothingness? Has it not become colder? Does not night come on continually, darker and darker? Do we not hear the noise of the gravediggers who are burying God? God is dead! God remains dead! *And we have killed him*!"[3]

IS GOD DEAD?

This shocking scenario was conceived in 1882 by the German philosopher Friedrich Nietzsche. Although the whole story is not often remembered, the phrase "God is dead" has left an indelible impression on Western society since Nietzsche's time. In fact, it is probably Nietzsche's most famous quote, even if through the words of one of his characters. But what did Nietzsche, through the mouth of the madman, mean by the phrase "God is dead"?

Several years later, Nietzsche himself explained his point. In 1887 he wrote, "The greatest recent event—that God is dead [means] that the belief in the Christian God has become unbelievable."[4] His point

---

[3]Story adapted from Friedrich Nietzsche, *The Gay Science*, 1882, sections 125–126.
[4]Nietzsche, *The Gay Science*, second edition, 1887, section 343.

was not that God had literally died, but rather that, due to advances in science and philosophy, the Christian concept of God (which had undergirded European thinking for centuries) had become logically untenable. It could no longer be honestly believed by intelligent individuals. Therefore, the very idea of God was dead.

Nietzsche, of course, saw the Christian understanding of God as inherently distasteful. He rejected the possibility of a personal, all-powerful deity who demanded repentance and worship from sinful human beings. In 1888 he wrote, "The Christian conception of God . . . is one of the most corrupt conceptions of God arrived at on earth."[5] And Nietzsche was not alone in his conclusions. Along with him, many of Europe's cultural and intellectual elite also rejected the biblical notion of God because they considered it indefensible.

TEN REASONS WE BELIEVE IN GOD

So, is God dead? Is belief in Him unreasonable? Or does the Bible offer us credible reasons to put our faith in His existence? Thankfully, the answer to that final question is *yes*. Nietzsche and his contemporaries may have rejected God. They may have denied His existence and even discounted His influence within society. Yet, in so doing, they rejected the clear evidence that God Himself provides. As the Bible says, "Claiming to be wise, they became fools" (Romans 1:22). "The fool says in his heart, 'There is no God'" (Psalm 14:1).

With that as a backdrop, let's consider some of the many reasons we as Christians believe that God exists and we can know Him.

---

[5]Nietzsche, *The Anti-Christ*, 1888, section 18.

Reason 1:
We Believe in God

Because He Has Revealed Himself to Us

At the most foundational level, we believe in God because He has made Himself known to us, both through His creation (cf. Psalm 19:1–6) and through His Word (cf. Psalm 19:7–11). "Whatever we know about God has been revealed to us by God Himself," explains Christian author William Brown. "Christians do not claim to have found God; rather *we claim that God found us.* . . . If God had not revealed Himself, we would have no hope of ever truly knowing Him."[6]

On the one hand, God has revealed certain things about Himself through the natural world (that He is the Creator and Sustainer of the universe—Acts 14:15–17; Romans 1:20) and through the human conscience (that He is the ultimate Lawgiver and Judge—Romans 1:19; 2:14–15). Such revelation is called *general* revelation because it is inescapably available to everyone (being all around us and even inside of us) and because the truths it reveals about God are quite general or basic.

On the other hand, God has also revealed truths about Himself that are much more specific. This *special* revelation comes from two sources of information—the Bible (which is the written Word of God) and Jesus Christ (who is the incarnate Word of God—John 1:1).[7] Both in the Scriptures and through His Son, God has revealed Himself to us in a detailed and personal way. If He had not done so, we would have no way of knowing who He is or what He expects.

It would be no help to us at all in our human predicament if God were silent, but happily this is not the case. God not only exists, but also

---

[6]William E. Brown, *Making Sense of Your Faith* (Wheaton, IL: Victor Books, 1989), 62. Emphasis in the original.

[7]In the past God has also spoken through dreams, visions, prophecies, and the like. But now that the canon of Scripture is complete, it is no longer necessary for God to speak outside of the Bible.

He has communicated that fact to us. He has told us all about who
He is, what He is like, and what His plan is for planet earth. He has
revealed these things to mankind through the Bible.[8]

The Bible begins by presupposing God's existence with the words
"In the beginning, God . . . " (Genesis 1:1). Other passages such as
2 Samuel 22:47 and 1 Kings 8:60 echo this claim, stating that "the
LORD lives" and that "the LORD is God." The Bible goes on to
explain that God is the absolute Ruler and Sustainer of everything in
the universe (Nehemiah 9:6). He is personal (Exodus 3:14–15), intelligent (Psalm 147:5), and purposeful in His actions (Ephesians 3:11).
Unlike His creation, He is eternal (Deuteronomy 33:27), unchanging
in His character (Malachi 3:6), everywhere present (Psalm 139:7–10),
all-knowing (Hebrews 4:13), all-wise (Romans 11:33–34), and all-
powerful (Job 42:2). He is perfectly righteous (Deuteronomy 32:4),
just (Genesis 18:25), true (Daniel 4:37), loving (1 John 4:7–8), and holy
(Isaiah 6:3). As God's self-testimony, the Bible enables us to learn things
about its Author we would never have known otherwise.

God has also revealed Himself to us through His Son, Jesus Christ.
The apostle John noted this when he wrote, "No one has ever seen
God; the only God [referring to Christ], who is at the Father's side, he
has made him known" (John 1:18). The author of Hebrews made the
same point at the beginning of his letter: "Long ago, at many times
and in many ways, God spoke to our fathers by the prophets, but in
these last days he has spoken to us by his Son, whom he appointed the
heir of all things, through whom also he created the world" (1:1–2).
As the incarnate Word of God, Jesus Christ revealed God in a way that
people could see, hear, and touch (1 John 1:1–3). Though He is now in
heaven, a record of what Jesus was like during His ministry on earth is
preserved for us in the New Testament Gospels.

We will discuss more about the authenticity of both the Bible and
Jesus Christ later in this book. At the outset, however, it is important
to establish the two primary pillars of Christian belief—that the Bible is
God's Word and that Jesus Christ is His Son. Because God has revealed
Himself to us through them, we are able to believe in Him.

---

[8]Josh McDowell and Don Stewart, *Answers to Tough Questions* (Nashville: Thomas Nelson,
1993), 71.

Reason 2:
We Believe in God

Because the Existence of Our Universe Points to a Creator

The Bible repeatedly asserts that God created the universe and that without His creative work nothing outside of Him would exist. The apostle John stated it like this: "All things were made through him, and without him was not any thing made that was made" (John 1:3). The apostle Paul echoed those words in Colossians 1:16, where he said of Jesus Christ, "For by him all things were created, in heaven and on earth, visible and invisible, whether thrones or dominions or rulers or authorities—all things were created through him and for him." Many other passages could be cited (such as Genesis 1:1; Psalm 8:1–3; 19:1; 95:3–6; 115:15; Romans 11:36; 1 Corinthians 8:6; and Hebrews 1:2), but the simple point remains: The Bible answers the age-old question, *Where did everything come from?* by pointing to God. There could be no universe, no time, space, matter, energy, or intelligence, without a Creator.

If there is no God, then we must attempt to explain why there is something at all rather than nothing. "In light of the evidence, we are left with only two options: either *no one* created something out of nothing, or else *someone* created something out of nothing," explain evangelical scholars Norman Geisler and Frank Turek. "If you can't believe that nothing caused something, *then you don't have enough faith to be an atheist.* The most reasonable view is God."[9]

Historically, this line of evidence has been called the cosmological argument. Though sometimes nuanced in different ways, Christian apologist William Lane Craig (a PhD from the University of Birmingham, England) uses a helpful syllogism that demonstrates its basic premise. Craig's argument follows three simple points:

---

[9]Norman Geisler and Frank Turek, *I Don't Have Enough Faith to Be an Atheist* (Wheaton, IL: Crossway Books, 2005), 94. Emphasis in original.

1. Everything that begins to exist has a cause.
2. The universe began to exist.
3. Therefore, the universe must have a cause.[10]

Scripture tells us who this cause is. "In the beginning, *God* created the heavens and the earth" (Genesis 1:1, emphasis added).

Recognizing that our universe had a definite beginning, secular scientists have attempted to account for its origins in terms of a massive explosion of matter and energy. But what caused this *big bang* is something they have not been able to adequately explain. As Stanford University physics professor Andrei Linde wrote in *Scientific American*:

> The first, and main, problem is the very existence of the big bang. One may wonder, What came before? If space-time did not exist then, how could everything appear from nothing? What arose first: the universe or the laws determining its evolution? Explaining this initial singularity—where and when it all began—still remains the most intractable problem of modern cosmology.[11]

In other words, scientists don't know what sparked the big bang. They also don't know where the matter and energy involved came from or what the universe was like beforehand. It's little wonder then that even some prominent scientists, such as Sir John Maddox of England's Royal Society, have called it a "view of the origin of the Universe [that] is thoroughly unsatisfactory."[12]

Although science cannot answer the question of ultimate origins,[13]

---

[10]Known more precisely as the Kalaam Cosmological Argument, this is explained by Craig in *Reasonable Faith* (Wheaton, IL: Crossway Books, 1994), 91–122. Gary R. Habermas and Michael R. Licona, *The Case for the Resurrection of Jesus* (Grand Rapids: Kregel, 2004), 330 add: "Some skeptics respond, 'Well, this argument also requires God to have a beginning too.' Not at all, because this argument only applies to what begins to exist. We know the universe began to exist. However, there are no good arguments that require God to have had a beginning. Indeed, precisely the opposite can be argued: there must be a final and uncaused Cause that is eternal." Interested readers may also benefit from Craig's in-depth study, *The Cosmological Argument from Plato to Leibniz* (Eugene, OR: Wipf and Stock Publishers, 2001).

[11]Andrei Linde, "The Self-Reproducing Inflationary Universe," *Scientific American*, Vol. 271 (November 1994), 48. Cited from Henry Morris, *That Their Own Words May Be Used Against Them* (Green Forest, AR: Master Books, 1997), 15.

[12]John Maddox, "Down with the Big Bang," *Nature*, Vol. 340 (August 10, 1989), 425. Maddox is a trained chemist and physicist who was the editor of *Nature* for twenty-two years. Cited from Morris, *Their Own Words*, 16.

[13]Richard Swinburne, in "Evidence for God," 229–238, in *Does God Exist?* by Terry Miethe and Richard Flew (San Francisco: Harper, 1991), 229 notes: "Personal explanation and scientific explanation are the two ways we have of explaining the occurrence of phenomena. Since there cannot

the Bible can and does: God is the one who created the world. "The words of Genesis 1:1 are precise and concise beyond mere human composition. They account for everything evolution *cannot* explain."[14]

Of course, the Bible gives credence to a big bang of sorts. God spoke, and *bang* it was created. As former NASA scientist Robert Jastrow observes, "The essential elements in the astronomical and biblical accounts of Genesis are the same: the chain of events leading to man commenced suddenly and sharply at a definite moment in time, in a flash of light and energy."[15] He further admits, in a moment of remarkable honesty, "For the scientist who has lived by his faith in the power of reason, the story ends like a bad dream. He has scaled the mountain of ignorance; he is about to conquer the highest peak; as he pulls himself over the final rock, he is greeted by a band of theologians who have been sitting there for centuries."[16]

Brought face-to-face with the inexplicable origins of our universe, scientists like Jastrow have come to consider the necessary existence of a divine First Cause. As physicist and Nobel Prize winner Arno Penzias notes, "Astronomy leads us to a unique event, a universe which was created out of nothing, one with the very delicate balance needed to provide exactly the conditions required to permit life, and one which has an underlying (one might say 'supernatural') plan."[17] His implication is clear: the existence of our orderly, life-sustaining universe cannot be accounted for in purely naturalistic terms.

By pointing to a Creator, the biblical view of origins not only explains what naturalism cannot, it also corresponds to our everyday experience. The law of cause and effect is something we all understand as human beings: everything that happens has a cause, and everything in our universe, including the universe itself, has a source. The television set in our living room is on because someone turned it on. It exists because someone designed and constructed it. The same is true for

be a scientific explanation of the existence of the universe, either there is a personal one or there is no explanation at all."

[14]John MacArthur, *The Battle for the Beginning* (Nashville: W Publishing Group, 2001), 40.

[15]Robert Jastrow, *God and the Astronomers*, 1978. Jastrow played a prominent role at NASA and also taught science at Dartmouth College and Columbia University. Cited from Donald B. DeYoung, *Astronomy and the Bible* (Grand Rapids, MI: Baker, 2000), 127.

[16]Ibid.

[17]Arno Penzias, in *Cosmos, Bios, Theos: Scientists Reflect on Science, God, and the Origin of the Universe, Life and Homo Sapiens*, ed. Henry Margenau and Roy Abraham Varghese (LaSalle, IL: Open Court, 1992), 83; cited from John Ankerberg and John Weldon, *Fast Facts on Defending Your Faith* (Eugene, OR: Harvest House, 2002), 24.

our universe: something or someone outside of it must be the cause and grounds of its existence. The Bible tells us who this First Cause is (Genesis 1:1). We know, then, that God exists because without Him it is impossible to explain the origin and existence of anything else.[18]

So why would secular scientists deny the existence of God? The answer is found in what they *believe* (namely, that nothing outside of the material universe exists) and has little, if anything, to do with true science. As much as any religion, atheistic naturalism is built on faith. "Evolution has deep religious connections," explains philosophy professor Alvin Plantinga. "A good deal more than reason goes into the acceptance of such a theory as the Grand Evolutionary Story."[19] Robert Jastrow agrees:

> There is a kind of religion in science. . . . The religious faith of the scientist is violated by the discovery that the world had a beginning under conditions in which the known laws of physics are not valid, and as a product of forces or circumstances we cannot discover.[20]

Because of its prior "faith" commitment to a materialistic world-view, naturalism denies the existence of God even in the face of contrary evidence. Speaking candidly, Richard Lewontin, former professor of zoology and biology at Harvard, admits:

> We take the side of science *in spite* of the patent absurdity of some of its constructs . . . because we have a prior commitment, a commitment to materialism. It is not that the methods and institutions of science somehow compel us to accept a material explanation of the phenomenal world, but, on the contrary, that we are forced by our *a priori* adherence to material causes . . . no matter how counter-intuitive, no matter how mystifying to the uninitiated. Moreover, that materialism is an absolute, for we cannot allow a Divine foot in the door.[21]

---

[18]Cf. Paul E. Little, *Know Why You Believe* (Downers Grove, IL: InterVarsity Press, 2000). On 24–25 he notes that "we come eventually to an uncaused cause, who is God. . . . God, the Creator, the Beginner, by definition is eternal. He is self-existent. Were God a created being, he would not be a cause, he would be an effect. He would not and could not be God."

[19]Alvin Plantinga, "When Faith and Reason Crash," 113–145, in *Intelligent Design Creationism and Its Critics*, ed. Robert T. Pennock (Cambridge, MA: The MIT Press, 2001), 125–126. In short, "the theory of evolution is by no means religiously or theologically neutral" (123). Plantinga is currently the John A. O'Brien Professor of Philosophy at the University of Notre Dame.

[20]Robert Jastrow, *God and the Astronomers* (New York: Norton, 1978), 113–114; cited from Geisler and Turek, *I Don't Have Enough Faith to Be an Atheist*, 89.

[21]Richard Lewontin, "Billions and Billions of Demons," *The New York Review* (January 9, 1997), 31.

More succinctly, immunologist Scott Todd notes, "Even if all the data point to an intelligent designer, such a hypothesis is excluded from science because it is not materialistic."[22] Such admissions confirm that evolution, in actuality, "isn't science. [It] is dogmatism."[23]

When the "faith" of naturalism, and the faith of biblical Christianity are compared, only one can adequately answer the question of origins. There is "a possible explanation of equal intellectual respectability— and to my mind, greater elegance," notes theoretical physicist John Polkinghorne, former president of Queen's College, Cambridge. It is "that this one world is the way it is because it is the creation of the will of a Creator who purposes that it should be so."[24]

Thus the existence of our universe points to God, because without a creator there can be no creation. In the words of eminent British philosopher Richard Swinburne, longtime professor at Oxford University, "Why believe that there is a God at all? My answer is that to suppose that there is a God explains why there is a world at all . . . and so much else. In fact, the hypothesis of the existence of God makes sense of the whole of our experience, and it does better than any other explanation which can be put forward, and that is the grounds for believing it to be true."[25]

Lewontin was still an active Harvard professor when he made these comments. Cited from Jonathan Sarfati, *Refuting Compromise* (Green Forest, AZ: Master Books, 2004), 43.

[22]Scott Todd, correspondence to *Nature*, 410 (6752): 423 (September 30, 1999); cited from Jonathan Sarfati, *Refuting Compromise*, 43. Scott Todd is an immunologist at Kansas State University.

[23]William A. Dembski, *The Design Revolution* (Downers Grove, IL: InterVarsity Press, 2004), 279. Dembski is a leading proponent of intelligent design and holds a PhD in mathematics from the University of Chicago, a PhD in philosophy from the University of Illinois, Chicago, and an MDiv from Princeton Theological Seminary.

[24]John Polkinghorne, *One World* (London: SPCK, 1986), 79–80. Cited from Ravi Zacharias, *The Real Face of Atheism* (Grand Rapids, MI: Baker, 2004), 48. Polkinghorne's quote was specifically in response to the idea that life could have risen from purely naturalistic causes.

[25]Richard Swinburne, in "Evidence for God," 229–238, in *Does God Exist?* ed. Miethe and Flew, 229.

Reason 3:
We Believe in God

Because the Order and Design of Life Point to a Designer

God's creative power is seen not only in the mere existence of the universe, but also in the incredible complexity with which He designed the life therein. God did not stop with simply forming our earth; He also created the life that fills it. The book of Genesis records God's creation of plants, animals, and people (Genesis 1:11–30), and the Bible repeatedly views the design of that life as a testimony to His creative power (Job 38–41; Psalm 104:1–35). Reflecting on the wonder of God's design, King David wrote these words of praise to God: "For you formed my inward parts; you knitted me together in my mother's womb. I praise you, for I am fearfully and wonderfully made. Wonderful are your works; my soul knows it very well" (Psalm 139:13–14).

Modern medical and biological science has only deepened our understanding of the design of life. Even the "simplest" forms of life, from the millions of species on our planet, are incredibly complex. Richard Dawkins, professor of zoology at Oxford and renowned atheist, has noted that the DNA information contained in just the cell nucleus of one amoeba exceeds that of an entire thirty-volume set of the *Encyclopedia Britannica*. Moreover, the DNA of the entire amoeba contains as much information as one thousand such encyclopedia sets.[26] The astonishing fact is that this DNA information is not random. Rather, it consists of very specific sequences of data (in the form of four bases—adenine, thymine, guanine, and cytosine), all specifically ordered to produce the amoeba's genetic code.

As amazing as they are, amoebas are certainly not the most impressive of God's creatures. The Bible points to mankind as the crown jewel of God's earthly creation. In fact, God fashioned human beings in His image, creating them to rule over and cultivate the earth (Genesis

---

[26]See Geisler and Turek, *I Don't Have Enough Faith*, 116.

1:26). Unlike the animals, God gave man the ability to reason and the intellectual capacity to ponder the profound truths of the universe. As Christian apologist John Gerstner keenly observes: "There is more in the universe than mere life. There is intelligent life. There is a kind of life which not only lives but which thinks about living. . . . How could matter, which has no life in itself, actually produce a life which can reflect on matter and tell it that it has no life in itself?"[27] Ironically, even when men use their rational ability to defy the existence of God, their level of intelligence still testifies to God's creative greatness.

Atheists will contend that no designer is necessary, arguing that everything in the universe including complex life on Planet Earth is the product of two naturalistic mechanisms: random chance and natural selection. But such beliefs are held contrary to the evidence. As William Dembski explains, "There are some entities and events [in nature] that we cannot and, indeed, do not explain by reference to these twin modes of materialistic causation."[28] Elsewhere he expands on this thought:

> Naturalistic mechanisms are incapable of generating the highly specific, information-rich structures that pervade biology. Organisms display the hallmarks of intelligently engineered high-tech systems— information storage and transfer, functioning codes, sorting and delivery systems, self-regulation and feedback loops, signal-transduction circuitry—and everywhere, complex arrangements of mutually interdependent and well-fitted parts that work in concert to perform a function.[29]

The origins of such intricate and complex life forms leave the atheist with more unanswered questions. Consider the following quotes from some of today's leading scientists:
  • "In the speculations on the origin of life, the most difficult conceptual problems deal with the complexity of the first organism." (Hyman Hartman, biologist from the University of California, Berkeley)[30]

---

[27]John Gerstner, *Reasons for Faith* (Grand Rapids, MI: Baker, 1967), 31.
[28]William Dembski, "The Third Mode of Explanation," 17–45, in Michael Behe, William Dembski, and Stephen Meyer, *Science and Evidence for Design in the Universe* (San Francisco: Ignatius Press, 2000), 44.
[29]William Dembski, *The Design Revolution*, 63. Earlier Dembski writes, "The claim that the Darwinian mechanism of chance variation and natural selection can generate the full range of biological diversity strikes people as an unwarranted extrapolation from the limited changes that mechanism is known to effect in practice" (53).
[30]Hyman Hartman, *Journal of Molecular Evolution*, Vol. 4, 1975, 359. Cited from Nathan Aviezer, *In the Beginning* (Hoboken, NJ: KTAV Publishing House, 1995), 70.

• "Science, you might say, has discovered that our existence is infinitely improbable, and hence a miracle." (John Horgan, director of the Center for Science Writings at the Stevens Institute of Technology)[31]

• "Precious little in the way of biochemical evolution could have happened on the Earth. It is easy to show that the two thousand or so enzymes that span the whole of life could not have evolved on the Earth." (Sir Fred Hoyle, famed British astronomer, and Nalin Chandra Wickramasinghe, professor of mathematics and astronomy at Cardiff University)[32]

• "It is extremely improbable that proteins and nucleic acids, both of which are structurally complex, arose spontaneously in the same place at the same time. Yet it also seems impossible to have one without the other. And so, at first glance, one might have to conclude that life could never, in fact, have originated by chemical means." (Leslie Orgel, professor of chemistry at the Salk Institute and the University of California, San Diego)[33]

• "Although at the beginning the paradigm was worth consideration, now the entire effort in the primeval soup paradigm is self-deception [maintained solely] on the ideology of its champions." (Hubert Yockey, physicist and information theorist from the University of California, Berkeley)[34]

Even the late Francis Crick, co-discoverer of DNA and winner of the 1962 Nobel Peace Prize, made this astonishing admission: "An honest man, armed with all the knowledge available to us now, could only state that in some sense, the origin of life appears at the moment to be almost a miracle, so many are the conditions which would have had to have been satisfied to get it going."[35]

Statements such as these have led some, such as Princeton-trained mathematician and molecular biologist David Berlinski, to doubt whether atheistic naturalism is really an adequate explanation after all. Berlinski writes:

> Unable to say *what* evolution has accomplished, biologists now find themselves unable to say *whether* evolution has accomplished it. This leaves evolutionary theory in the doubly damned position of having compromised the concepts needed to make sense of life—complexity,

---

[31]John Horgan, in 2002; cited by Lee Strobel, *The Case for the Creator* (Grand Rapids, MI: Zondervan, 2004), 42.

[32]Fred Hoyle and Chandra Wickramasinghe, "Where Microbes Boldly Went," *New Scientist*, 412–415, Vol. 91 (August 13, 1991), 415. Cited from Morris, *Their Own Words*, 55.

[33]Leslie E. Orgel, "The Origin of Life on the Earth," *Scientific American*, Vol. 271, 77–83 (October 1994), 78. Cited from Morris, *Their Own Words*, 49.

[34]Hubert Yockey, *Information Theory and Molecular Biology* (Cambridge: Cambridge University Press, 1992), 336.

[35]Francis Crick, *Life Itself: Its Origin and Nature* (New York: Simon & Schuster, 1981), 88.

adaptation, design—while simultaneously conceding that the theory does little to explain them.[36]

As Peter J. Bowler, historian of biology, has rightly observed, "So many (and not just the creationists) remain skeptical of the [evolutionary] theory's scientific credentials."[37]

After extensively studying how Darwin's theories correspond to the complexity of the human body, medical doctor Geoffrey Simmons concludes: "There are no conclusive facts that reliably support Darwin's theories—yet there are millions of facts that challenge them. Maybe billions. Some people may always have difficulty accepting that there is a Designer . . . but an alternative explanation for the exquisite design and complexity of the human body has yet to be found."[38] Malcolm A. Jeeves, former president of the Royal Society of Edinburgh, and R. J. Berry, a geneticist, agree: "In no way can the human body be properly seen as the simple consequence of a set of random chemical specifications."[39]

As we noted earlier regarding the amoeba, the information in DNA and proteins is especially strong evidence of a designer. So much so, in fact, that Stephen Meyer (a PhD from Cambridge) observes that "most biologists who specialize in origin-of-life research now reject chance as a possible explanation for the origin of the information in DNA and proteins."[40] None other than Bill Gates has compared the information in DNA to a software program much more complex than anything human beings have ever developed.[41] We would never conclude that a Microsoft program came into existence without a designer. So why would we think this about DNA?[42]

---

[36]David Berlinski, "The Deniable Darwin," *Commentary*, 19–29, Vol. 101 (June 1996), 28. Cited in Morris, *Their Own Words*, 123. Berlinski is a leading proponent for intelligent design.

[37]Peter J. Bowler, "The Status of Evolutionism Examined," review of *Monad to Man* by Michael Ruse (Harvard University Press, 1996), in *American Scientist*, Vol. 85 (May/June 1997), 274. Cited in Morris, *Their Own Words*, 113.

[38]Geoffrey Simmons, *What Darwin Didn't Know: A Doctor Dissects the Theory of Evolution* (Eugene, OR: Harvest House, 2004), 309. In his book, Simmons lists over eighty factors in the human body that convincingly point to purposeful design, including DNA, cellular complexity, self-identity, and memory.

[39]Malcolm A. Jeeves and R. J. Berry, *Science, Life, and Christian Belief* (Grand Rapids, MI: Baker, 1998), 160.

[40]Stephen Meyer, "Evidence for Design in Physics and Biology," 53–111, in *Science and Evidence for Design in the Universe*, 73. Meyer is a leading proponent of intelligent design.

[41]Reference to Bill Gates adapted from Lee Strobel with Jane Vogel, *The Case for a Creator*, student edition (Grand Rapids, MI: Zondervan, 2004), 75–76.

[42]See C. L. Cagan with Robert Hymers, *From Darwin to Design* (New Kensington, PA: Whitaker House, 2006), 56.

Christian author Lee Strobel summarizes why DNA is so amazing.

> As scientists have studied the six feet of DNA tightly coiled inside every one of our body's one hundred trillion cells, they have marveled at how it provides the genetic information necessary to create all of the different proteins out of which our bodies are built. In fact, each one of the thirty thousand genes that are embedded in our twenty-three pairs of chromosomes can yield as many as 20,500 kinds of proteins.[43]

The highly-organized data contained in DNA leads us to only one possible conclusion: "All we can say is that given the information in a DNA molecule, it is certainly reasonable to posit that an intelligent agent made it. Life came from a 'who' instead of a 'what.'"[44]

It is noteworthy, also, to realize that DNA links all known life in our universe together. "Whether we are studying a blade of grass, a bacterium, or a human all base their existence on the same 20 amino acids," notes Gerald Schroeder, former professor of nuclear physics at MIT. He continues, "In spite of the complexity of individual proteins, often containing specific combinations of as many as 300 individual amino acids, there are several nearly identical proteins that appear in most forms of life. This equivalence among all life forms is strong evidence for a single source of all life. It is not plausible that this similarity arose by chance."[45] Thus, as British astronomer Sir Frederick Hoyle so graphically illustrated, "The chance that higher life forms arose by evolutionary processes is comparable with the chance that a tornado sweeping through a junkyard might assemble a Boeing 747 from the materials therein."[46]

Again the Bible provides answers for what naturalism cannot; and what it reveals to us is in keeping with what we see in the world around us. If there is a God, and if the Bible describes Him accurately,

---

[43]Strobel with Vogel, *The Case for the Creator*, student edition, 75.
[44]Walter L. Bradley and Charles B. Thaxton, "Information & the Origin of Life," 173–210, in *The Creation Hypothesis*, ed. J. P. Moreland (Downers Grove, IL: InterVarsity Press, 1994), 209. Stephen Meyer, "Evidence for Design in Physics and Biology," 93 agrees: "The specifically arranged nucleotide sequences—the complex but functionally specified sequences—in DNA imply the past action of an intelligent mind, even if such mental agency cannot be directly observed."
[45]Gerald Schroeder, *Genesis and the Big Bang* (New York: Bantam Books, 1992), 113.
[46]Sir Frederick Hoyle, *Nature*, November 12, 1981; cited from Donald B. DeYoung, *Astronomy and the Bible*, 127.

then we would expect to find that the world operates according to fixed laws, exhibiting signs of both purpose and design. "Everything we find in nature that points to harmony, design, purpose, and intelligence is consistent with the Christian presupposition that God exists and provides supporting evidence for it."[47] An insightful article from *Newsweek* explains:

> Physicists have stumbled on signs that the cosmos is custom-made for life and consciousness. It turns out that if the constants of nature—unchanging numbers like the strength of gravity, the charge of an electron, and the mass of a proton—were the tiniest bit different, the atoms would not hold together, stars would not burn, and life would never have made an appearance.[48]

In other words, our earth was purposely designed for life. Its distance from the sun, atmosphere, and natural resources (including water) are all perfectly fine-tuned for the life that's here.[49] The weight of this evidence has caused many secular thinkers to change their minds about atheistic naturalism. Consider the following account from the Associated Press:

> A British philosophy professor who has been a leading champion of atheism for more than 50 years has changed his mind. Antony Flew, 81, [of Oxford University] said scientific evidence has now convinced him that a super-intelligence is the only explanation for the origin of life and the complexity of nature. . . . If his newfound belief upsets people, Flew said, "that's too bad"—but he's always been determined to "follow the evidence wherever it leads."[50]

Paul C. Davies (physics professor at Arizona State University) was also convinced by the evidence: "[There] is for me powerful evidence that there is something going on behind it all. . . . It seems

[47]Ronald Nash, *Faith and Reason* (Grand Rapids, MI: Zondervan, 1988), 142.

[48]Sharon Begley, "Science Finds God," *Newsweek*, July 20, 1998, 46–51.

[49]Such evidence has caused secular scientists such as astronomer Robert Jastrow to realize that the statistical probability of all the necessary factors for life occurring in the same place is infinitesimally small: "All these numbers are so small that, even when multiplied by the vast number of planets probably present in the universe, they force us to conclude that the Earth must be the only planet bearing life." Robert Jastrow, "What Are the Chances for Life?," review of *The Biological Universe* by Steven J. Dick (Cambridge: Cambridge University Press, 1996), in *Sky and Telescope* (June 1997), 62–63. Cited by Morris, *Their Own Words*, 47.

[50]"Leading Atheist Says Science Has Changed His Mind," Associated Press, December 10, 2004. Cited from C. L. Cagan, *From Darwin to Design*, 23.

as though somebody has fine-tuned nature's numbers to make the Universe. . . . The impression of design is overwhelming."[51] The makeup of our universe and our world, as well as the life that inhabits it, provides compelling evidence that we are not here by accident.[52]

[51]Paul C. Davies, *The Cosmic Blueprint: New Discoveries in Nature's Creative Ability to Order the Universe* (New York: Simon & Schuster, 1988), 203. Cited from John Ankerberg and John Weldon, *Fast Facts*, 24.
[52]In the words of naturalist philosopher David Hume: "A purpose, an intention, or design strikes everywhere the most careless, the most stupid thinker; and no man can be so hardened in absurd systems, as at all times to reject it." Cited from *The New Encyclopedia of Christian Quotations*, ed. Mark Water (Grand Rapids, MI: Baker, 2000), 408.

Reason 4:
We Believe in God

Because the Continuation of the Universe Points to a Sustainer

The Bible explains that God not only created the universe and the life therein, He is also the One who keeps it going, for "he himself gives to all mankind life and breath and everything" (Acts 17:25; cf. 1 Timothy 6:13). In fact, "he upholds the universe by the word of his power" (Hebrews 1:3). He established the laws of nature and set in motion the seasons and the tides (Jeremiah 5:22–24). He not only created the stars, He keeps track of each one of them (Isaiah 40:26). He set the earth in its orbit (Job 26:7) and faithfully ensures its rotation (Psalm 74:16–17). He causes the grass and trees to grow (Psalm 104:14), provides shelter and food for the animals (Psalm 104:16–18, 27–30), and even determines the rise, fall, and boundaries of the nations (Acts 17:26). From the weather to the stars to animals and people, God continually oversees every detail of His creation (cf. Matthew 10:30).

In this sense, God is not only the creator and designer of the universe, He is also the foundation upon which our universe rests. "God is the necessary condition of the world in two senses," explains Christian philosopher Ronald Nash. "(1) Had God not created the world in the first place, it would never have come into existence; and (2) should God ever will to withdraw his sustaining power, the world would cease to exist."[53] If there were no God, then there would be no explanation for why the universe and everything in it continues as it does.

Why does everything in our universe hold together? Why does it keep working? Why doesn't it fall apart, explode, or simply stop? These are questions that random chance and natural selection are again unable to answer, even at the molecular level. Former Stanford physicist Lambert Dolphin notes, "The nucleus of the atom contains positively-charged and neutral particles—to use a simplistic model.

---

[53]Nash, *Faith and Reason*, 125.

Mutual electrostatic repulsion between the like-positive protons would drive the nucleus apart if it were not for the 'strong force' which binds the nucleus together."[54] Since physicists cannot adequately explain this "strong force," Dolphin believes there is only one way to account for it: "God is behind the mysterious strong force that holds every atomic nucleus together"[55] (cf. Colossians 1:17; 2 Peter 3:10).

In fact, the Bible associates the power behind everything in our universe, from the atomic to the galactic, with God's creative and sustaining work. At creation God spoke the universe into existence. Since then, He continues to uphold it, and He does this in a personal and intimate way.

Though He created everything perfectly, the Bible explains that shortly thereafter mankind rebelled against God, which brought about a curse on the whole of creation (Genesis 3:14–19; Romans 5:12; 8:20–22). Because of that curse, the universe is slowly winding down— a fact that scientists explain by the Second Law of Thermodynamics (the law of increasing entropy, that everything in the universe tends toward death and disorder). Amazingly, even this points to God, especially when it is seen in concert with the First Law of Thermodynamics (the law of conservation, that the total energy of the universe remains constant). Creation scientist Henry Morris explains why this is:

> Now, since it [the universe] has not yet died, it must not be infinitely old, and therefore it must have had a beginning. As time goes on, the available power [in the universe] decreases (by the Second Law) even though the total power in the universe remains constant (by the First Law). Therefore the source of the tremendous power manifest throughout the universe must be outside and above the universe. It cannot be temporal power; it must be *eternal* power. The universe had a beginning, brought about by a great First Cause, a Prime Mover, an omnipotent God! The basic laws of the universe thus witness with great power to the fact of God.[56]

The atheist, on the other hand, is left with yet more unanswered questions. "Where did it all start?" asks the renowned biochemist Isaac

---

[54]Lambert Dolphin, "What Holds the Universe Together?" Article online at http://www.ldolphin. org/cohere.shtml. Accessed February 4, 2007. Dolphin worked for thirty years as a physicist at Stanford Research Institute (eventually renamed SRI International).
[55]Ibid.
[56]Henry Morris, *Many Infallible Proofs* (San Diego: Creation-Life Publishers, 1974), 107–108.

Asimov. "If the universe is running down into utter disorder, what made it orderly to begin with? Where did the order come from that it is steadily losing? What set up the extremes that are steadily being chipped away?"[57] Ironically, the answers to such modern queries are found in the first few chapters of Genesis, a book written almost 3,500 years ago.

The cycles of nature, and the laws that undergird those cycles, all point to the sustaining power of the Creator. And the evidence is not just around you, it is *in* you as well. God has done more than program your DNA and walk away. He sustains every moment of your life. The fact that your heart continues to beat (at seventy-two beats per minute) and that your lungs continue to draw air (at between twelve and twenty breaths per minute), that your brain continues to work (with its complex network of a hundred billion neurons) is all testimony to the sustaining power of the One who made you. Hence our lives, along with the continuation of everything else in our universe, from the vastest galaxy to the smallest atomic particle, bear witness to the upholding work of God. From the infinitely large to the infinitely small, the testimony of the sustaining power of God is clearly manifest and undeniably evident.

---

[57]Isaac Asimov, "In the Game of Energy and Thermodynamics You Can't Even Break Even," *Smithsonian Institute Journal* (June 1970), 10–11. Cited in Morris, *Their Own Words*, 66.

Reason 5:
We Believe in God

Because the Human Sense of Morality Points to a Lawgiver

God has not only given human beings the ability to think and reason, He has also created each of us with an intrinsic awareness of right and wrong. The Bible refers to this awareness as *conscience*. Because men and women have consciences, we are not just rational beings. We are also moral beings.

The book of Romans describes the conscience as "the work of the law [that] is written on [people's] hearts" (2:15) because "what can be known about God is plain to them" (Romans 1:19; cf. 1:32). Along with the created world *around* us (which points to God as the Creator, Sustainer, and Designer), the conscience *within* us reveals that there is a higher moral order, of which God is both the Standard and the Judge (Ecclesiastes 12:14). As a result, "there is built into every man the deep awareness that love and justice and holiness constitute a higher order of reality than do hate and injustice and wickedness. Even men who do not believe in a God of love and righteousness at all seem to be continually troubled at the hatred and cruelty that abound in the world."[58]

Some may argue that our awareness of God's moral law is simply the product of our Western, Judeo-Christian society; that the guilt we feel (when we violate this law) has less to do with a transcendent moral code and more to do with the cultural rules and regulations that have characterized Western thought since medieval times. But such protests cannot explain away the conscience since, as apologist Paul Little explains, "there is a surprising consensus from civilization to civilization about what is moral decency. And we all do agree some moralities are better than others."[59] God's moral law is universal, and its awareness has been built into all of us. We naturally understand that it is wrong to steal, lie, and murder (Exodus 20:13–17) and that it is right

---

[58]Henry Morris, *Many Infallible Proofs*, 105.
[59]Paul Little, *Know Why You Believe*, 32.

to show love and kindness (Mark 12:31). In the words of C. S. Lewis, "If no set of moral ideas were truer or better than any other, there would be no sense in preferring civilized morality to savage morality, or Christian morality to Nazi morality."[60]

Biblical Christianity not only articulates the common ethical standards that transcend culture, it also explains the origins of mankind's moral awareness. It "helps make sense out of how [our] moral faculties could have come about in the first place," notes Christian philosopher J. P. Moreland. "How is it that humans can have intuitional insight into the nature of morality? God has created us to know moral values."[61]

It is true, of course, that our consciences are affected by the knowledge they receive. The Bible explains that they can malfunction if not given the right information or if ignored for too long (1 Corinthians 8:7; 1 Timothy 4:2; Titus 1:15). Nonetheless, at its core, the conscience bears witness to the fact that deep within ourselves we know some things are right and other things are wrong. Such moral cognizance cannot be adequately explained in purely biological terms. If "survival of the fittest" were all that mattered, who could say that the Nazis were wrong?[62]

At this point, some may ask, "But how can God exist when there is so much evil in this world?"[63] The Bible answers that question by pointing to sin and the resulting curse (Genesis 3:14–19; Romans 5:12). Much of the evil and suffering in our world is the immediate result of sinful actions, as people do and say things that wrongfully inflict pain on those around them (cf. Galatians 5:19–21), while other forms of "evil," such as natural disasters and diseases, are part of what it means to live in a sin-stained world under the judgment of a righteous God (cf. Luke 13:2–5). Though we do see evil and injustice in this world, the Bible teaches that God will one day create new heavens and a new earth free from any sin or curse (Revelation 21:4; 22:3).

But, coming back to the question itself (*how can God exist when*

---

[60]C. S. Lewis, *Mere Christianity* (New York: Macmillan, 1960), 25.

[61]J. P. Moreland, "Ethics Depend on God," 111–126, in *Does God Exist?*, a debate between J. P. Moreland and Kai Nielsen (Nashville: Thomas Nelson, 1990), 119.

[62]Sir Arthur Keith, in *Evolution and Ethics* (New York: G.P. Putnam's Sons, 1947) directly linked the Nazi regime to Darwin's theories: "The German Fuhrer, as I have consistently maintained, is an evolutionist; he has consciously sought to make the practice of Germany conform to the theory of evolution" (230). Cited from Morris, *Their Own Words*, 427.

[63]Many Christian works have been written on the "problem" of evil in a world created by a good God. For those interested, Brian Morley's *God in the Shadows* (Ross-shire, Scotland: Christian Focus, 2006) is a helpful introduction to the topic.

there is so much evil in this world?), it should be noted that such a question presupposes the existence of God. *Evil* cannot exist unless there is also a standard of *good*. Something cannot be *wrong* unless it violates what we know to be *right*. Deep in our hearts we understand when something is unrighteous or unjust—it offends us, saddens us, and causes us to cry out for justice. We rejoice when good triumphs over evil, and we feel violated when it does not.

According to the Bible, that inner awareness was built into us by God, and it points us back to Him as the ultimate Lawgiver and Judge. As Ronald Nash explains, "God is the ground of the laws that govern the physical universe and that make possible the order of the cosmos. God is also the ground of the moral laws that ought to govern human behavior and that make possible order (or peace) between humans and within humans."[64] Our innate understanding of right and wrong (on a personal level), as well as our society's general concern with preserving and protecting justice (on a collective level), both point to something (or more accurately Someone) for which naturalism cannot account.

When renowned geneticist Francis Collins, head of the Human Genome Project, came to realize these truths about God's moral law, his naturalistic presuppositions were shattered. Reflecting on his departure from atheism, he writes:

> I had started this journey of intellectual exploration to confirm my atheism. That now lay in ruins as the argument from the Moral Law (and many other issues) forced me to admit the plausibility of the God hypothesis. Agnosticism, which had seemed like a safe second-place haven, now loomed like the great cop-out it often is. Faith in God now seemed more rational than disbelief.[65]

Later he concludes:

> After twenty-eight years as a believer, the Moral Law still stands out for me as the strongest signpost to God. More than that, it points to a God who cares about human beings, and a God who is infinitely good and holy.[66]

---

[64]Nash, *Faith and Reason*, 40.
[65]Francis S. Collins, *The Language of God* (New York: Free Press, 2006), 30.
[66]Ibid., 218.

Reason 6:
We Believe in God

Because Eternity Is Written on the Hearts of People

In addition to an innate moral awareness, God has also placed a sense of the eternal within us. Human beings, unlike animals, are able to contemplate not only their day-to-day existence but also the very concepts of time, history, and eternity. That is because God "has put eternity into man's heart" (Ecclesiastes 3:11).

Eternity is a recurring theme in Scripture. God alone is eternal (Psalm 93:2), having always existed, without beginning and without end (Psalm 90:2). Human beings, on the other hand, are mortal (Psalm 90:10)—our lives start at birth and end physically at death, when our bodies are no longer able to sustain life. Physical death, however, is not the end of our existence (cf. 2 Corinthians 5:8). Because God created us with a soul, we will continue to live forever (Ecclesiastes 12:5; Matthew 10:28). In fact, the Bible says that one day God will give us new resurrected bodies that, unlike our bodies now, will last eternally (John 5:29; 1 Corinthians 15:35–49).

After death, human beings go to one of two places, depending on how they respond in this life to Jesus Christ (Hebrews 9:27–28). Those who embrace Christ in saving faith will live forever in the joyful presence of God. They stand forgiven because the penalty for their sin is covered by Christ's sacrifice on the cross (Romans 6:23; Colossians 1:20). But those who have rejected Jesus Christ will face the never-ending consequences of their sin (cf. Matthew 25:46). Having rebelled against an eternal God, and having refused His offer of salvation, they will receive the eternal punishment they rightly deserve (Revelation 20:11–15).

Instead of trying to prove that eternity exists and that life after death is a reality, the Bible presupposes that men already know this. It is part of the fabric of their being. Of course, in recent times some have tried to deny a belief in any such afterlife. But they represent the vast minority. In every age and in every culture, belief in life after death pervades the human race. As Christian author Morris Inch observes:

> What would it mean to live forever? One of the most persisting beliefs of humankind from antiquity has been with regard to an afterlife. Artifacts found buried with the departed were meant to equip them for the life to come. The Egyptians succeeded in preserving the deceased's body to accommodate future life. Ancient texts describe in vivid detail events thought to transpire once one had passed on. There has been a near universal hope, even if not confidence, that life survives death.[67]

This remains true in the United States, in spite of being heavily influenced by atheistic naturalism, where recent statistics show that over 80 percent of people openly admit they believe in an afterlife of some sort.[68] Even in societies where Christianity or other "mainstream" religions have been historically absent, belief in the eternal persists. "Anthropological research has indicated there is a universal belief in God among the most remote peoples today," explains Paul Little.[69] While such universal testimony does not ultimately *prove* the existence of God, it certainly corresponds to what the Bible says (cf. Romans 1:19–20). The dying words of even some noted atheists underscore this point. One such individual, Sir Thomas Scott, reportedly exclaimed on his deathbed, "Until this moment I thought there was neither a God nor a hell. Now I know and feel that there are both, and I am doomed to perdition by the just judgment of the Almighty."[70]

If eternity is indeed written on the hearts of men, we would expect the great majority of human beings (throughout history and from every culture) to recognize and affirm that belief. When we survey the data, that is exactly what we find.

---

[67]Morris Inch, *A Case for Christianity* (Wheaton, IL: Tyndale House, 1997), 75.
[68]Based on statistics derived from the Barna Research Group (www.barna.org/FlexPage.aspx?Page=BarnaUpdate&BarnaUpdateID150).
[69]Paul E. Little, *Know Why You Believe*, 23.
[70]Sir Thomas Scott, cited from John W. Lawrence, *The Seven Laws of the Harvest* (Grand Rapids, MI: Kregel, 2003), 56. On 54–57, Lawrence gives the dying words of ten well-known atheists (including Scott) who confessed their belief in God.

Reason 7:
We Believe in God

Because Life Without God Is Ultimately Meaningless

A month before he died, the famous atheist and existential philosopher Jean-Paul Sartre made an astounding admission: "Despair returns to tempt me again. . . . The world seems ugly, bad, and without hope. There, that's the cry of despair of an old man who will die in despair. But that's exactly what I resist. I know I shall die in hope. But that hope needs a foundation."[71] A few years earlier, Sartre had written, "I do not feel that I am the product of chance, a speck of dust in the universe, but someone who was expected, prepared, prefigured. In short, a being whom only a Creator could put here; and this idea of a creating hand refers to God."[72]

Though he remained an atheist to the end of his life, Sartre's words underscore the hopelessness of the atheistic worldview. In a world without God, men and women are nothing more than the biological results of random mutations and naturalistic chance. In the grand scheme of things, individual lives have no ultimate purpose or significance. People are simply highly-evolved protoplasm with legs and brains—here today and gone tomorrow.

The biblical view of human life could not be more opposite. As the caretakers of God's creation (Genesis 2:15), human beings were created to love God (Mark 12:30) and live for Him (1 Corinthians 8:6), enjoying fellowship with Him forever (Revelation 22:3–4). In a world marred by sin, God still gives men and women the opportunity to be in a right relationship with Him—to be reconciled through His Son Jesus Christ (2 Corinthians 5:18–21; 1 John 4:13–17). By trusting in Christ and His work on the cross, they can be forgiven and restored to God (Romans 10:9–10).

[71]Jean-Paul Sartre, "Today's Hope," 180–181, cited from Martin Jay, *Marxism and Totality* (Berkeley, CA: University of California Press, 1986), 360.
[72]Sartre cited in Norman L. Geisler, *Is Man the Measure? An Evaluation of Contemporary Humanism* (Grand Rapids, MI: Baker, 1983), 46–47.

At conversion, God gives believers new hearts, with new desires and new purposes (Colossians 3:10; Titus 3:5–6). They yearn to glorify God in everything they do (1 Corinthians 10:31), to obey Him out of their love for Him (John 14:15), and to love other people as a testimony of His grace (John 13:34–35). Pleasing God, then, becomes their greatest aim (2 Corinthians 5:9). Because they love Him more than anything else, Christians find worshiping and serving God to be a profound joy.

All of the other pursuits and purposes of this life are empty without God. The search for satisfaction apart from Him will always end in disappointment. Consider King Solomon, the wealthiest, most successful, most famous, and most powerful person of his day (1 Kings 10:23–25). He had endless resources at his disposal; yet his pursuit of happiness proved utterly futile. Though he tried to find satisfaction in things like romance, accomplishment, alcohol, material possessions, and even wisdom, Solomon finally realized that life without God is vanity (Ecclesiastes 2:1–11, 25; 12:13–14).

Other wealthy, famous, and powerful individuals throughout history have come to understand the same hard lessons that Solomon learned. "Millionaires seldom smile," said Andrew Carnegie;[73] and elsewhere, "Wealth lessens rather than increases human happiness. Millionaires who laugh are rare."[74] William Vanderbilt's comment was, "The care of 200 million dollars is too great a load for any brain or back to bear. It is enough to kill anyone. There is no pleasure in it."[75] Henry Ford concluded, "I was happier when doing a mechanic's job,"[76] and John D. Rockefeller admitted, "I have made many millions, but they have brought me no happiness. I would barter them all for the days I sat on an office stool in Cleveland and counted myself rich on three dollars a week."[77] Benjamin Franklin had it right when he said,

---

[73]Andrew Carnegie, cited from Bob Kelly, *Worth Repeating: More Than 5000 Classic and Contemporary Quotes* (Grand Rapids, MI: Kregel, 2003), 229.

[74]Andrew Carnegie, cited from "Andrew Carnegie at 80," *The New York Times*, November 21, 1915. This article can be accessed online in the archives section of *The New York Times* web site (http://nytimes.com/mem/archive-free/pdf?_r=1&res=9B01E5DB153BE233A25752C2A9679D04 6496D6CF&oref=slogin).

[75]William Vanderbilt, cited from James Burnley, *Millionaires and Kings of Enterprise* (Philadelphia: J. B. Lippincott, 1901), 500.

[76]Henry Ford and John D. Rockefeller, cited from Randy Alcorn, *Money, Possessions & Eternity* (Wheaton, IL: Tyndale House, 2003), 47.

[77]John D. Rockefeller, cited from *The Speaker's Quote Book*, comp. Roy B. Zuck (Grand Rapids, MI: Kregel, 1997), 260.

"Money never made a man happy yet, nor will it. There is nothing in its nature to produce happiness. The more a man has, the more he wants. Instead of it filling a vacuum, it makes one. If it satisfied one want, it doubles and trebles that want another way. That was a true proverb of the wise man; rely upon it: 'Better a little with the fear of the Lord, than great treasure, and trouble therewith.'"[78]

Echoing the words of Franklin, Christian theologian Cornelius Plantinga explains what the rich and famous of our world often learn the hard way:

> The truth is that nothing in this earth can finally satisfy us. Much can make us content for a time, but nothing can fill us to the brim. The reason is that our final joy lies "beyond the walls of the world," as J. R. R. Tolkien put it. Ultimate beauty comes not *from* a lover or a landscape or a home, but only *through* them. These earthly things are solid goods, and we naturally relish them. But they are not our final good. They point to what is "higher up" and "further back."[79]

In other words, they point to God. As the famous church father Augustine prayed, "O Lord, you have made us for yourself, and our heart is restless until it rests in you."[80]

God created us for a purpose. When we deny His existence, we simultaneously deny the purpose for which He created us. Thus, to deny God is to embrace despair and hopelessness. On the flip side, to embrace God is to discover the source of hope, satisfaction, purpose, and fulfillment (cf. Acts 14:17).

At a more foundational level, even the very idea of *meaning* bears witness to God. The existence of logic, and the universal rules that apply to it, is evidence of a divine Logos. The laws of math, science, aesthetics, and ethics, and the fact that there are elements of universal consistency among these and other disciplines, all point to a transcendent intelligence that makes such uniformity possible. It is not enough to say, "My life would be meaningless without God." We must also conclude, "All life, and even life itself and everything that comprises life, becomes meaningless without God." Even circumstances that may

---

[78]Benjamin Franklin, cited from *Treasury of Wisdom, Wit and Humor, Odd Comparisons and Proverbs*, comp. Adam Wooléver (D. McKay, 1891), 72.
[79]Cornelius Plantinga, Jr., *Engaging God's World* (Grand Rapids, MI: Eerdmans, 2002), 6.
[80]Augustine, *Confessions*, trans. Henry Chadwick (New York: Oxford, 1992), 145 (8.7.17); 3 (1.1.1). Cited from Cornelius Plantinga, *Engaging God's World*, 6.

seem random to us do so only because they contrast with the order and design we constantly observe. "The only reason the sorrow and tragedy stand out is because there is also much joy and gladness. The only reason we recognize the ugliness is that God has given us so much beauty. The only reason we feel the disappointment is that there is so much that satisfies."[81]

We could not even have a logical discussion about the existence of God (or about any other topic) if God did not exist. To do so presupposes that laws of logic exist. But if all is a product of random chance, then there is no rhyme or reason to our existence; there are no laws of logic or reason unless something greater than chance is at work.

In fact, it is God who is at work. He created us to love and worship Him. That is our purpose. And we will never find true fulfillment or joy apart from pursuing Him. French philosopher Blaise Pascal was exactly right when he observed, "There is a God shaped vacuum in the heart of every man which cannot be filled by any created thing, but only by God, the Creator, made known through Jesus."[82]

[81]John MacArthur, *The God Who Loves* (Nashville: Thomas Nelson, 2003), 118.
[82]Blaise Pascal, cited from *The New Encyclopedia of Christian Quotations*, comp. Mark Water (Grand Rapids, MI: Baker, 2000), 407.

Reason 8:
We Believe in God

*Because the Flow of Human History Conforms to
a Divine Plan*

The Bible not only presents each individual with his or her
God-given purpose, it also underscores the fact that God has an overarching purpose for all of human history. It really is *His story*, in the sense
that everything is working according to His plans. Psalm 135:6 states,
"Whatever the LORD pleases, he does, in heaven and on earth, in the seas
and all deeps" (cf. Psalm 115:3). Nothing can thwart His purposes (Job
42:2). Thus He declares, "There is none who can deliver from my hand; I
work, and who can turn it back?" (Isaiah 43:13). And again, "Remember
the former things of old; for I am God, and there is no other; I am God,
and there is none like me, declaring the end from the beginning and from
ancient times things not yet done, saying, 'My counsel shall stand, and I
will accomplish all my purpose'" (Isaiah 46:9–10). He is the one who has
appointed the times and boundaries of all nations (Acts 17:26); and He is
orchestrating all of human history for His eternal glory.

God's sovereign working in history is most clearly seen in fulfilled
prophecy. The tremendous "success" of biblical prophecy cannot
be explained as simple luck. The only adequate explanation is that
Someone is actively fulfilling biblical predictions. Biblical prophecy
is 100 percent accurate, not by happenstance, but because God is
orchestrating the events of human history to fit His plan perfectly. We
will look at biblical prophecy more in upcoming sections, but for now
consider just a handful of fulfillments.

The Old Testament foretold numerous historical events, including
the fall of Tyre (Ezekiel 26:3–14), the Babylonian captivity and return
of Israel (Jeremiah 29:10–14), the rise of King Cyrus (Isaiah 45:1–7),
the destruction of Nineveh (Nahum 1:10; 2:8–13; 3:17–19), and the
rise and fall of Babylon, Persia, Greece, and Rome (Daniel 2:39–40;

7:17–24). Time after time, these and other biblical prophecies have been confirmed by modern archaeology. "The prophets of the Old Testament, and Jesus in the New, pronounced [prophetic] judgments that the archaeologist's spade has revealed were fulfilled," affirms archaeologist Randall Price.[83] Not including messianic prophecies, the Bible contains nearly two thousand prophecies concerning almost every nation within a thousand miles of Israel (such as Egypt, Ethiopia, Philistia, and the other nations listed above). Some of these prophecies will yet take place in the future, but many of them have already been literally fulfilled in history.[84] (See Section 3 for more on archaeology's confirmation of the Bible.)

When it comes to the many messianic prophecies in the Old Testament, the evidence is equally compelling. Long before Jesus was born, the prophets predicted that He would be a descendant of Abraham (Genesis 22:18; cf. Galatians 3:16), from the tribe of Judah (Genesis 49:10), from the line of David (Psalm 110:1). They named the place of His birth (Micah 5:2) and also described the violent nature of His death (Psalm 22:16–18; Isaiah 53:5–8). "Hundreds of other details were predicted in minute detail," explains Christian apologist Hank Hanegraaff. "These prophecies do not deal with vague generalities (as is so often the case with modern-day 'prophets' and psychics); they are specific and verifiable. Each was literally fulfilled down to the smallest detail in the person of Jesus Christ."[85] It has been calculated that the chance of only forty-eight prophecies coming true in one person is 10 to the 157th power, making it a statistical impossibility.[86] Yet Jesus fulfilled many more than that. Even the timing of His coming was accurately foretold by the prophet Daniel half a millennium before

---

[83]Randall Price, *The Stones Cry Out* (Eugene, OR: Harvest House, 1997), 252. The author discusses prophecies about Cyrus, Nineveh, Tyre, and the Temple Mount as examples of those that have been confirmed by archaeology. He adds, "The same is true for prophecies made against many other ancient sites such as Babylon, Memphis, Thebes, Moab-Ammon, and Petra (Edom)" (255).

[84]For an assessment of the critical response to biblical prophecy, see Robert C. Newman, "Fulfilled Prophecy as Miracle," 214–225, in *In Defense of Miracles*, ed. Douglas Geivett and Gary R. Habermas (Downers Grove, IL: InterVarsity Press, 1997). On 224–225 Newman concludes, "Even when critical scholarship has done its best to redate Old Testament texts so as to avoid fulfilled prophecy, the constraints provided by the translation of the Old Testament into Greek (250–150 B.C.) and the rise of the Christian church leave a substantial residue of clear examples [of fulfilled prophecies]."

[85]Hank Hanegraaff, "Fulfilled Prophecy as an Apologetic," Christian Research Institute, Statement DA151 (January 30, 2007); http://www.equip.org/site/c.muI1LaMNJrE/b.2711713/k.AD9B/DA151.htm.

[86]John Ankerberg with John Weldon and Walter Kaiser, *The Case for Jesus the Messiah* (Eugene, OR: Harvest House, 1989), 21.

Jesus was born (Daniel 9:24–27).[87] (For more on messianic prophecies, see Sections 4–5.)

Since the life of Christ, other prophecies have also been fulfilled, including the destruction of the temple and of Jerusalem by the Romans (Daniel 9:26; cf. Luke 21:6, 24), the dispersion of the Jews among the nations (Deuteronomy 28:64; cf. Ezekiel 22:14–15; Hosea 9:17), the persecution of the Jews throughout much of history (Deuteronomy 28:65–67), and the subsequent return of Israel to the land (Ezekiel 20:34; Hosea 3:4–5; Amos 9:14–15; cf. Isaiah 11:11). Nearly two millennia after Rome destroyed Jerusalem, the Jews again established a nation in the Promised Land in 1948. Commenting on Israel's recent history, Jewish-Christian scholar Arnold Fruchtenbaum notes, "The restoration of the Jewish State is a fulfillment of those prophecies that spoke of a regathering [of the nation] in unbelief in preparation for judgment"[88] (cf. Ezekiel 22:17–22; 36:22–24; Zephaniah 2:1–2). Thus, evangelical theologian John F. Walvoord concludes:

> The fact is that the world as a whole has recognized Israel as a political state and has assigned her certain territories in the Middle East. The people of Israel are very conscious of their lineage, their history, their religion, and their culture, and all of this combines to make the nation Israel what it is today. Up to the present time a literal fulfillment of the promises given to Abraham has been clearly confirmed by history.[89]

The very preservation of the Jewish people, along with the reestablishment of their nation, corresponds exactly with what the Bible has foretold.

All of this is in keeping with God's divine purpose and timetable. History is not the sum of chance events, chaotically ordered in random sequence. It is instead the outworking of a pre-designed and deliberate plan. God is at work in history. Biblical prophecy is but one evidence that His sovereign purposes are being realized.

---

[87]Stephen R. Miller, *Daniel*, New American Commentary (Nashville: Broadman & Holman, 1994), 265–266 has a helpful discussion of the various evangelical views of Daniel 9:25. This author prefers the views of Harold Hoehner, "Daniel's Seventy Weeks and New Testament Chronology," 171–186, in *Vital Old Testament Issues*, ed. Roy B. Zuck (Grand Rapids, MI: Kregel, 1996).

[88]Arnold G. Fruchtenbaum, *The Footsteps of the Messiah* (San Antonio, TX: Ariel Press, 2003), 104. Fruchtenbaum converted to Christianity from Judaism at age thirteen.

[89]John F. Walvoord, *Major Bible Prophecies* (Grand Rapids, MI: Zondervan, 1991), 61.

Reason 9:
We Believe in God

Because Miraculous Events Confirm the Supernatural

The Bible unapologetically reports that God has, in certain instances, specially intervened in the natural world in a miraculous and supernatural way. Furthermore, the Bible presents these miracles as evidence that God exists and that He is actively involved in His creation. Thus, the true God has given testimony to Himself through His supernatural intervention at various points in history, such as during the Exodus (Deuteronomy 6:20–23; Psalm 78:40ff.; 105:25ff.), the events on Mount Carmel (1 Kings 18:20–40), and the ministry of Jesus (John 5:36; 10:38; cf. Acts 2:22). According to Scripture, such wondrous works are reason to recognize His power and worship Him (cf. Jeremiah 32:17–20; Psalm 77:13–14; 98:1; Isaiah 25:1).

Miracles are, by definition, events that are extraordinary and supernatural—they do not require natural explanations because if natural explanations sufficed, they would cease to be miracles. Thus they point to Someone outside of the natural realm. Though none of us were present for the miracles recorded in the Bible, we can accept them for several reasons.

First, because the Bible is the Word of God (a topic we will look at in the next section), its description of miraculous events can be accepted as true. Second, because Jesus is the Son of God (a topic we will look at in Section 5), His affirmation of supernatural events in the Old Testament can be trusted (e.g., Matthew 12:40; 19:4; 24:37). Third, eyewitness testimony confirms biblical miracles. In the words of Christian theologian William Shedd:

> The historical reality of a miracle is proved in the same manner that any historical event is proved, namely, by human testimony. Testimony is another man's memory. We trust our own memory as we trust our own senses, because memory is a remembered sensation

or consciousness. If therefore another person is honest and possesses as good senses as ourselves, there is no more reason for disbelieving his remembered sensations than for disbelieving our own. . . . It is the common human testimony, such as is accepted in a court of law, that is relied upon to establish the historical reality of a miracle.[90]

As we will see in Section 5, the human testimony confirming the miracles of Jesus is particularly strong, even being admitted by His enemies. We will also find, in Section 4, that the New Testament Gospels are accurate records of the life of Christ. Thus, because the Gospels demonstrate themselves to be historically reliable in all other matters, their testimony regarding Jesus' miracles can be fully trusted. After all, "the only way we in fact have of evaluating the reliability of a witness's testimony concerning extraordinary events is to evaluate the reliability of that witness's testimony concerning events that admit of external support." [91]

Fourth, the effect of many miracles can be seen in human history. The existence of our universe is the effect of God's miraculous creation (Genesis 1:1). The various language families point back to God's miraculous intervention at the Tower of Babel (Genesis 11:8–9). The presence of Old Testament Israel in the Promised Land bears witness to their miraculous exodus from Egypt (Exodus 15:11–19; Psalm 135:8–12). The sudden appearance of the church on the Day of Pentecost attests to Jesus' miraculous resurrection and the subsequent coming of the Holy Spirit (Acts 2:41, 47). Without such supernatural events, biblical history becomes meaningless.

> Take away the miraculous events of Genesis 1–2, for example, and the message about the Creator evaporates with it. Likewise, the story of Noah and his faithfulness to God in a day of violence and unbelief makes no sense apart from God's intervention to save him and destroy the world by a flood. And Israel's call of God and special deliverance from Egypt is meaningless apart from the supernatural intervention by which these things were accomplished. The same is true of the miracles of Elijah, Elisha, and Jonah. Each is an inseparable part of the very fabric of history they record.[92]

[90]William G. T. Shedd, *Dogmatic Theology*, 3 volumes in 1 (Phillipsburg, NJ: P&R Publishing, 2003), 128.
[91]Robert A. Larmer, "Miracles and Testimony: A Reply to Wiebe," 121–131, in *Questions of Miracle*, ed. Robert A. Larmer (Buffalo, NY: McGill-Queen's University Press, 1996), 123.
[92]Norman L. Geisler, *Miracles and the Modern Mind* (Grand Rapids, MI: Baker, 1992), 142.

Other examples could be added to this list. In more modern times, the establishment of the Jewish nation in 1948, in spite of the odds, testifies to the miraculous promise of God to once again establish the nation of Israel (Deuteronomy 30:3–5; Amos 9:14–15).

Fifth, the miracle of regeneration in the human heart has been the experience of every born-again Christian (John 3:3; Ephesians 2:1–5; Titus 3:3–7). As David Hume once antagonistically quipped, "The Christian religion not only was at first attended with miracles, but even at this day cannot be believed by any reasonable person without one."[93] Though he meant it pejoratively, Hume was exactly right. The regenerative work of the Holy Spirit in the heart of a sinner is nothing short of a miracle (John 3:1–8). When that sinner's life is transformed from rebellion to righteousness, God's miraculous work of salvation is vividly put on display (Romans 6:17–18; 2 Corinthians 5:17).[94]

Finally, it should be noted that the miraculous events of Christianity are unique to it, because they are central to it. Boston College professor Peter Kreeft makes this important point:

> In fact, all the essential and distinctive elements of Christianity are miracles: creation, revelation (first to the Jews), the giving of the law, prophecies, the Incarnation, the Resurrection, the Ascension and the Second Coming and Last Judgment.
>
> Subtract miracles from Islam, Buddhism, Confucianism, or Taoism, and you have essentially the same religion left. Subtract miracles from Christianity, and you have nothing but the clichés and platitudes most American Christians get weekly (and weakly) from their pulpits.[95]

Miracles, then, provide additional support for the fact that God exists and that He is actively involved in our world and our lives.

---

[93]David Hume, cited from *The Encyclopedia of Christian Quotations*, comp. Mark Water (Grand Rapids, MI: Baker, 2000), 193. David Hume was admittedly an opponent of biblical miracles. For a critique of Hume's views, see C. John Collins, *The God of Miracles* (Wheaton, IL: Crossway Books, 2000), 147–151.

[94]Along these lines, we do not disagree with Stephen T. Davis, *God, Reason, & Theistic Proofs* (Grand Rapids, MI: Eerdmans, 1997), 192–193 who states, "[T]he reason I am a theist has almost nothing to do with theistic proofs." Instead it has to do with the fact that God has worked a miracle in our hearts, having revealed Himself in His Word and made Himself personally known to us through His Holy Spirit.

[95]Peter Kreeft, *Christianity for Modern Pagans* (San Francisco: Ignatius Press, 1993), 273. Cited from Josh McDowell, *The New Evidence That Demands a Verdict* (Nashville: Thomas Nelson, 1999), 358.

Reason 10:
We Believe in God

Because Other Belief Systems Are Inadequate Alternatives

A final reason we believe in the God of the Bible is because it is folly to believe otherwise. As David rightly declared, "The fool says in his heart, 'There is no God.' They are corrupt, doing abominable iniquity; there is none who does good" (Psalm 53:1; cf. Psalm 10:4; 14:1). Later in the Psalms, Asaph expressed similar thoughts: "Remember this, O LORD, how the enemy scoffs, and a foolish people reviles your name" (Psalm 74:18). Those who deny the true God (whether they serve false gods or deny the existence of God altogether) are those who walk in darkness (Acts 26:18; Ephesians 5:8). They are "foolish," as Paul described them in Romans 1:31. "Since they did not see fit to acknowledge God, God gave them up to a debased mind" (Romans 1:28). Moreover, they are under God's wrath for their disobedience (Romans 1:18; Ephesians 5:6; Colossians 3:6). Their folly will lead them to destruction, for "there is a way that seems right to a man, but its end is the way to death" (Proverbs 14:12; cf. 16:25).

On the other hand, true wisdom begins with belief in the true God. "The fear of the LORD is the beginning of knowledge," wrote Solomon in Proverbs 1:7. Later he reiterated this point: "The fear of the LORD is the beginning of wisdom, and the knowledge of the Holy One is insight" (Proverbs 9:10). That is not to say that non-Christians cannot know anything (in terms of collecting information), but they will never understand the real purpose and meaning of life. The sad reality is that though they profess to be wise, they are really playing the part of the fool (Romans 1:21–23). They think they can find happiness and success without acknowledging the Creator, but they will ultimately find that their pursuits are empty without Him (Ecclesiastes 2:1–11, 24–26; 12:13–14).

The Bible clearly asserts that God exists, that He is one

(Deuteronomy 6:4), and that He is personal. All other supposed "gods" are nothing more than non-existent, demonic figments of the imagination (Psalm 115:4–8; 135:5–18; cf. 1 Timothy 4:1). This, of course, directly contrasts with the philosophical tenets of atheism (that God does not exist), polytheism (that there are many gods), and pantheism (that "god" is an impersonal force, synonymous with the universe).

The true God is incomparable and stands apart from any other supposed deity. At the end of his study of comparative religions, theology professor Robert Lightner concludes:

> The God of the Bible is altogether unique and separate from all other gods. As the one true and only God, He has manifested Himself in three separate and distinct divine Persons. The God of the Bible is infinite and eternal. He is the Creator and the Sustainer of humanity and all things. His knowledge and power are limitless, and His love is boundless and measureless. The goodness, glory, and grace of the God of the Bible are fathomless; these virtues are beyond description or comparison.[96]

We have discussed naturalistic atheism to some extent in this section, showing that it runs contrary to everything that creation reveals about itself (cf. Psalm 19:1–6; Acts 14:17). In fact, "the evidence is so strong for intelligence and against naturalism that [some] prominent evolutionists have actually suggested aliens deposited the first life here."[97] But it takes more faith to believe that than to believe in God, which again underscores the point that faith is at the heart of the atheistic worldview. "The atheist and the Christian believe very different things about whether there is a God," observes Oxford theology professor Alister McGrath, a former atheist. "But they both take their positions as a matter of faith."[98]

Because naturalists necessarily *believe* that our universe and the life therein spontaneously generated from nothing, "it turns out that faith

---

[96]Robert Lightner, *The God of the Bible and Other Gods* (Grand Rapids, MI: Kregel, 1998), 173.

[97]Norman Geisler and Frank Turek, *I Don't Have Enough Faith*, 121. The authors add this point: "Fred Hoyle . . . invented this far-out theory (called "panspermia," for "seeds everywhere") after calculating that the probability of life arising by spontaneous generation was effectively zero. Of course, panspermia doesn't solve the problem—it simply puts it off another step: who made the intelligent aliens?"

[98]Alister E. McGrath, *What Was God Doing on the Cross?* (Grand Rapids, MI: Zondervan, 1992), 92.

in naturalistic evolution is tantamount to faith in the miraculous."[99] And that is only one of the many ironic inconsistencies the atheist must face. As Douglas Wilson pointed out to atheist Christopher Hitchens, there are "two fundamental tenets of *true* atheism. One: There is no God. Two: I hate Him."[100]

Polytheistic and pantheistic religions are equally unreasonable. The order of the universe and the design of life cannot be explained as the result of competing deities. To quote again from creation scientist Henry Morris:

> The universe is not a "multiverse." Its intrinsic unity as a vast and glorious space-mass-time "continuum" is explicable only in terms of a unified First Cause, not as a conglomerate of First Causes. The very notion of a vast assemblage of individual "gods" gathering together to apportion out their several segments of creative responsibility is its own refutation.[101]

Morris continues by noting that pantheism, "which identifies God with the universe, and is experienced primarily as animism," is also untenable because "a God who is essentially synonymous with the universe and its components could never be the *Cause* of the universe."[102]

Only the biblical identification of God as a monotheistic, personal deity is consistent with the testimony of creation (Psalm 96:5; Isaiah 40:18–26, Romans 1:20) and of the conscience (Romans 2:15).[103] Referring to the God of the Bible, Baylor University philosophy professor C. Stephen Evans notes, "Belief in God is genuinely coherent with all we know about ourselves and our universe. It contradicts no known facts and it makes sense of many things that would otherwise

---

[99]John Ankerberg and John Weldon, *Fast Facts*, 23. It should be noted that Ankerberg and Weldon are proponents of old-earth creationism, a point on which we would disagree. For articles defending the young-earth creationist position, from a scientific perspective, visit the Institute for Creation Research online at www.icr.org

[100]Douglas Wilson, "Is Christianity Good for the World?" Part 5. Posted May 25, 2007. Accessed September 17, 2007 from the online archives of *Christianity Today* (http://www.christianitytoday.com). Theologian Addison Leitch agrees: "Even an atheist has a hard time here. Unless he is carrying on his fight against absolute nothingness, and this makes us wonder about his zeal, then he must be marshalling his arguments against something he finds ingrained in himself and in others" (Addison Leitch, *Interpreting Basic Theology* [New York: Channel Press, 1961], 10–11).

[101]Henry Morris, *Many Infallible Proofs*, 104.

[102]Ibid.

[103]Other monotheistic religions (Islam specifically) will be addressed in Section 2, as we consider the reasons we believe that the Bible, not the Qur'an, is God's book.

be inexplicable."[104] The universe God made, the people He created in His own image, and the self-revelation He gave us in His Word all bear witness to the fact that He exists and that we can know Him.

Though some may deny that God exists, they do so in spite of the obvious. C. S. Lewis graphically described their futile attempts with these words: "A man can no more diminish God's glory by refusing to worship him than a lunatic can put out the sun by scribbling the word darkness on the walls of his cell."[105]

---

[104]C. Stephen Evans, *Quest for Faith*, 131. Cited from Nash, *Faith & Reason*, 284.
[105]C. S. Lewis, cited from *The New Encyclopedia of Christian Quotations*, 419.

REASONS WE BELIEVE IN THE BIBLE

PART ONE

The Bible Is the Word of God

In regard to this Great Book, I have but to say, I believe the Bible is the best gift "God has given to man." All the good the Savior gave to the world was communicated through this "Book." All things most desirable for man's welfare, here and hereafter, are to be found portrayed in it.

ABRAHAM LINCOLN[1]

He that shall collect all the moral rules of the philosophers and compare them with those contained in the New Testament will find them to come short of the morality delivered by our Saviour and taught by His disciples: a college made up of ignorant but inspired fishermen.

JOHN LOCKE[2]

---

[1]Abraham Lincoln, cited from Don Hawkinson, *Character for Life: An American Heritage* (Green Forest, AZ: New Leaf Press, 2005), 103.
[2]John Locke, *The Works of John Locke* (London: C. Baldwin, 1824), 6:140.

INTRODUCTION

Christianity, if false, is of no importance and if true, of infinite importance," noted the famed Oxford professor C. S. Lewis. "The only thing it cannot be is moderately important."[3] Though spoken of the whole of Christian belief, those words certainly apply to the Bible, since "the foundation of our faith is a book."[4] As Christians, we stake not only our entire lives but also our eternity on the Scriptures. Why we believe the Bible, then, is a subject that deserves serious consideration.

Not everyone, of course, believes the Bible is God's Word. A quick visit to the "Celebrity Atheist List" web site demonstrates just how many of society's rich and famous reject God and the Bible.[5] Television host and comedian Bill Maher is one such example. In a June 2006 article from SlashFilm he quips, "I don't believe God is a single parent who writes books. I think that the people who think God wrote a book called The Bible are just childish." Actor Bruce Willis (in a July 1998 *George* magazine interview) shares similar sentiments:

> Organized religions in general, in my opinion, are dying forms. They were all very important when we didn't know why the sun moved, why weather changed, why hurricanes occurred, or volcanoes happened. Modern religion is the end trail of modern mythology. But there are people who interpret the Bible literally. Literally! I choose not to believe that's the way.

Sir Ian McKellen, who starred alongside Tom Hanks in *The Da Vinci Code* (the 2006 conspiracy-themed film by Columbia Pictures), revealed his views about the Bible during a May 17, 2006 appearance on the NBC *Today Show*. When asked if the film needed a disclaimer

---

[3]C. S. Lewis, cited from *The New Encyclopedia of Christian Quotations*, comp. Mark Water (Grand Rapids, MI: Baker, 2000), 193.
[4]Harry Rimmer, *Internal Evidence of Inspiration* (Grand Rapids, MI: Eerdmans, 1938), 17. Alan F. Johnson and Robert E. Webber, in *What Christians Believe* (Grand Rapids, MI: Zondervan, 1989), 17 add, "Christianity stands or falls with one's understanding of Scripture."
[5]The "Celebrity Atheist List" is online at www.celebatheists.com. The quotes from various celebrity atheists in this chapter were taken from this source. Accessed October 9, 2007.

noting it was fictional, as some religious groups had requested, McKellen responded, "Well, I've often thought the Bible should have a disclaimer in the front saying this is fiction. I mean, walking on water— it takes an act of faith. And I have faith in this movie. Not that it's true, not that it's factual, but that it's a jolly good story."

But does the Bible need such a disclaimer? Is it childish to believe it? In an increasingly skeptical world, believers must be ready to answer those kinds of questions, giving good reasons for the veracity of the Christian faith (1 Peter 3:15).

Over a century ago, a young man named Reuben A. Torrey found himself confronted with doubts about whether or not the Bible was true. His uncertainty launched him on a quest to investigate the teachings of the Bible, to see whether his childhood beliefs could hold up under critical scrutiny. Torrey would later recount his experience:

> I was brought up to believe that the Bible was the Word of God. In early life I accepted it as such upon the authority of my parents, and never gave the question any serious thought. But later in life my faith in the Bible was utterly shattered through the influence of the writings of a very celebrated, scholarly and brilliant skeptic. I found myself face to face with the question, *Why* do you believe the Bible is the Word of God?
>
> I had no satisfactory answer. I determined to go to the bottom of this question. If satisfactory proof could not be found that the Bible was God's Word I would give the whole thing up, cost what it might. If satisfactory proof could be found that the Bible was God's Word I would take my stand upon it, cost what it might. I doubtless had many friends who could have answered the question satisfactorily, but I was unwilling to confide to them the struggle that was going on in my own heart; so I sought help from God and from books, and after much painful study and thought came out of the darkness of skepticism into the broad daylight of faith and certainty that the Bible from beginning to end is God's Word.[6]

Torrey's investigation led him to the sure conclusion that the Bible was indeed what it claimed to be. Armed with God-given assurance, he would go on to become one of the leading evangelists and pastors of the early twentieth century.

---

[6]R. A. Torrey, "Ten Reasons I Believe the Bible Is the Word of God," cited from Roger Martin, *R. A. Torrey: Apostle of Certainty* (Murfreesboro, TN: Sword of the Lord, 2000), 281.

As a result of his intensive study, Torrey wrote an article entitled "Ten Reasons I Believe the Bible Is the Word of God," a helpful overview of his reasons for embracing the Scriptures as God's Word. In this section we will survey a similar list, in part based on Torrey's work. Though not exhaustive, we trust the ten reasons presented here will encourage Christians to rest confidently in their Bibles.

TEN REASONS WHY WE BELIEVE IN THE BIBLE

There is no question that the Bible claims to be the Word of God. "The Bible is the word of God," writes Christian theologian H. D. McDonald. "Such is the verdict to which our considerations have led us. And this verdict has the certain witness and warrant of the Bible itself."[7] In fact, over two thousand times in the Old Testament alone, from the beginning (Genesis 1:3) to the end (Malachi 4:3), the assertion is made that God Himself spoke what is written within its pages (cf. Exodus 24:4; Deuteronomy 4:2; 2 Samuel 23:2; Psalm 119:89; Jeremiah 26:2).

This theme continues into the New Testament, where the phrase "the word of God" occurs over forty times (cf. Luke 11:28; Hebrews 4:12). Without apology or qualification, the Bible declares that it was written by men under the inspiration of the Holy Spirit (2 Timothy 3:16–17; 2 Peter 1:21), making it the Word of God (cf. 1 Thessalonians 2:13; 2 Peter 1:16–21; 1 John 4:6). It further claims that its message is true because its divine author is incapable of falsehood (John 17:17; cf. Titus 1:2; Hebrews 6:18). "In effect, God signed every page of the Bible," writes pastor Erwin Lutzer. "We have every reason to believe that His signature was not forged. God has spoken and He has told us so."[8]

But how can we, as Christians, be confident in accepting such claims? As the famous Protestant Reformer John Calvin said, "We cannot rely on the doctrine of Scripture until we are absolutely convinced that God is its author."[9] *So how do we know that the Bible came from God?* That is the question that Reuben A. Torrey asked himself nearly a century ago. It is the question we will address in this section.

---

[7]H. D. McDonald, *What the Bible Teaches about the Bible* (Wheaton, IL: Tyndale House, 1979), 46.
[8]Erwin W. Lutzer, *Seven Reasons Why You Can Trust the Bible* (Chicago: Moody Press, 1998), 44.
[9]John Calvin, cited from *The New Encyclopedia of Christian Quotations*, 118.

Reason 1:
We Believe the Bible Is the Word of God

Because the Holy Spirit Confirms It to Be the Word of God

The Bible claims that its ultimate author is God, being penned by men who wrote and "spoke from God as they were carried along by the Holy Spirit" (2 Peter 1:21). Its writings are therefore *inspired* because they were "breathed out by God" (2 Timothy 3:16), having been superintended by "the Spirit of Christ" (1 Peter 1:11). Thus, both the Old Testament (Zechariah 7:12) and the New Testament (John 14:26; 16:13) find their source in the Holy Spirit.

Because the Spirit of God is alive and active in the world (John 14:16–17; 16:8), it follows that His Word is also actively at work (cf. Ephesians 6:17). It "is living and active, sharper than any two-edged sword, piercing to the division of soul and of spirit, of joints and of marrow, and discerning the thoughts and intentions of the heart" (Hebrews 4:12). Though verified by every external standard, the Word itself cannot produce belief unless it is accompanied by the Holy Spirit's power (cf. 1 Thessalonians 1:5). Only He can reveal the truth to those who are spiritually blind and give life to those who are spiritually dead (cf. 2 Corinthians 4:3–4; Ephesians 2:1–4).

Unless the Spirit intervenes, non-Christians will reject the Bible as foolishness, no matter how much evidence to the contrary is presented. In the words of Paul, "The natural person does not accept the things of the Spirit of God, for they are folly to him, and he is not able to understand them because they are spiritually discerned" (1 Corinthians 2:14). Christians, on the other hand, have received "the Spirit who is from God, that we might understand the things freely given us by God" (v. 12). We have been given "the mind of Christ" (v. 16b), meaning that God Himself, through His Spirit, has enabled us to understand and embrace the Scriptures in faith. The Holy Spirit thereby heightens "the mind's awareness of the marks of divinity present in the text in such a way as to produce the conviction that this text is indeed the product of the divine mind and therefore to be relied on utterly."[10] Or put more simply, the Holy Spirit bears witness to the truthfulness of His Word, opening the hearts of those who are children of God so that they can know and obey the truth (John 10:27; cf. Romans 8:16).

To the non-Christian reader, it may sound arbitrary to say that the primary reason we believe the Bible is because the Holy Spirit has opened our eyes to the truth. Yet that is precisely the case. The evidence for the Bible's divine authorship is certainly substantial; but in the end "there is only one argument that can prove to us that the Bible is true and authoritative for our lives: the work of the Holy Spirit in our hearts and minds."[11] After all, "this question of the authority of the Scriptures is a matter of faith and not of argument," observes British preacher D. Martyn Lloyd-Jones. "You may convince a man intellectually of what you're saying, but he still may not of necessity believe in and accept the authority of Scripture."[12]

The Word of God, of course, welcomes those who are spiritually thirsty to come drink of its deep reservoirs. The Lord of the Scriptures can quench any spiritual thirst and satisfy any spiritual hunger (Deuteronomy 8:3; Job 23:12; John 4:10–14; 6:35; 7:37–38). He invites sinners with these words, "Come to me, all who labor and are heavy laden, and I will give you rest" (Matthew 11:28), and "Whoever comes to me I will never cast out" (John 6:37b). All who embrace Him in faith will be made righteous before God and sealed by the Holy Spirit (Romans 3:21–26; Ephesians 1:13–14). As a result, they will "have peace with God" (Romans 5:1) and will experience "the love of God in Christ Jesus our Lord" (Romans 8:39).

Those who come to the Bible in sincerity and humility will not leave empty-handed (cf. Isaiah 55:6–11). "If we follow the directions of the Word of God, we will find salvation, contentment, joy, and eternal life," writes James Montgomery Boice.[13] The God of the Bible does not disappoint (Romans 5:5; cf. Psalm 22:5). The pleading promise of Psalm 34:8 still rings true: "Oh, taste and see that the LORD is good!

[10]Paul Helm, "Faith, Evidence, and the Scriptures," in *Scripture and Truth*, ed. D. A. Carson and John Woodbridge (Grand Rapids, MI: Baker, 1992), 313.
[11]John MacArthur, *Why Believe the Bible* (Ventura, CA: Regal Books, 1980), 23.
[12]D. Martyn Lloyd-Jones, "Authority of the Scripture," *Decision* (June 1963). Cited in MacArthur, *Why Believe*, 23.
[13]James Montgomery Boice, *Psalms 1–41* (Grand Rapids, MI: Baker, 1994), 172.

Blessed is the man who takes refuge in him!" Those who genuinely taste of the kindness and mercy of God, having been nourished on the substance of His Word (Psalm 119:103; 1 Peter 2:1–3), will find Him to be true. Jesus said of His own words, "My teaching is not mine, but his who sent me. If anyone's will is to do God's will, he will know whether the teaching is from God" (John 7:16–17). Thus, as theologian Paul Helm observes, "God is proved by hearing and obeying Him and finding that He is as good as His word. . . . The claims of the Scriptures bear the weight of experience."[14] This is true because the Spirit of God empowers the Scriptures and bears witness in the human heart to the fact that the Bible is indeed the very Word of God.

---

[14]Paul Helm, "Faith, Evidence, and the Scriptures," 312. Thus, "the chief evidence or reason for taking the Scriptures to be the Word of God is their own evidence, found to hold good in the life and experience of those who are serious and 'open'" (319).

Reason 2:
We Believe the Bible Is the Word of God

*Because It Explains Life in a Way That Corresponds
to Reality*

Whether they recognize it or not, everybody has a worldview—a personal set of values, attitudes, and beliefs that govern the way in which they perceive themselves and the world around them (cf. Proverbs 27:19). For the Christian, these presuppositions and priorities come from the Bible and involve "beliefs about 1) God (theology); 2) ultimate reality (metaphysics); 3) knowledge (epistemology); 4) ethics (axiology); and 5) human nature (anthropology)."[15] Thus, a biblical worldview asserts that God exists (Genesis 1:1; Hebrews 11:6), that He offers eternal life (Titus 1:2; 1 John 5:11), that He is the source of knowledge (Proverbs 1:7; 2:6; 9:10), that He is the standard of morality (Psalm 89:14; 111:7; 1 Peter 1:15–16), and that men have been created in His image (Genesis 1:26–27; 9:6; James 3:9), though they have sinned against Him (Romans 3:23).

But does the biblical worldview actually correspond to reality? Is it consistent with the way things really are? Christian philosopher Ronald Nash frames the discussion this way:

> Christian theism is only one of a number of competing conceptual systems. . . . When faced with a choice among competing touchstone propositions of different world-views, we should choose the one that, when applied to the whole of reality, gives us the most coherent picture of the world.[16]

When we look at the world around us, we see both beauty and ugliness, order and chaos, happiness and pain, growth and decay. We find ourselves confronted with questions about the origin of the

---

[15]Brian Morley, "Understanding Our Postmodern World," 135–154, in *Think Biblically*, ed. John MacArthur (Wheaton, IL: Crossway, 2003), 222.
[16]Ronald Nash, *Faith and Reason* (Grand Rapids, MI: Zondervan, 1988), 51.

universe, the meaning of life, the existence of evil, and the inevitability of death. But how can all of this be explained in a way that is both comprehensive and internally consistent?

As we saw in the previous section of this book, the atheistic worldview is beset with unanswerable questions.

> The vast array of insurmountable problems for the naturalist begins at the most basic level. What was the first cause that caused everything else? Where did matter come from? Where did energy come from? What holds everything together and what keeps everything going? How could life, self–consciousness, and rationality evolve from inanimate, inorganic matter? Who *designed* the many complex and interdependent organisms and sophisticated ecosystems we observe? Where did *intelligence* originate?[17]

In contrast to atheistic naturalism, the Bible is more than able to answer such questions and any others that arise from our observations of the world around us. "The Bible answers the questions which nature raises," observes theologian John Gerstner (a PhD from Harvard). "This seems to be an initial presumption in favor of the Bible's being the very word of God, namely, it answers the questions that only God can answer."[18]

The Bible explains the existence and order of the universe (which was created by God—Acts 14:15; Revelation 4:11), the personhood and dignity of men and women (who were made in the image of God—Genesis 5:1; 9:6), the origins of reason and knowledge (which come from the mind of God—Job 28:28; Psalm 111:10; James 1:5), the reality of evil and pain (which was introduced into the world when Adam and Eve sinned—Genesis 3:1–24; Romans 5:12, 17; 8:20–22), mankind's innate awareness of morality (which arises from the conscience—Romans 2:14–15), and the reason human beings cannot find ultimate satisfaction in the things of this life (since they were created to find ultimate satisfaction only in God—Psalm 16:11; Ecclesiastes 2:25–26; 1 Timothy 6:17).

The Bible alone gives us credible answers to life's most profound questions. "There is [but] one worldview which can explain the existence of the universe, its form, and the uniqueness of people—the

---

[17]John MacArthur, *The Battle for the Beginning* (Nashville: W Publishing Group, 2001), 31.
[18]John Gerstner, *Reasons for Faith* (Grand Rapids, MI: Baker, 1967), 69.

worldview given to us in the Bible," explains Christian philosopher Francis Schaeffer. "The Bible tells us that the universe is ordered, because God made it to cohere in all sorts of amazing ways. At the same time it tells us that we are persons. We are able to know what is around us; the subject can know the object."[19] Reality as we observe it, both in relation to ourselves and our universe, is most adequately explained by the biblical worldview.

If the Scriptures are true, and if the worldview they present is true, then their explanation of reality must correspond to the world around us. After all, the God of Scripture (Psalm 19:7–14) is also the God of the universe (Psalm 19:1–6). The specific revelation of the Bible must therefore be consistent with the general revelation of nature. And indeed it is.

The Bible presents the only worldview truly consistent with reality, and that is evidence of its divine authorship.

---

[19]Francis Schaeffer and C. Everett Koop, *Whatever Happened to the Human Race?* (Wheaton, IL: Crossway Books, 1983), 82, 111.

Reason 3:
We Believe the Bible Is the Word of God

Because It Has Been Tested and Found Trustworthy

The Bible repeatedly claims to be true (Psalm 119:142, 151, 160; John 17:17; cf. James 1:18) because it comes from the "God of truth" (Isaiah 65:16; cf. 2 Samuel 7:28; Psalm 31:5). In fact, the truthfulness of Scripture "is the starting point for a true Christian worldview—and it is the point to which Christians must inevitably return to evaluate and discern every competing opinion and philosophy. Scripture is true. It is reliable."[20] Because God cannot lie (Numbers 23:19; 2 Timothy 2:13; Titus 1:2; Hebrews 6:18), we can put our trust in what He has said. "If God is a God of truth, He must speak only that which is consistent with His character," explains Erwin Lutzer. "It would be unthinkable to have an untruthful message from a truthful God."[21]

The Bible describes itself as pure (Psalm 12:6; 119:140; Proverbs 30:5), perfect (Psalm 19:7), precious (Psalm 19:10), and powerful (Hebrews 4:12). Because it expresses the will of God, it cannot fail or be broken (Luke 16:17; John 10:35), nor will any part of it pass away without being fulfilled exactly as God intended (Matthew 5:17–18).

In claiming to be true, the Bible invites scrutiny. Though it certainly speaks to issues of faith, it also speaks to issues of history and science. This is important, because it means the Bible is a testable document. Its truthfulness in the areas of history, geography, and science can be examined and validated. Were it found to be unreliable in the places where it *can* be tested, we would have serious reason to doubt its trustworthiness in areas where it *cannot* be tested (such as its teachings regarding God, sin, salvation, and the spiritual world).

On the other hand, the fact that the Bible is continually vindicated

---

[20]John MacArthur, "Embracing the Authority and Sufficiency of Scripture," 21–36, in *Think Biblically*, ed. John MacArthur, 35.
[21]Lutzer, *Seven Reasons*, 53.

by history, archaeology, geography, and science does much to increase our confidence in its credibility. "Taken collectively, the many bits of data from these sources that confirm the factual accuracy of both the Old and New Testaments go far in removing a person's reluctance to believe that the Bible is from God."[22] Rather than being undermined by external evidence, the case for the Bible's truthfulness is only strengthened.

Recent interviews with leading archaeologists in Israel have again confirmed the historical and geographical trustworthiness of the Bible.[23] "Serious scholars, even if they're not believers, even if they do not think this is a sacred text, still consider it to be history, because things match up so well," says archaeologist Steven Ortiz. He continues, "[T]here isn't anything to contradict or anything to make me wary of the testimony of Scripture."[24] Speaking specifically of the Old Testament, Denis Baly notes that "the historical material in the [Old] Testament must be taken with great seriousness. It is primary evidence for the history of the time, and no honest historian or archaeologist should treat it as anything else."[25] Echoing this sentiment, Aren Maier of Bar Ilan University acknowledges the fact that "You can't do archaeology in Israel without the Bible."[26]

Their consensus on the importance of the biblical text to Middle-Eastern archaeology echoes the words of Yale archeologist Millar Burrows, who wrote over a half-century ago, "On the whole, archeological work has unquestionably strengthened confidence in the reliability of the scriptural record. More than one archeologist has found his respect for the Bible increased by experience of excavation of Palestine."[27] More recently, after an extensive study of Old Testament data, renowned archaeologist and Egyptologist Kenneth Kitchen (of the University of Liverpool) has written:

> What can be said of historical reliability? Here our answer—on the evidence available—is more positive. The periods most in the glare of

---

[22]Rubel Shelly, *Prepare to Answer* (Grand Rapids, MI: Baker, 1990), 101.

[23]Cf. "The Archaeologists I," video presentation, SourceFlix Productions (uploaded August 10, 2007); http://www.sourceflix.com/vid_arch_1.htm. Accessed September 2, 2007. This clip highlights the testimony of a number of archaeologists who are currently working in Israel and who affirm the importance of the Bible to their work. It is part of a larger documentary to be released in 2008.

[24]Steven Ortiz, transcribed from "The Archaeologists I," video presentation.

[25]Denis Baly, *God and History in the Old Testament* (New York: Harper & Row, 1976), 19.

[26]Aren Maier, transcribed from "The Archaeologists I," video presentation.

[27]Millar Burrows, *What Mean These Stones?* (New Haven, CT: American Schools of Oriental Research, 1941), 1.

contemporary documents—the divided monarchy and the exile and return—show a very high level of direct correlation (where adequate data exist) and of reliability. . . . In terms of general reliability . . . the Old Testament comes out remarkably well.[28]

The testimony of archaeology continually confirms the trustworthiness of the Bible. As Norman Geisler points out, "While many have doubted the accuracy of the Bible, time and continued research have consistently demonstrated that the Word of God is better informed than its critics."[29] Henry Morris presses the point even further, asserting that there is "not one unquestionable find of archaeology that proves the Bible to be in error at any point."[30] On the other hand, notes Josh McDowell, "numerous discoveries have confirmed the historical accuracy of the biblical documents, even down to the occasional use of obsolete names of foreign kings."[31] No other religious book can make those statements. Yet they correspond directly to the Bible's own claim to be true.

The Bible is equally compatible with science and has played an important role in scientific developments throughout history.[32] After all, "modern science arose within a culture saturated with Christian faith. It was Christianized Europe that became the birthplace of modern science—there and nowhere else."[33] Referring to Copernicus, Galileo, Kepler, and Newton, authors Kenneth Boa and Robert Bowman observe that "the four individuals who did the most to pioneer modern science were pious men whose belief in God was integral to their view of science."[34] It was Isaac Newton himself who said, "We account the

---

[28]Kenneth A. Kitchen, *On the Reliability of the Old Testament* (Grand Rapids, MI: Eerdmans, 2003), 499–500.

[29]Norman Geisler, *Baker Encyclopedia of Christian Apologetics* (Grand Rapids, MI: Baker, 1998), 52. Cf. Thomas Lea's commentary on *1, 2 Timothy, Titus*, New American Commentary (Nashville: Broadman Press, 1992), 239, where he notes that "any errors in the field of history would undermine the confidence of the reader in the theological trustworthiness of Scripture."

[30]Henry Morris, *The Bible and Modern Science* (Chicago: Moody, 1956), 95. Cited from Josh McDowell, *The New Evidence That Demands a Verdict* (Nashville: Thomas Nelson, 1999), 98.

[31]McDowell, *New Evidence That Demands a Verdict*, 89. Along these lines, Jens Bruun Kofoed in *Text and History* (Winona Lake, IN: Eisenbrauns, 2005), 4–5 responds to skeptics of the Old Testament by arguing that it is much more historically reliable than many scholars claim, and that "it must be *included in* rather than *excluded from* the pool of reliable data for a reconstruction of the origin and history of ancient Israel."

[32]Obviously, we would exclude an atheistic evolutionary view of origins from true science. The naturalistic understanding of origins is faith-based, not science-based, as we saw in Section 1.

[33]Nancy Pearcey and Charles Thaxton, *The Soul of Science: Christian Faith and Natural Philosophy* (Wheaton, IL: Crossway Books, 1994), 19.

[34]Kenneth D. Boa and Robert M. Bowman Jr., *20 Compelling Evidences That God Exists* (Colorado Springs: Cook, 2005), 108–109.

Scriptures of God to be the most sublime philosophy. I find more sure marks of authenticity in the Bible than in any profane [secular] history whatsoever."[35]

Though it is not a science textbook, the Bible harmonizes with the facts of science when it speaks to such issues, including the great number of stars in our universe (Jeremiah 33:22), the uniqueness of those stars (Isaiah 40:26; 1 Corinthians 15:41), the suspension of earth in space (Job 26:7), different species of plants and animals (Genesis 1:11–12, 20–22), the importance of blood to life (Leviticus 17:11), and certain medical precautions such as lip covering (Leviticus 13:45), quarantine (Leviticus 13:45–46; 14:8–9), and disinfection (Leviticus 15:13, 25–27).[36]

> You can find many other examples of how the Bible matches up with discoveries of modern science. Of course the precise technological language is not there, and for good reason. God wrote the Bible for men of all ages and while His Word never contradicts science, it also never gets trapped into describing some precise scientific theory that becomes outdated in a few years, decades or centuries.[37]

The Bible sometimes uses poetic language (depending on the genre) and often speaks from a human point of reference (such as when it refers to the rising or setting of the sun). But once that is taken into account, there is nothing in Scripture that is not reconcilable with what the scientific method reveals about the world.

Before becoming a Christian, astronomer Hugh Ross, the former director of observations for Vancouver's Royal Astronomical Society, studied the various holy books of the major world religions. Time and again he found himself disappointed with the scientific foolishness, myth, legends, and ignorance of these texts. But when he came to the Bible he realized something was different. Thinking back on his experience, he wrote:

> I was amazed with the quantity of historical and scientific references and with the detail in them. I committed myself to spend at least

[35]Isaac Newton, cited from Robert Witty, *The Bible: Fact or Fiction?* (Fort Washington, PA: CLC Publications, 2001), 90.
[36]Robert T. Boyd, *Boyd's Handbook of Practical Apologetics* (Grand Rapids, MI: Kregel, 1997), 73–94 lists a number of scientific illustrations and facts that are represented in Scripture.
[37]John MacArthur, *Why Believe the Bible?*, 21.

an hour a day going through the Bible to test the accuracy of all its statements on science, geography, and history. At the end of eighteen months, I had to admit to myself that I had been unsuccessful in finding a single provable error or contradiction. I was now convinced that the Bible was supernaturally accurate and thus supernaturally inspired.[38]

Whether science or history, the Scriptures always speak the truth. Wayne Grudem (a PhD from Cambridge) explains, "This is because God, who speaks in Scripture, knows all facts. He has not spoken in a way that would contradict any true fact in the universe."[39] Though critics have repeatedly tried to undermine its message, the Bible has stood the test of time. Its truthfulness has been vindicated again and again; yet "no error has ever been proven in the Bible."[40] In the words of British pastor Brian H. Edwards:

God's word has stood against its critics for hundreds of years. They come, they criticize, they disagree among themselves and they disappear—leaving only a paper trail of unbelief as their legacy. But for those who believe the Bible to be without error, and who believe it is God's clear revelation for modern man, it consistently proves to be a reliable guide to the way of salvation and for every aspect of the Christian life.[41]

For a text that is thousands of years old, that is an amazing testimony to its supernatural authorship. In the places where it can be tested, it has been tried and found true.

---

[38]Hugh Ross, *The Creator and the Cosmos* (Colorado Springs: NavPress, 1993). Cited from Robert J. Morgan, *Evidence and Truth* (Wheaton, IL: Crossway Books, 2003), 41. Though Ross is an old-earth creationist (a point with which we would not agree), we appreciate the sentiments he expresses here about the Bible. For a helpful critique of Ross's old-earth views, visit the Institute for Creation Research at www.icr.org.
[39]Wayne Grudem, *Systematic Theology* (Grand Rapids, MI: Zondervan, 1994), 275.
[40]John Ankerberg and John Weldon, *Fast Facts on Defending Your Faith* (Eugene, OR: Harvest House, 2002), 79.
[41]Brian H. Edwards, *Nothing but the Truth* (Webster, NY: Evangelical Press, 2006), 465. For more on specific attacks against Scripture throughout history, see *Challenges to Inerrancy*, ed. Gordon Lewis and Bruce Demarest (Chicago: Moody Press, 1984).

Reason 4:
We Believe the Bible Is the Word of God

Because It Has Been Validated by Hundreds of Fulfilled Prophecies

The Bible claims to be a true document that comes from God Himself. But if this is the case, the Bible must be reliable not only when speaking of past or present events, but also when predicting the future. This is an important point, since "a staggering 27 percent of the Bible deals with predictions about the future."[42] According to Old Testament professor J. Barton Payne, who produced the *Encyclopedia of Bible Prophecy*, 8,352 of the Bible's 31,124 verses are predictive. When duplicates are removed, Dr. Payne counted 1,817 predictions in the Bible, far more than any other religious text.[43]

Referring to itself as "the prophetic word" (2 Peter 1:19), the Bible makes predictive prophecy a means by which we can measure its trust-worthiness. In Deuteronomy 18, for example, God delineates the way in which His people can differentiate between false prophets and His true spokesmen. "When a prophet speaks in the name of the Lord, if the word does not come to pass or come true, that is a word that the Lord has not spoken" (v. 22). Put simply, if the prediction fails, it did not come from God. The Lord further issues this challenge to false gods and those who worship them: "Tell us what is to come hereafter, that we may know that you are gods" (Isaiah 41:23). Their inability to do so indicates they are "nothing" (v. 24).

On the other hand, the God of the Bible is able to predict events "before they spring forth" (Isaiah 42:9). It is He who proclaims, "I

---

[42]Walter C. Kaiser, citing the work of J. Barton Payne in *A Biblical Introduction to Hermeneutics*, ed. Walter C. Kaiser and Moisés Silva (Grand Rapids, MI: Zondervan, 1994), 139. On balance, Carl Edwin Armerding in "Prophecy in the Old Testament," 61–71, in *A Guide to Biblical Prophecy*, ed. Carl E. Armerding and W. Ward Gasque (Peabody, MA: Hendrickson, 1999), 61 notes that "biblical prophecy has a much broader scope than simply the prediction of future events."
[43]Cited from Robert G. Witty, *The Bible: Fact or Fiction?* (Fort Washington, PA: CLC Productions, 2001), 46. Payne's work in *The Encyclopedia of Bible Prophecy* (New York: Harper & Row, 1973), 257 is one of the most exhaustive treatments of the subject.

am God, and there is none like me, declaring the end from the begin-ning and from ancient times things not yet done" (Isaiah 46:9b–10a). Because He knows everything, including the future (Psalm 139:1–6; Matthew 6:8; Romans 11:33–36), God stakes His own reputation on the accuracy of His predictive prophecies (cf. Isaiah 45:3; Jeremiah 28:9; 44:28–29; Ezekiel 6:10). Thus "God Himself points to prophecy as an absolute proof that it is He who speaks."[44]

In addition to messianic prophecies (which we will consider in upcoming sections), the Bible records many God-given predictions that have been fulfilled in history. Here are just a few:

• God promised Abraham that he would have a son in his old age and would be the father of a great nation (Genesis 15:4; 17:19, 21), and it came to pass (Genesis 21:1–5). Moreover, He promised Abraham's descendants a homeland (Genesis 15:18–21; Exodus 6:8) following their captivity in Egypt (Genesis 15:13). This prediction was fulfilled centuries later (Joshua 21:43–45).

• Ezekiel 26:1–21 predicted that the city of Tyre would be destroyed (which it was in two stages, first by Nebuchadnezzar [in 585–573 B.C.] and later by Alexander the Great [in 332 B.C.]). Though it was a thriving port city in Ezekiel's day, the prophet declared that its eventual demise would be so great that it would not be rebuilt (Ezekiel 26:14). "Today this once-great commercial center lies in ruins," notes Bible commentator Charles Dyer. "Though the sur-rounding area has been rebuilt, the original site is a mute testimony to God's awesome judgment."[45]

• Around 910 B.C. the prophets of God predicted the fall and captivity of the northern kingdom of Israel (1 Kings 14:15–16), events that came to pass 180 years later in 722 B.C. (2 Kings 17:6, 22–23). The fall and captivity of the southern kingdom of Judah was also predicted (Isaiah 39:5–7) some 150 years before it happened (2 Chronicles 36:15–17).

• The length of Israel's captivity (lasting for seventy years) was fore-told by the prophet Jeremiah (Jeremiah 29:10) and precisely fulfilled (2 Chronicles 36:21). The role of the Persian King Cyrus in Israel's release from captivity was depicted by Isaiah more than a century beforehand (Isaiah 44:28–45:7).

• That Israel would reject her Messiah (Isaiah 53:1–12), that the temple would be destroyed (Daniel 9:24–27; Matthew 24:1–2), and that the Jews

---

[44]Boyd, *Boyd's Handbook*, 97.
[45]Charles H. Dyer, "Ezekiel," in *The Bible Knowledge Commentary*, ed. John F. Walvoord and Roy B. Zuck (Wheaton, IL: Victor Books, 1985), Chapter 26. After Alexander's conquest, Tyre was rebuilt and was a city of some influence during New Testament times. Later, in A.D. 1291, it was completely destroyed, never to be rebuilt. Thus the final fulfillment of Ezekiel's prophecy came to pass nineteen hundred years after his prophecy.

would be dispersed around the world (Deuteronomy 28:64; 30:3) were also all prophesied. Even Israel's recent return to the land was foretold by the prophets (Ezekiel 36:22–24).[46]

Many more prophecies could be added to this list.[47] The book of Daniel, for instance, contains astonishing predictions about the rise of the Medo-Persian, Greek, and Roman empires. In the eleventh chapter alone there are over one hundred prophecies that were fulfilled years and even centuries after they were predicted.[48] "The detail of this history as presented [in Daniel 11] provides one of the most remarkable predictive portions of all Scripture," writes Old Testament scholar Leon Wood.[49] Bible commentator Stephen R. Miller agrees, noting that "The historical details set forth in this prophecy are astounding."[50] Daniel's prophecies are so precise, in fact, that critical scholars have argued that it could not have been written until *after* the events it describes (usually ascribing it a date in the second century B.C.). But archaeological discoveries (such as the Dead Sea Scrolls) have made this dating impossible. Old Testament scholar Gleason Archer (a PhD from Harvard) explains:

> The linguistic evidence from Qumran makes the rationalistic explanation for Daniel no longer tenable [i.e., that it was written after the events it predicts]. It is difficult to see how any scholar can defend this view and maintain intellectual respectability. . . . There is no evading the conclusion that the prophecies of the Book of Daniel were inspired by the same God who later fulfilled them, or who will fulfill them in the last days.[51]

Hebrew professor Bruce K. Waltke (who also earned his PhD from Harvard) reveals why critical scholarship is unwilling to accept

---

[46]Robert Boyd's *Handbook* details these and other prophecies on 97–129.

[47]John F. Walvoord, *Daniel: The Key to Prophetic Revelation* (Chicago: Moody Press, 1971), 253 gives several additional examples. "The Median conquest of Babylon as a result of the drying up of the Euphrates River and the Babylonian drunken feast is anticipated in detail in Jeremiah 50–51 (note especially 50:38; 51:32, 36, 39, 57). Other illustrations include Isaiah 13:17–18; 21:1–10. In a similar way, prophecies concerning Syria, Phoenicia, Tyre, Gaza, Ashkelon, Ashdod, and the Philistines are given in Zechariah 9:1–8."

[48]Cf. John MacArthur's introduction to Daniel in *The MacArthur Study Bible* (Nashville: Thomas Nelson, 2006), 1200 (in the NASB edition).

[49]Leon Wood, *A Commentary on Daniel* (Grand Rapids, MI: Zondervan, 1973), 280.

[50]Stephen R. Miller, *Daniel*, New American Commentary (Nashville: Broadman & Holman, 1994), 290.

[51]Gleason L. Archer, *Encyclopedia of Bible Difficulties* (Grand Rapids, MI: Zondervan, 1982), 24–26. Cited from John Ankerberg and John Weldon, *Ready with an Answer* (Eugene, OR: Harvest House, 2007), 241–242.

the actual date of Daniel's authorship—in the sixth century B.C.—even after linguistic and archaeological evidence has confirmed it.

> If evidence for a sixth-century date of composition is so certain, why do scholars reject it in favor of an unsupportable Maccabean hypothesis? The reason is that most scholars embrace a liberal, naturalistic, and rationalistic philosophy. Naturalism and rationalism are ultimately based on faith rather than on evidence; therefore this faith will not allow them to accept the supernatural predictions.[52]

When the evidence is honestly considered, biblical prophecies (like those in Daniel) cannot be explained away. They are neither lucky guesses nor post-fulfillment forgeries, making it hard to disagree with the words of Paul Little: "One cannot deny the force of fulfilled prophecy as evidence of divine guidance."[53]

Thus, the Bible defends its claim to be the Word of God by calling its critics to consider this amazing fact: it repeatedly and accurately predicts the future. "In world literature, the Bible is unique in this respect. At best, other religions' scriptures contain a small number of vague predictions, or their predictions fail, but nothing anywhere is comparable to the large number of detailed prophecies in Scripture."[54] As Christian theologian Bernard Ramm points out, "Real prophecy is peculiar to the Bible. This does not mean that other religions do not have prophetic elements. But whereas prophecy is an occasional phenomenon of non-Christian religions, it is part and parcel of Biblical religion."[55] Among books that claim to come from God, the Bible stands alone—not only because it contains so many predictions, but because those predictions repeatedly come true. "Nowhere is the uniqueness of the Bible more evident than in the supernatural nature of its prophecies."[56]

---

[52]Bruce K. Waltke, "The Date of the Book of Daniel," 194–203, in *Vital Apologetic Issues*, ed. Roy B. Zuck (Grand Rapids, MI: Kregel, 1995), 203.
[53]Paul E. Little, *Know Why You Believe* (Downers Grove, IL: InterVarsity Press, 2000), 70.
[54]Ankerberg and Weldon, *Ready with an Answer*, 232.
[55]Bernard Ramm, *Protestant Christian Evidences* (Chicago: Moody Press, 1972), 84–85.
[56]Robert L. Saucy, "How Else Is the Bible Unique?," 43–49, in *Understanding Christian Theology*, ed. Charles R. Swindoll and Roy B. Zuck (Nashville: Thomas Nelson, 2003), 43.

Reason 5:
We Believe the Bible Is the Word of God

Because It Is Marked by a Clear and
Consistent Message

Spanning from the law of Moses (written around 1400 B.C.) to the final epistles of the New Testament (completed around A.D. 100), the sixty-six books of the Bible were written by some forty different human authors. They were written on three different continents (Asia, Europe, and Africa) in three different languages (Hebrew, Aramaic, and Greek) by men, many of whom did not know each other, and most of whom came from very different walks of life. For example, Moses was a prince (Exodus 2:10; cf. Hebrew 11:24–25) who became a shepherd (Exodus 3:1); David was a shepherd (1 Samuel 16:11–13) who became the king (2 Samuel 2:4). Jonah preached repentance to an enemy nation, and they listened (Jonah 3:4–5); Jeremiah preached repentance to his own nation, and they rejected him (cf. Jeremiah 32:1–15). Daniel was a government official (Daniel 5:29); Ezra was a priest (Ezra 7:11); Isaiah was a prophet (2 Kings 20:1). Matthew was a tax collector (Matthew 9:9); Paul was a former Pharisee (Philippians 3:5); Luke was a Gentile physician (Colossians 4:14); and Peter was a Jewish fisherman (Matthew 4:18).

The men who wrote Scripture were a diverse group. Yet, in spite of those differences, including the various types of literature they wrote (from historic narrative to religious poetry to didactic treatises), the writings they produced express a perfect unity of thought. As F. F. Bruce, emeritus Professor of Biblical Criticism and Exegesis at the University of Manchester, rightly observed, "The Bible is not simply an anthology; there is a unity which binds the whole together. An anthology is compiled by an anthologist, but no anthologist compiled the Bible."[57]

---

[57]F. F. Bruce, *The Books and the Parchments* (Grand Rapids, MI: Fleming H. Revell, 1984), 88.

The divine origin of the Bible is further seen in considering the continuity of its teaching despite the unusual nature of its composition. It stands distinct from other religious writings. For example, the Islamic Koran was compiled by an individual, Zaid ibn Thabit, under the guidance of Mohammed's father-in-law, Abu-Bekr. Additionally, in A.D. 650, a group of Arab scholars produced a unified version and destroyed all variant copies to preserve the unity of the Koran. By contrast, the Bible came from some forty different authors from diverse vocations in life.[58]

Yet the message of Scripture is both consistent and coherent. "One way in which the Bible substantiates its own authority is its amazing coherency and symmetry," writes R. C. Sproul. "Its consistency over centuries and through the pens of multiple authors is nothing less than astonishing."[59]

The remarkable continuity of Scripture, in spite of its diverse composition, points to the fact that God is its ultimate author. "There is no real diversity [in the Bible]," explains Martin Womack of Pepperdine University, "but only diverse ways through which the majestic and unified message of God has been revealed to man."[60] Because their writings were inspired by the Spirit of God, the various writers of Scripture all conveyed the message of the divine author, God Himself (cf. 1 Thessalonians 1:5; 2:13; 2 Peter 1:19–21). The revelation they received was always consistent with what had been previously revealed, since it all came from the one and only God (cf. 1 Samuel 15:29; Malachi 3:6).

If the Scriptures are the Word of God, then, properly interpreted, the sentences of Scripture will at least be logically consistent with each other. This follows from the fact that if the Scriptures are the word of God, then properly interpreted, the sentences are true. And if a set of propositions is true, the propositions must be consistent with each other.[61]

In New Testament times, that consistency was underscored by Jesus and the apostles, who saw their teachings as complementing what

---

[58]Paul P. Enns, *The Moody Handbook of Theology* (Chicago: Moody, 1997), 154–155.
[59]R. C. Sproul, *Defending Your Faith* (Wheaton, IL: Crossway Books, 2003), 169.
[60]Morris M. Womack, "The Unity of the Bible," 35–46, in *Pillars of Faith*, ed. Herman O. Wilson and Morris M. Womack (Grand Rapids, MI: Baker, 1973), 45.
[61]Paul Helm, "Faith, Evidence, and the Scriptures," 317.

God had already revealed in the Old Testament (cf. Luke 18:31–33; 24:27, 44–45; John 5:39, 46; Acts 10:43; 1 Peter 1:10–12). Thus, the apostle Paul could say that "*all* Scripture is breathed out by God and profitable for teaching, for reproof, for correction, and for training in righteousness" (2 Timothy 3:16, emphasis added).

The Bible presents a unified picture of God, mankind, sin, salvation, and every area of doctrine. In fact, wherever theological or doctrinal topics are discussed in Scripture (such as creation, the nature of man, the way of salvation, or the end of the world), the specific passage is always consistent with the whole. [62] This unity is specifically seen in reference to the gospel of Jesus Christ, since He is the one to whom the entire Bible points (from Genesis 3:15 to Revelation 22:16). "The Old Testament is the preparation (Isaiah 40:3). The Gospels are the manifestation (John 1:29). The Book of Acts is the propagation (Acts 1:8). The epistles give the explanation (Colossians 1:27). The Book of Revelation is the consummation (Revelation 1:7). The Bible is all about Jesus."[63]

No matter the Testament, the author, the genre, or the historical background, every teaching of every passage of Scripture is consistent with the rest of Scripture. The message always remains the same. This again provides strong support for the Bible's claim that God is its author.

> In unity these books teach the triunity of God, the deity of Jesus Christ, the personality of the Holy Spirit, the fall and depravity of man, as well as salvation by grace. It quickly becomes apparent that no human being(s) could have orchestrated the harmony of the teachings of the Scripture. The divine authorship of the Bible is the only answer.[64]

---

[62]For those interested in studying interpretive difficulties and apparent contradictions in Scripture, we would recommend Gleason L. Archer, *An Encyclopedia of Bible Difficulties* (Grand Rapids, MI: Zondervan, 1982).

[63]Josh McDowell and Don Stewart, *Answers to Tough Questions Skeptics Ask about the Christian Faith* (Wheaton, IL: Tyndale House, 1986), 18–19.

[64]Ibid.

Reason 6:
We Believe the Bible Is the Word of God

Because It Is Unsurpassed in Its Moral Ethic and Social Impact

Throughout its pages, the Bible presents itself as a supreme book, being given by God Himself. Two Psalms in particular, 19 and 119, exalt the supernatural character of God's Word. From these Psalms alone we learn that the Word of God is perfect (19:7a), complete (19:7b), right (19:8a), pure (19:8b), timeless (19:9a), and true (19:9b). By following the light of Scripture (119:105), men and women can walk in a way that is blameless (119:1), free from wrongdoing (119:3), upright (119:7), pure (119:9), and righteous in the eyes of God (119:11). Moreover, it is through God's Word that blessing (119:1), comfort (119:76), wisdom (119:98–99, 130), peace (119:165), and salvation (119:174) are all found. Because they are God's own revelation, the Scriptures possess infinite value—their worth is incalculable because their wisdom is incomparable. As the Psalmist understandably exclaims, "More to be desired are they than gold, even much fine gold; sweeter also than honey and drippings of the honeycomb . . . in keeping them there is great reward" (19:10–11).

One way in which the unequalled excellence of Scripture is clearly seen is in the Bible's transcendent moral code. In revealing both the character and commandments of the Creator, God's Word provides the supreme standard for human morality—a standard that starts with loving God and subsequently includes loving other people (Mark 12:29–31). The Bible assumes that those who love God will also love righteousness and justice (Psalm 33:5; Proverbs 21:3; Micah 6:8), that they will work hard for His glory (1 Corinthians 10:31; Colossians 3:17, 23), and that they will reflect His merciful love in their dealings with others (Proverbs 14:21, 31; Romans 12:9–21). Scripture thereby establishes the basic principles of human rights and social responsibility—such as racial equality (Acts 17:26; Galatians 3:28; Revelation 5:9), the sanctity of human life (Deuteronomy 5:17; Romans 13:9), social justice (Exodus 20:1–13; Deuteronomy 16:19–20), the golden rule (Matthew 7:12; Luke 6:31), good citizenship (Romans 13:1–7; 1 Timothy 2:1–2; 1 Peter 2:13–14), care for the poor and destitute (Deuteronomy 15:11; James 1:27), selfless service (Mark 10:43; Philippians 2:1–4), and individual integrity and responsibility (Psalm 15:1–2; 1 Thessalonians 4:11; 1 Peter 1:14–16).

Kenneth Boa and Robert Bowman highlight the Bible's exceptional ethical value.

> Its teachings and principles are the wisest of all literature. Its laws exalt justice, according dignity to all human beings. Its insights into the human condition are both realistic and hopeful. The Bible offers sound principles concerning marriage and the family, money and possessions, character development, and reconciliation. From the Ten Commandments to the Golden Rule, the Bible continues to be the greatest and wisest book ever written.[65]

It's no wonder, then, that "civilization has been influenced more by the Judeo-Christian Scriptures than by any other book or series of books in the world."[66] Even the United States Constitution, and its Bill of Rights, were highly influenced by biblical Christianity.[67]

The Bible's superior moral ethic is heightened when one compares it with other religious texts. "The moral character produced by New Testament Christianity is higher than that produced by other religions," notes theologian William G. T. Shedd. "The Vedas, the Koran, and the still better writings of Plato and Aristotle do not transform human nature as do the Scriptures."[68] Shedd's observation, though written a century ago, remains true today.[69]

---

[65]Boa and Bowman, *20 Compelling Evidences*, 106.

[66]Norman L. Geisler and William E. Nix, *A General Introduction to the Bible* (Chicago: Moody Press, 1996), 196.

[67]Jeffrey Donley, *The Everything History of the Bible Book* (Avon, MA: Adams Media, 2006), 245 notes, "Of the fifty-five people drafting the Constitution, fifty-two were Christians. . . . Of the fifty-six signers of the Declaration of Independence, twenty-seven had Bible seminary degrees. . . . Ninety-four percent of all quotes by the Founding Fathers were based on the Bible."

[68]William G. T. Shedd, *Dogmatic Theology*, one-volume edition (Phillipsburg, NJ: P & R Publishing, 2003), 127.

[69]G. Coleman Luck, "Christian Ethics," 228–238, in *Bibliotheca Sacra* 118:471 (July 1961), 231. Referring to the ethics of atheism, Luck writes: "Non-Christian systems of ethics must be rejected as utterly inadequate. They provide no objective standard [of morality]. Indeed they are not actually realistic, since they view natural man as perfectible. In none of them is there a recognition of the

It was also true in the times of the Old Testament. After an extensive study of how ancient pagan writings compare to the Bible, Garry K. Brantley concludes that "the Bible's ethical and spiritual concepts are unparalleled by pagan sacred literature."[70] He further explains that while pagan deities were morally degenerate and difficult to appease, the true God is infinitely righteous and quick to forgive and bless His people. "Thus, the similarities between biblical and pagan literature are eclipsed by the enormous differences. Actually, there is no better indicator of the Bible's inspiration than to put it side by side with its pagan counterparts."[71] That stark contrast is often pointed out by the writers of the Bible themselves, who recognized the deep moral chasms that existed between what the pagan nations practiced and what the true God required (cf. Leviticus 18:24; Deuteronomy 18:14; Psalm 106:35–40; cf. 1 Corinthians 6:9–11). No religious writings from Israel's pagan neighbors remain relevant today; yet the Bible speaks to the modern man as clearly and applicably as it did to men living thousands of years ago.[72]

Even today, the contemporary philosophies of popular culture, having rejected the Bible, cannot cure the ills of human society. "The departure from divine revelation has brought our culture to chaos in the area of ethics," notes R. C. Sproul.[73] After all, any system of morality without God's Word as its foundation becomes groundless. "The flexuous modern outlook offers no solid basis whatever for ethical norms," writes Carl Henry. "Moreover, it inevitably leads to nihilism, to the loss of the worth and meaning of human existence."[74] On the other hand, "the answer to our moral crisis and the way out of our ethical dilemma lies in the acceptance of Christ and in the revelation of the nature of God that He has shown us. His standard of goodness, finding its source in God rather than man, provides the only adequate standard to guide us

---

sinful nature which all men possess—a nature which lacks the ability to do that which is right. None of these systems provide the individual with spiritual power to live a righteous life."

[70]Garry K. Brantley, "Pagan Mythology and the Bible," *Reason & Revelation* 13/7 (July 1993), 49–53.

[71]Ibid.

[72]Referring to the early Christian church, Philip Schaff in his *History of the Christian Church*, 8.94, notes: "The superiority of the principles of Christian ethics over the heathen standards of morality even under its most favorable forms is universally admitted."

[73]R. C. Sproul, *Following Christ* (Wheaton, IL: Tyndale House, 1996), Chapter 15.

[74]Carl F. H. Henry, "Preface," *Wycliffe Dictionary of Christian Ethics* (Peabody, MA: Hendrickson, 2000), v.

through our problems."[75] That perfect standard is revealed for us in Scripture.

In a postmodern world, the Bible remains the only real answer for the moral problems of our day. "Only Christ's church, blessed with His Word, can speak to [mankind's] truest needs."[76] While other religious and philosophical systems merely effect external changes of behavior, the Bible is able to transform people's hearts and minds through the power of the Holy Spirit. As Arthur Rendle Short of Bristol University points out, "If it be true that the Book is divinely inspired, we shall expect to find that it is in quite a different category from all other books whatsoever."[77] When we study the Bible from an ethical standpoint, that is just what we find.

---

[75] J. P. Sanders, "Our Moral Crisis," 237–254, in *Pillars of Faith*, ed. Herman O. Wilson and Morris M. Womack, 252.
[76] James R. White, *Scripture Alone* (Minneapolis: Bethany House, 2004), 215–216.
[77] A. Rendle Short, *Why Believe?* (London: Inter-Varsity Fellowship, 1958), 59.

Reason 7:
We Believe the Bible Is the Word of God

*Because It Possesses an Inexhaustible and
Supernatural Richness*

The Bible claims that its divine author possesses infinite
intelligence, insight, and wisdom. The God of the Bible "knows everything" (1 John 3:20); He is "perfect in knowledge" (Job 37:16), and
"his understanding is beyond measure" (Psalm 147:5). The universe
He created puts His wisdom on daily display (Psalm 104:24; Proverbs
3:19; Jeremiah 10:12), as does His Word (Proverbs 2:6). His understanding is such that He is intimately familiar with everything (Psalm
147:4; Proverbs 15:3; Matthew 10:29), everyone (Psalm 33:13–15;
139:1; Proverbs 5:21), and everything everyone has done or will do
(Psalm 139:2–4; Isaiah 46:9–10; cf. James 4:13–15). In response to
God's infinite wisdom, the prophet Isaiah cries out, "Have you not
known? Have you not heard? The LORD is the everlasting God, the
Creator of the ends of the earth. He does not faint or grow weary;
his understanding is unsearchable" (Isaiah 40:28; cf. Job 12:13). The
apostle Paul, overwhelmed by those same thoughts, asks rhetorically,
"For who has known the mind of the Lord, or who has been his counselor?" (Romans 11:34). The obvious answer is, no one.

In light of the infinite depth of God's wisdom and knowledge, it
follows that the Bible (if it comes from God) should be characterized
by profound depth and insight. God, of course, revealed His truth in
a way that was understandable to human beings (cf. Deuteronomy
29:29). But His Word is nonetheless marked by a profundity that
no other book possesses. It not only imparts wisdom to the simple-
minded (Psalm 19:7; 119:98–100; 2 Timothy 3:15) but also provides
the wisest of men with an endless treasure trove of spiritual understanding (cf. Deuteronomy 17:18–19; Psalm 1:2). Moreover, those
who heed its teachings will find true success in this life (Psalm 1:3;

cf. Joshua 1:8; 1 Kings 2:2–4) as they walk in the path of wisdom (cf. Proverbs 3:13; 19:8).

The profound wisdom of the Bible is evidenced by the fact that its depths remain unexhausted, even after centuries of study and examination. Reuben A. Torrey, the man with whom we began this section, made the following observation:

> Not only individual men but generations of men for eighteen hundred years have dug into it and given to the world thousands of volumes devoted to its exposition, and they have not reached the bottom of the quarry yet. A book that man produces man can exhaust, but all men together have not been able to get to the bottom of this book. How are you going to account for it? Only in this way—that in this book are hidden the infinite and inexhaustible treasures of the wisdom and knowledge of God.[78]

Many others have agreed. Thomas Scott, a nineteenth-century Bible commentator and friend of John Newton (author of "Amazing Grace"), noted, "The most learned, acute and diligent student cannot, in the longest life, obtain an entire knowledge of this one Volume—The Bible."[79] Renowned preacher Charles Spurgeon similarly declared, "Nobody ever outgrows Scripture; the book widens and deepens with our years."[80] Statements such as these could be multiplied a thousand times over. Yet in the end, "all of the various tributes paid to the Bible are in reality one tribute: *the Bible is able perennially to grip profoundly the human soul.*"[81]

Millennia after it was composed, the Bible continues to grip the souls of billions from all around the globe. "The Bible has been translated into over one thousand languages representing more than ninety percent of the world's population. It has been published in billions of copies. There are no close seconds to it on the all-time bestseller list."[82] It has inspired millions of books, influenced thousands of organizations (both secular and sacred), and instructed countless individuals in ways no human book ever could. No single person has

[78]R. A. Torrey, "Ten Reasons I Believe the Bible Is the Word of God," 289.
[79]Thomas Scott, *Essays* (London: L. B. Seely and Sons, 1830), 19. This individual should not be confused with the Sir Thomas Scott noted in Section 2.
[80]Charles Spurgeon, cited from *The New Encyclopedia of Christian Quotations*, 116.
[81]Ramm, *Protestant Christian Evidences*, 224.
[82]Norman L. Geisler and William E. Nix, *A General Introduction to the Bible* (Chicago: Moody Press, 1996), 196.

ever uncovered all of its treasures; nor have all the people in all of history exhausted its wealth. From this we conclude that the wisdom of Scripture is inexhaustibly rich. The only reasonable explanation for its ageless profundity is that it comes from the mind of the eternal God, which is exactly what it claims (cf. 1 Corinthians 2:10–16; 2 Timothy 3:16–17).

Reason 8:
We Believe the Bible Is the Word of God

Because It Changes the Lives of People through the
Power of the Spirit

The Bible not only inspires people with its inexhaustible richness—it changes them through the life-transforming power of the Spirit. It describes itself as a living book that, being empowered by the Spirit of God (Ephesians 6:17), is able to penetrate the deepest parts of the soul (Hebrews 4:12). It is through the Word of truth that men and women can find true life (Psalm 119:50, 93; John 20:31). It sanctifies those who embrace it (John 17:17; Ephesians 5:26), illuminates their path (Psalm 119:105, 130), gives them hope (Psalm 119:49; Romans 15:4), and motivates their obedience (cf. Deuteronomy 17:19–20). It purifies them (Psalm 119:9), protects them (Psalm 17:4; 19:11), nourishes them (Deuteronomy 8:3; Matthew 4:4; 1 Peter 2:2), comforts them (Psalm 19:8; 119:76; Romans 15:4), and encourages them in the faith (Acts 20:32; 1 Corinthians 10:11).

The same word that created the universe (Hebrews 11:3; 2 Peter 3:5; cf. Genesis 1:3, 6, 9, etc.), is able to create new life in the human heart (James 1:18; 1 Peter 1:23). It is through meditating on "the word of Christ" that believers are "filled with the Spirit" (compare Colossians 3:16–17 with Ephesians 5:18–20), the result of which is a total transformation of heart and life (John 14:17; Romans 8:2–5, 13–14; 15:13; Galatians 5:22–25; Titus 3:5). Without exception, the Word of God works effectively in the hearts and minds of those who believe (1 Thessalonians 2:13), conforming them into the likeness of Christ (cf. Romans 8:29; Colossians 1:25–29). Even the worst sinner can be transformed by the power of this book, since it is in the Scriptures that the gospel of God's grace through Jesus Christ is revealed, and "the gospel . . . is the power of God for salvation to everyone who believes" (Romans 1:16).

Countless examples of men and women throughout history could be recounted here, evidencing the fact that the Bible, through the power of the Holy Spirit, can radically change people's lives. Josh McDowell tells how his alcoholic father was dramatically changed by the gospel:

> It was like someone reached down and switched on a light inside him. He touched alcohol only once after that. He got the drink only as far as his lips and that was it—after forty years of drinking! He didn't need it any more. Fourteen months later, he died from complications of his alcoholism. But in that fourteen-month period over a hundred people in the area around my tiny hometown committed their lives to Jesus Christ because of the change they saw in the town drunk, my dad.[83]

A million other stories could be added about those who, running away from God, found that they could not outrun His grace. Lives that were previously captivated by sin were miraculously transformed through the gospel. In writing to the Corinthians, Paul outlined some of the sins that had previously characterized those Christians: sexual immorality, idolatry, adultery, homosexuality, theft, greed, drunkenness, slander, and swindling. "Such were some of you," the apostle wrote. "But you were washed, you were sanctified, you were justified in the name of the Lord Jesus Christ and by the Spirit of our God" (1 Corinthians 6:11). When the Spirit of God empowers the Word of God, any heart can be changed (cf. Ezekiel 36:26–27; 2 Corinthians 5:17).

The story is told of pastor and theologian Harry Ironside, who was publicly preaching the gospel in San Francisco when an antagonist in the crowd shouted, "Atheism has done more for the world than Christianity!"[84] W. A. Criswell recounts the event, noting that the atheist further challenged Ironside to a debate:

> Dr. Ironside, God's wonderful preacher, said, "I would be happy to debate with you. This time. This hour. This place. I will meet with you."
> "Fine," said the infidel, "I'll debate with you."
> And Ironside said, "I just have one thing that I want us to do. Tomorrow, this very hour, I am going to bring with me 100 men and

---

[83]McDowell, *Evidence That Demands a Verdict*, xxvii.
[84]Cited from Little, *Know Why You Believe*, 145–146.

women who have been saved out of the gutter and out of the darkness and despair of life, who have been lifted up into the brightness of
God. I am going to bring 100 of them. And they will be here, standing
beside me tomorrow—this place, this time.

"And you, you bring 100 men and women who have been
saved out of the gutter and the darkness of life, by the gospel of
infidelity."[85]

Needless to say, the debate never happened. When asked to produce those whose lives had been radically improved by atheism, the
antagonist knew he could not do so. In contrast to "the gospel of infidelity," the gospel of Jesus Christ has transformed the lives of millions.
With each life that is changed, the power of God through the means of
the Bible is vividly put on display.

---

[85]W. A. Criswell, "The Truth of the Faith," sermon on John 6:66–69, preached July 26, 1987; http://www.wacriswell.com/index.cfm/FuseAction/Search.Transcripts/sermon/713.cfm. Accessed September 4, 2007. Parts of this excerpt were slightly edited to improve readability.

Reason 9:
We Believe the Bible Is the Word of God

*Because It Stands Alone among Books That Claim
to Come from God*

The God of the Bible describes Himself as one who is incomparable. "To whom then will you liken God, or what likeness compare with him? . . . To whom then will you compare me, that I should be like him? says the Holy One" (Isaiah 40:18, 25). And again, "To whom will you liken me and make me equal, and compare me, that we may be alike?" (Isaiah 46:5; cf. Exodus 15:11; Psalm 89:6–8).

Though the answer is obvious, the Bible answers those questions without hesitation: "There is none holy like the LORD; there is none besides you; there is no rock like our God" (1 Samuel 2:2). "Therefore you are great, O LORD God. For there is none like you, and there is no God besides you" (2 Samuel 7:22). "O LORD, God of Israel, there is no God like you, in heaven above or on earth beneath" (1 Kings 8:23a). "There is none like you, O LORD; you are great, and your name is great in might" (Jeremiah 10:6). Many other passages could be cited, but the point is clear: The God of the Bible is unlike anything in His creation or any other supposed deity. In the words of David, "There is none like you among the gods, O Lord, nor are there any works like yours. . . . For you are great and do wondrous things; you alone are God" (Psalm 86:8–10).

It follows, then, that because God is unique (being infinitely greater than any other imagined "god"), His Word would also be unique among all other religious books. An examination of Scripture should "leave little question about the uniqueness of the Bible among all human writings, including the most revered scriptures of other religions."[86] If the supreme and matchless God is truly its source, the Bible should be clearly superior to any supposed rival. And in fact it

---

[86]Robert L. Saucy, "How Else Is the Bible Unique?" 48–49.

is. When "we compare the Bible with other claimants, that is exactly what we find. The Scriptures [alone] bear the marks of a supernatural book."[87]

To make the point, we will briefly consider the Qur'an, a book that some regard as the Bible's closest "competitor" (and which over one billion Muslims believe to be the word of God). Made up of 114 chapters (each known as a *sura*), the Qur'an is the central religious book of Islam. It is believed by Muslims to be "the last book of guidance from Allah, sent down to Muhammad (*pbuh*) through the angel Gabriel (*Jibra'il*). Every word of the Qur'an is the word of Allah."[88] But did the Qur'an truly come from God?

The Qur'an teaches that previous revelation also came from God, including the writings of Moses (sura 2:87; 3:3), David (4:163), and the gospel of Jesus (5:46–48).[89] Elsewhere the Qur'an affirms these previous scriptures (2:91; 3:14, 84; 4:47), asserting that God has protected his revelation in them (5:48; 18:28). It also teaches that "Muhammad is to consult the scriptures already revealed if he is in doubt about what is revealed to him" (10:94–95).[90] Thus, the Qur'an claims to be in perfect harmony with the revelation that God gave earlier through Moses, David, and Jesus (2:136).

When confronted with the fact that the Qur'an is at odds with the Old and New Testaments, Muslims contend that it is the Bible that has been corrupted.[91] Hence, it is argued, the Jewish and Christian Scriptures have been tainted, not the Qur'an. But there are significant problems with this claim.

For starters, the Qur'an implies that the Old Testament was trustworthy at the time of Mary (sura 66:12), John the Baptist (19:12), Jesus (3:48–50; 5:113; 61:6), and even at the time of its own composition, since it commands Jews and Christians to follow what had been revealed to them in their Scriptures (5:47, 68). The Qur'an also claims that the gospel confirms the truth of the Torah (5:49) and calls Jews and

---

[87]Robert L. Saucy, *Is the Bible Reliable?* (Wheaton, IL: Victor Books, 1978), 31.

[88]Ghulam Sarwar, *Islam: A Brief Guide*. Cited from Colin Chapman, *Cross and Crescent* (Downers Grove, IL: InterVarsity Press, 2003), 84.

[89]The parenthetical references here and in the following paragraphs refer to chapters and verses within the Qur'an. They should not be confused with biblical references, which are preceded by a book of the Bible.

[90]Chapman, *Cross and Crescent*, 92.

[91]For a full discussion on this topic, see Chawkat Moucarry, *The Prophet and the Messiah* (Downers Grove, IL: InterVarsity Press, 2001).

Christians "People of the Scripture" (2:44, 113, 121; 3:78–79; 5:43; 6:92; 7:157; 10:95). Steven Masood, who converted to Christianity from a Muslim background, notes:

> The Qur'an testifies that its main purpose is to provide a revelation for Arabic speaking people, who could not understand (or did not have access to) the Scriptures of the Jews and Christians (Surah 46:11–12; 41:2–3; 20:112; 39:29; 12:2). There is no suggestion that this new revelation (the Qur'an) was needed to *replace* any corrupted Scripture. In fact, the Qur'an claimed to be a *verification* of the earlier revelations such as in the Torah and the Gospel, that went before it (Surah 10:37; 12:111).[92]

The Qur'an thus implies that the Old and New Testaments had not yet been "corrupted" when the Qur'an was completed in the late sixth or early seventh century.

Moreover, the Qur'an claims "to be the guardian of previous Scriptures, therefore any Muslim who claims that there has been a corruption of the text of the Torah [of Moses] or the Injil [Gospel] also, inevitably, charges the Qur'an with failure in its role in 'guarding' them (Surah 5:48)."[93] The Qur'an therefore bears witness to the veracity of the Old and New Testaments, at least as they existed in the sixth century A.D.

> The Qur'an says that no one can change the Word of God. If the Jews did corrupt the Word of God then it would mean that the Qur'anic statement is unreliable, a concept that would be blasphemy to Muslims. The only possible conclusion in the light of the Qur'an is therefore that the copies of the pre-Islamic Scriptures (known as the Torah and the Injil) were available in the days of Muhammad as they are available today, i.e. that they are valid. Since Christians have ample documentary evidence from before Muhammad's time, they can confidently assert that their Scriptures are trustworthy.[94]

This, then presents a major problem for those who hold to the inerrant inspiration of the Qur'an, especially when one considers the textual evidence for the Bible. The papyri and older manuscripts of

---

[92]Steven Masood, *The Bible and the* Qur'an (Cumbria, UK: Authentic Media, 2002), 70–71.
[93]Ibid., 72.
[94]Ibid., 80–81.

the New Testament, as well as the translation of the Latin Vulgate, the work of Origen on the Old Testament text, the Syriac Peshitta translation of both testaments, the Greek translations of the Old Testament in the Septuagint, the Dead Sea Scrolls, and the Samaritan Pentateuch all predate the Qur'an and demonstrate that the texts of the Old and New Testaments that existed when the Qur'an was written are the same texts we still have today. No major changes (especially of the nature demanded by Muslim beliefs) have been made to the Bible in its entire history, either before or after the Qur'an.[95]

By its own admission, the Qur'an must be consistent with previous revelation from God. But it does not take long to see that the Bible and the Qur'an are not compatible. This "should come as no surprise to well-informed Muslims who know that, in the final analysis, the claims of Christianity and Islam are incompatible," writes Syrian-born scholar Chawkat Moucarry, who earned his doctorate in Islamic studies from the University of Sorbonne, Paris. "This incompatibility is behind the Islamic assumption that, in one way or another, the Bible has been corrupted."[96] When it is demonstrated that the Bible has not been corrupted, both from the claims of the Qur'an and from the textual evidence for the Bible, it is the Qur'an—not the Bible—that is discredited.

In addition to being incompatible with previous revelation from God, the Qur'an contains its own internal contradictions, such as urging religious tolerance in one place (sura 2:256) and then commanding Muslims to fight and kill those who do not believe (9:29; 9:5). In other places (7:54 and 32:4) the Qur'an claims that the earth was made in six days. But in sura 41:9–12, it teaches that eight days were needed to create the world.[97]

The Qur'an also purports certain scientific inaccuracies, claiming that human beings are formed from a clot of blood (sura 23:14), that the sun rests in a muddy spring in the west (18:86), that mountains were created to hold down the earth and prevent earthquakes (31:10–11; cf. 16:15; 21:31; 78:6–7; 88:17, 19), that there are literally

---

[95]This paragraph was adapted from correspondence with William D. Barrick, Professor of Old Testament at The Master's Seminary. Dr. Barrick spent two decades as a missionary in Bangladesh, a predominantly Muslim country, and has given seminars on Islamic teachings and practice.
[96]Moucarry, *The Prophet and the Messiah*, 264.
[97]For more on this point, see Norman L. Geisler and Abdul Saleeb, *Answering Islam* (Grand Rapids, MI: Baker, 2002), 201–203.

seven heavens (2:29; 17:44; 41:12; 23:17, 86; 67:3; 71:15–16), and that meteors are a form of divine retribution being hurled at devils who might try to spy on the heavenly council (37:6–10; 72:8–9; cf. 15:16–18; 67:5; 86:2–3).[98]

The Qur'an contains historical errors as well. As one non-Christian author explains,

> At sura 40.38; the Koran mistakenly identifies Haman, who in reality was the minister of the Persian King Ahasuerus (mentioned in the book of Esther), as the minister of the Pharoah [sic] at the time of Moses.
>
> We have already noted the confusion of Mary, the mother of Jesus, with the Mary who was the sister of Moses and Aaron. At sura 2.249, 250 there is obviously a confusion between the story of Saul as told therein, and the account of Gideon in Judg. 7.5.
>
> The account of Alexander the Great in the Koran (18.82) is hopelessly confused historically; we are certain it was based on the Romance of Alexander. At any rate, the Macedonian was not a Muslim and did not live to an old age, nor was he a contemporary of Abraham, as Muslims contend.[99]

Examples such as these undermine the Qur'an's claim to be the Word of God.

If space permitted, we could also consider other religious texts, such as the Hindu Veda or the Book of Mormon. In each case, we would again find that the supposedly inspired text falls far short of the Bible. Consider, as just one example, the test of predictive prophecy. Norman Geisler and William Nix explain: "Other books claim divine inspiration, such as the Koran, the Book of Mormon, and parts of the [Hindu] Veda. But none of those books contains [genuine] predictive prophecy. As a result, fulfilled prophecy is a strong indication of the unique divine authority of the Bible."[100]

Perhaps the greatest difference between the Bible and all other religious books is that the Bible teaches a message of salvation by grace,

---

[98]Ibid., 203–205. Several examples also taken from William Campbell, *The Qur'an and the Bible in the Light of History & Science* (Middle East Resources, 2002), Section 4, Chapter 2; http://www.answering-islam.org/Campbell/index.html.

[99]Ibn Warraq, *Why I Am Not a Muslim* (Amherst, NY: Prometheus Books, 1995), 158–159. In *What the Koran Really Says* (Amherst, NY: Prometheus Books, 2002), Warraq shows additional evidence of contradictions, obscurities, and inaccuracies in the Qur'an.

[100]Geisler and Nix, *A General Introduction to the Bible*, 196. Cited from Josh McDowell, *New Evidence That Demands a Verdict*, 13.

whereas every other religious system teaches salvation by human works (cf. Micah 7:18; Ephesians 2:4–10; Titus 3:3–7). "All other religions we know of teach salvation by meritorious works. Christianity is the only religion that teaches salvation solely by grace through faith alone."[101] This again is evidence of the uniqueness of the true God and His true Word, the Bible. "Such salvation is so strange to the natural man and yet so grand and satisfying to the deep aspirations in the hearts of all people that it cannot have been authored by mere humans."[102]

---

[101]Ankerberg and Weldon, *Fast Facts on Defending Your Faith*, 32.
[102]Robert L. Saucy, "Are the Bible's Teachings Unique?," 35–42, in *Understanding Christian Theology*, ed. Charles R. Swindoll and Roy B. Zuck (Nashville: Thomas Nelson, 2003), 42.

Reason 10:
We Believe the Bible Is the Word of God

Because Jesus Affirmed the Bible as the Word of God

We began with the testimony of the Holy Spirit, the third member of the Trinity. We will conclude with the testimony of the second member, Jesus Christ the Son of God. As God in human flesh (e.g., John 1:1–4; 5:18; Philippians 2:6; Hebrews 1:3), Jesus Christ provides divine witness to the inspiration and authority of His Word (cf. Colossians 3:16; 1 Peter 1:11). In the words of British theologian John Stott, "The chief reason why the Christian believes in the divine origin of the Bible is that Jesus Christ himself taught it."[103] It is appropriate, then, that the incarnate Word of God (John 1:1) should stand as our final, authoritative witness to the written Word of God.

> In fact, the greatest testimony to the authenticity of the Bible as God's inspired and inerrant Word is the Lord Jesus. Why is His testimony so important? Because God authenticated and proved Him to be His own divine Son by the resurrection (cf. Acts 2:22-36; 4:8-12; 17:30-31; Rom. 1:4). Christ not only clearly confirmed the authority of the Old Testament, but He specifically promised the New Testament.[104]

Jesus spoke of the Old Testament Scriptures as "the word of God" and that which "cannot be broken" (John 10:35). He promised that no part of the Law would pass away "until all is accomplished" (Matthew 5:18). When tempted by Satan, Jesus answered by appealing to the Bible: "It is written, 'Man shall not live by bread alone, but by every word that comes from the mouth of God'" (Matthew 4:4). His condemnation of the religious leaders of His day centered on their distortion of God's Word, because they were "making void the word

---

[103]John Stott, cited from *The New Encyclopedia of Christian Quotations*, 124.
[104]J. Hampton Keathley III, "The Bible: The Inerrant Word of God"; www.bible.org/page.php?page_id=696. Accessed September 16, 2007.

of God by [their] tradition that [they had] handed down" (Mark 7:13). He continually undergirded his teaching with the phrase, "It is written" (e.g., Matthew 21:13; 26:31; Mark 7:6; 14:21).

Throughout His ministry, Jesus affirmed the Old Testament in its entirety (Matthew 5:17–18)—including its historical reliability (cf. Matthew 10:15; 12:40; 19:3–5; 24:38–39), prophetic accuracy (Matthew 26:54), sufficiency (Matthew 4:4; Luke 16:31), unity (Luke 24:27, 44), inerrancy (Matthew 22:29; John 17:17), infallibility (John 10:35), divine authorship (Matthew 22:31–32), and authority (Matthew 21:13, 16; Mark 7:6–13). "Our Lord used historical incidents in the Old Testament in a manner that evinced His total confidence in their factual historicity," explains Charles Ryrie. "Obviously, our Lord felt He had a reliable Bible, historically true, with every word trustworthy."[105]

Jesus also testified to the authority and inspiration of the New Testament, predicting that the Holy Spirit would come to complete His teaching ministry. In John 16:12–13, Jesus promised His disciples: "I still have many things to say to you, but you cannot bear them now. When the Spirit of truth comes, he will guide you into all the truth, for he will not speak on his own authority, but whatever he hears he will speak, and he will declare to you the things that are to come." These teachings were pre-authenticated by Christ Himself (John 14:26), authorizing the apostles to be His witnesses in the world (Matthew 28:18–19; Acts 1:8). The apostles, therefore, rightly recognized their own inspired writings as being part of the biblical canon, on par with the books of the Old Testament (1 Thessalonians 2:13; 2 Peter 3:15–16).

> How do we get to the sixty-six books from the slender base that has been established? The short answer to this is that we get to it through the authority of Christ. It is because He endorses the Old Testament and makes provision for the New that both Old and New have this authority.[106]

We will look more closely at the person and work of Jesus Christ in the following sections. Our goal here is to make one simple point: if we

---

[105]Charles C. Ryrie, *What You Should Know about Inerrancy* (Chicago: Moody Press, 1981), 77–78.
[106]Helm, "Faith, Evidence, and the Scriptures," 310.

accept the authority of Jesus Christ, we must also accept the authority of the Bible. "Christ's use of the Scriptures was constant and extensive. He relied solely upon the canonical Scriptures and expressed serious objections to the traditions of men which contradicted the Scriptures. His usage illustrates His profound respect for the inherent authority and irrevocable finality of Scripture."[107]

Clearly, God has given us many reasons that confirm what the Holy Spirit has already made known to us about His Word. The Bible's internal consistency, external verifiability, historical impact, and supernatural power all authenticate it as God's unique revelation. Additionally, as we will see in Section 4, it has been faithfully preserved throughout history, meaning that the text we read today is a faithful and accurate representation of the original. We can therefore rejoice in the privilege of hearing God speak each time we open the pages of His Word. As New Testament scholar William D. Mounce correctly concludes, "The entirety of Scripture comes from the mouth of God. To read it is to hear him speak. It is therefore true, and it can therefore be trusted."[108]

---

[107]Robert P. Lightner, *The Saviour and the Scriptures* (Philadelphia: Presbyterian & Reformed, 1973), 161.
[108]William D. Mounce, *Pastoral Epistles*, Word Biblical Commentary (Nashville: Thomas Nelson, 2000), 570.

REASONS WE BELIEVE IN THE BIBLE

PART TWO

The New Testament Gospels Are Historically Reliable

I esteem the Gospels to be thoroughly genuine, for there shines forth from them the reflected splendor of a sublimity proceeding from the person of Jesus Christ, and of as divine a kind as was ever manifested upon earth.

GOETHE[1]

Now as a literary historian, I am perfectly convinced that whatever else the Gospels are they are not legends. I have read a great deal of legend (myth) and I am quite clear that they are not the same sort of thing.

C. S. LEWIS[2]

---

[1]Goethe, *Conversations with Eckman*, 3:371. Cited from Grant R. Jeffrey, *Jesus: The Great Debate* (Toronto: Frontier Research, 1999), 172.
[2]C. S. Lewis. Cited from Armand M. Nicholi Jr., *The Question of God* (New York: Simon & Schuster, 2003), 87.

INTRODUCTION

Charles Dickens is a name most of us immediately recognize. Considered the foremost English novelist of the Victorian Era, his works—such as *The Adventures of Oliver Twist*, *David Copperfield*, *Great Expectations*, and *A Tale of Two Cities*—have become timeless classics. Centered around unforgettable characters, Dickens's stories have left an indelible mark on Western culture. It is difficult, for example, to imagine a Christmas season without some reference to *A Christmas Carol* or its stingy protagonist, Ebenezer Scrooge.

Though many readers are familiar with Dickens's novels, far fewer know that he also wrote a non-fiction account of the life and ministry of Jesus Christ. Entitled *The Life of Our Lord*, the book was written for his children (of whom he had ten), at a level they could understand. Because it was never intended for wider audiences to read, it was not published until after Dickens's death by the approval of his family. "It was written in 1849, twenty-one years before his death," explains Marie Dickens in the Foreword. She continues by noting that the work is a personal glimpse into Dickens's family life. "Charles Dickens frequently told his children the Gospel Story, and made mention of the Divine Example in his letters to them."[3]

The Life of Our Lord begins with this heartfelt introduction: "My dear children, I am very anxious that you should know something about the History of Jesus Christ. For everybody ought to know about Him." Then, beginning with Jesus' birth, Dickens follows the life of Jesus as portrayed by the four Gospels, in a manner suitable for young minds to comprehend.

That Charles Dickens accepted the historical veracity of the Gospel accounts is obvious throughout the entire volume. Consider just two short examples. At the end of the second chapter, he writes of Jesus' miracles:

---

[3]From Preface, Charles Dickens, *The Life of Our Lord* (Philadelphia: The Westminster Press, 1981). It was originally published in London newspapers in 1935.

> For God had given Jesus Christ the power to do such wonders; and he did them, that people might know he was not a common man, and might believe what he taught them, and also believe that God had sent him. And many people, hearing this, and hearing that he cured the sick, did begin to believe in him; and great crowds followed him in the streets and on the roads, wherever he went.

Later, after an overview of Jesus' death and resurrection, Dickens reports:

> After that time, Jesus Christ was seen by five hundred of his followers at once, and He remained with others of them forty days, teaching them, and instructing them to go forth into the world, and preach His Gospel and religion; not minding what wicked men might do to them. And conducting his disciples at last, out of Jerusalem as far as Bethany, he blessed them, and ascended in a cloud to Heaven, and took His place at the right hand of God.

Dickens's admiration for and "deep devotion to Our Lord," as Marie Dickens put it, was clearly evidenced in the high value he placed on the New Testament witness to Jesus Christ. Years later, Charles Dickens would again express his esteem in a letter he wrote to his son, who was leaving home in England to go live with his brother in Australia:

> I put a New Testament among your books, for the very same reasons, and with the very same hopes, that made me write an easy account of it for you, when you were a little child. Because it is the best book that ever was, or will be, known in the world; and because it teaches you the best lessons by which any human creature, who tries to be truthful and faithful to duty, can possibly be guided. . . . I now most solemnly impress upon you the truth and beauty of the Christian religion, as it came from Christ Himself, and the impossibility of your going far wrong if you humbly but heartily respect it.[4]

Beyond being a fascinating glimpse into the personal life of this notable author, the story of Charles Dickens raises some important questions, particularly regarding his view of the Gospels. Was Dickens

---

[4]Cited from John Forster, *The Life of Charles Dickens*, Vol. 3 (London: Chapman and Hall, 1874), 446. This letter was written in September 1868.

right to believe the New Testament accounts about Jesus, such that he would present them to his children as factual history? Or was he wrong to view *The Life of Our Lord* (and the biblical testimony on which it was based) as anything other than fiction? It is necessary that we answer such questions, not because they involve Charles Dickens (as notable as he was), but because they center on the person and work of someone much more significant—namely, Jesus Christ. How we respond to the Christ of the Gospels (whether we regard Him as fact or as fiction) makes a critical difference both for this life and the next.

TEN REASONS WE BELIEVE IN THE NEW TESTAMENT GOSPELS

Are the New Testament Gospels a reliable witness to the life and ministry of Jesus? It is a simple question, yet it is absolutely foundational to the Christian faith. If the Gospel accounts are reliable, then we have good reason to embrace Jesus Christ as Lord and Savior, based on His ancestry, birth, baptism, ministry, miracles, teaching, death, and resurrection. But if the Gospels are not reliable, then we face a massive theological dilemma, because if the Jesus of the Bible is not the real Jesus, then our faith in Him as Christians is surely misplaced.

For centuries, the universal understanding was that the Gospels were reliable documents. But since the rise of theological liberalism, some scholars have seriously questioned the historicity of the New Testament record. In the words of one liberal critic, "The narrative Gospels have no claim as historical accounts. The Gospels are imaginative creations."[5] The result of such negative assessments, which assume that the biblical accounts are inaccurate or convoluted, has been a search for the "historical Jesus" (meaning Jesus as He actually was), in contrast to the "Christ of faith" (meaning Jesus as He is presented in the Bible). But ironically, with the Gospels rejected, the liberal picture of the "historical Jesus" is itself nothing more than the subjective imaginations of this or that contemporary scholar, a person removed from the earthly life and setting of Jesus by two thousand years and often hundreds of miles.

Our contention, of course, is that there is no discrepancy between

---

[5]Burton Mack, cited by Richard N. Ostling, "Jesus Christ, Plain and Simple," *Time* magazine (January 10, 1994). Accessed online at www.time.com/time/magazine/article/0,9171,979938-2,00.html.

the Jesus of the Bible and the Jesus of history. That is because we believe the New Testament Gospels demonstrate themselves to be historically reliable documents. But what are our reasons for trusting them?

In the last section, we considered reasons we believe the whole Bible to be the Word of God. Those reasons, of course, apply to the New Testament Gospels as much as they do to any other part of Scripture. However, because the Gospels are our primary source of information about Jesus Christ, it is important that we look at them specifically. Unless we can trust their record of Jesus, we will never be able to examine His life and ministry with any level of confidence.

With that in mind, we will now consider ten factors that support the historical reliability of the New Testament Gospel accounts.[6]

---

[6]F. F. Bruce's *The New Testament Documents: Are They Reliable?* is a helpful overview of this topic and is recommended for further study.

Reason 1:
We Believe the New Testament Gospels Are Reliable

Because They Are Consistent with Previous Revelation from God

It follows that if the New Testament Gospels were written under the inspiration of the Holy Spirit (John 14:16–17, 26; 15:26–27; 16:12–15), they must harmonize with that which the Holy Spirit previously revealed in the Old Testament (cf. Zechariah 7:12). We would not be able to honestly embrace them if they were inconsistent with what had come before, since God cannot contradict His Word (Numbers 23:19; cf. John 10:35).

Because the Holy Spirit inspired both the Old and New Testaments (2 Timothy 3:16–17; 2 Peter 1:20–21; cf. 3:15–16), we should expect the doctrine and message of each Testament to be consistent with the other. And indeed that is the case. The New Testament is the perfect complement to the Old, a point that was underscored by Jesus and the apostles (cf. Luke 18:31–33; 24:27, 44–45; John 5:39, 46; Acts 3:18; 10:43; 1 Peter 1:10–12). The New Testament writers never suggested that their writings were in contradiction to those of the Old Testament. Rather, they continually appealed to the Old Testament in their writings and preaching. According to *Nelson's New Illustrated Bible Dictionary*:

> The number of quotations from and allusions to the Old Testament in the New varies with the counter. Direct quotations have been numbered from less than 150 to more than 300. When allusions are added to this number, the total number rises to anywhere from 600 to more than 4,000, again according to the person doing the counting.[7]

---

[7]Herbert Lockyer, ed., *Quotations in the New Testament,* in *Nelson's Illustrated Bible Dictionary* (Nashville: Thomas Nelson, 1986), 894.

Though scholars do not agree on the exact numbers, they do agree on the fact that the New Testament continually affirms and builds on the Old. In the Gospel accounts, this continuity becomes most clear when we consider what the Old Testament foretold about the Messiah, as there are hundreds of prophecies related to His coming.[8] In each case, the picture of the Messiah painted in the Old Testament matches perfectly with the description of Jesus in the four Gospels. The Evangelists (the Gospel writers) understood the importance of the Old Testament record, and they repeatedly emphasized the fact that "Moses and all the Prophets" (Luke 24:27) pointed to Jesus.[9]

According to the Old Testament, the coming Messiah would:

• be a descendant of Abraham (compare Genesis 22:18 with Galatians 3:16)

• be a descendant of Jacob (compare Numbers 24:17 with Luke 3:23, 34)

• be from the tribe of Judah (compare Genesis 49:10 with Luke 3:23, 33)

• be from the family of Jesse (compare Isaiah 11:1 with Luke 3:23, 32)

• be from the house of David (compare Jeremiah 23:5 with Luke 3:23, 31)

• be born at Bethlehem (compare Micah 5:2 with Matthew 2:1)

• be the preexistent one (compare Micah 5:2 with Colossians 1:17; cf. John 1:1)

• be the Lord (compare Psalm 110:1 with Matthew 22:43–45; Acts 2:34)

• be God with us (compare Isaiah 7:14 with Matthew 1:23)

• be a prophet (compare Deuteronomy 18:18 with Acts 3:22)

• be a priest (compare Psalm 110:4 with Hebrews 5:5–10)

• be anointed by the Spirit (compare Isaiah 11:1–2 with Luke 2:40; Matthew 3:16–17)

• be zealous for God's house (compare Psalm 69:9 with John 2:15–16)

• have a forerunner (compare Isaiah 40:3; Malachi 3:1 with Matthew 3:1–2)

• begin His ministry in Galilee (compare Isaiah 9:1 with Matthew 4:12–17)

• have a ministry of miracles (compare Isaiah 35:5–6 with Matthew 11:4–5)

• bring healing and spiritual life (compare Isaiah 61:1–2 with Luke 4:18–21)

---

[8]See passages such as Genesis 3:14–15; Deuteronomy 18:15–19; Psalm 22:1, 16, 18; 110:1–4; Isaiah 9:1–7; 42:1–4; 49:6; 53:1–12; 59:16–20; 61:1–3; Jeremiah 23:5–6; Daniel 7:13–14; 9:20–27; Zechariah 3:8–9; 6:12–13; 9:9–10; Malachi 3:1–3; 4:5–6.

[9]Cf. Matthew 2:15, 17, 23; 13:14, 35; 26:54, 56; 27:9; Mark 14:49; Luke 1:1–2; 18:31; 22:37; 24:44; John 17:12; 18:9; 19:24, 28, 36 and many others. We will discuss more about messianic prophecy in Section 5.

- enter Jerusalem on a donkey (compare Zechariah 9:9 with Matthew 21:5)
- be rejected by the Jews (compare Isaiah 53:3, 7–8 with Luke 18:31–33)
- be silent before His accusers (compare Isaiah 53:7 with Matthew 27:12)
- be wounded and bruised (compare Isaiah 53:5 with Matthew 27:26)
- be smitten and spat upon (compare Isaiah 50:6 with Matthew 26:67)
- be crucified with thieves (compare Isaiah 53:12 with Matthew 27:38)
- have His garments divided (compare Psalm 22:18 with John 19:23–24)
- have His side pierced (compare Zechariah 12:10 with John 19:34)
- be buried in a rich man's tomb (compare Isaiah 53:9 with Matthew 27:57ff.)
- come before Jerusalem and the temple were destroyed (compare Daniel 9:26 with Matthew 24:2)
- bring salvation to the world (compare Isaiah 49:6 with Acts 26:23)[10]

If we take messianic prophecy at all seriously, believing that it was historically fulfilled, then we are drawn immediately to the Christ of the New Testament Gospels. No other record of Jesus' life—whether from the early Gnostics or the more recent liberal theologians—is consistent with Old Testament revelation. On the other hand, because the New Testament Gospels are in perfect harmony with earlier revelation from God, they can be trusted.

The Old Testament, then, is our first witness to the authenticity of Matthew, Mark, Luke, and John.

---

[10]Robert T. Boyd outlines forty-eight such prophecies in *Boyd's Handbook of Practical Apologetics* (Grand Rapids, MI: Kregel, 1997), 125–127. Also cf. John Ankerberg and John Weldon, *Fast Facts on Defending Your Faith* (Eugene, OR: Harvest House, 2002), 65–67.

Reason 2:
We Believe the New Testament Gospels Are Reliable

Because They Were Written by Those Close to the Events of Jesus' Life

If the Gospels were written by men distantly removed from the events they recorded, we would have reason for concern. Thankfully, however, that is not the case. Two of the Gospels, Matthew and John, were penned by disciples of Jesus and provide eyewitness testimony to the events they discuss (cf. John 1:14; 21:20–25; 1 John 1:1–4). The Gospel of Mark was written by a close friend and associate of the apostle Peter (1 Peter 5:13; cf. Acts 12:12). As the early Christian leader Papias (c. 60–c. 130) explains, "Mark became an interpreter of Peter; as many things as he remembered he wrote down accurately (though certainly not in order) the things said or done by the Lord."[11] Thus Mark's Gospel reflects the memoirs of Peter (who was an eyewitness to Jesus' ministry), which Mark preserved by writing them down.

Luke (who wrote both the third Gospel and the book of Acts) was the traveling companion of the apostle Paul (2 Timothy 4:11; cf. Acts 16:10–17; 20:5–15; 21:1–18; 27:1–28:16) and was a careful researcher. Luke himself reports that he wrote his Gospel, "having followed all things closely for some time past . . . that you may have certainty concerning the things you have been taught" (Luke 1:3–4). The biblical Gospels, then, are the product of eyewitness testimony (Luke 1:1–4; Acts 1:21–22; Hebrews 2:3–4; 2 Peter 1:16), either firsthand (in the case of Matthew and John) or secondhand (in the case of Mark and Luke). As those who venerated Jesus (cf. Acts 2:36; Revelation 1:17), they took special care in giving solemn testimony to His life (Acts 2:40; 8:25; 10:42; 18:5; 20:21; 28:23; 2 Peter 1:16–20; 1 John 1:2; 4:14; Revelation 1:2).

---

[11]*Fragments of Papias*, 2.15.

Furthermore, the Gospels were not written in a vacuum. The events recorded by the Evangelists were at the heart and soul of their ministries. From the very beginnings of the church they had repeatedly recounted the details of Jesus' life and ministry, both to themselves and to those in the Christian community. That they would forget the very thing that defined them is difficult to imagine.[12] Yet, even if forgetting were possible, their eyewitness testimony was safeguarded by the Holy Spirit, whom Jesus promised would help His disciples remember His teachings (John 14:26; 16:13). As Robert Gromacki points out:

> . . . some have argued that even eye-witnesses would not have been able to remember the events accurately. Men, especially aging men, are prone to memory failure. If the Bible were nothing more than a mere human composition, then this argument would carry some weight. However, such critics disregard the promise of Christ to His apostles [in John 14:26].[13]

Thus the Holy Spirit guaranteed that what they remembered would be accurate.

That Matthew, Mark, Luke, and John were the actual authors of the Gospels that bear their names is overwhelmingly supported by the testimony of church history, with affirmation coming from early Christian leaders such as Papias (c. 60–c. 130), Justin Martyr (100–165), Polycrates (c. 130–196), Irenaeus (c. 140–c. 202) who cites Polycarp (c. 69–160), Clement of Alexandria (c. 150–c. 215), Tertullian (c.160–c. 220), Origen (c.185–c. 254), Eusebius (c. 263–c. 339), Jerome (c. 345–420), and others. Never is the fourfold Gospel seriously questioned.[14] In the words of Irenaeus (c. 140–c. 202):

---

[12]J. P. Moreland, *Scaling the Secular City* (Grand Rapids, MI: Baker, 2005), 143–145 explains how the Gospel writers' concern for accuracy would have been even greater in a Jewish oral tradition, where the students of leading rabbis (like Jesus) would take great care to memorize the teachings and deeds of their masters.

[13]Robert G. Gromacki, *New Testament Survey* (Grand Rapids, MI: Baker, 1992), 57. Gromacki assumes that the earliest Gospels were not written until A.D. 60, a point with which not all New Testament scholars agree.

[14]There is some discussion among scholars as to whether the fourth Gospel was penned by John the apostle or another John named "John the elder." D. A. Carson has shown that the two individuals were probably one and the same (D. A. Carson, *John*, Pillar New Testament Commentary [Grand Rapids, MI: Eerdmans, 1991], 69–70). Even if they were different, William Lane Craig, *Reasonable Faith* (Wheaton, IL: Crossway Books, 1994), 204 notes, "The clear majority [of church fathers] opts for the apostle." Craig goes on to demonstrate that based on the internal evidence in the book, the apostle John is the only plausible candidate for authorship.

It is not possible that the Gospels can be either more or fewer in number than they are. For, since there are four zones of the world in which we live, and four principal winds, while the Church is scattered throughout all the world, and the "pillar and ground" of the Church is the Gospel and the spirit of life; it is fitting that she should have four pillars, breathing out immortality on every side, and vivifying men afresh. . . . And therefore the Gospels are in accord with these things, among which Christ Jesus is seated.[15]

Irenaeus continues by listing the four Gospels as we know them today: Matthew, Mark, Luke, and John. Of course, nearly a century earlier, Papias had already given testimony to these same four books.[16] According to the church historian Eusebius, Irenaeus also received some of his information from Polycarp, who was taught these things by the apostles (cf. 2 Timothy 2:2).[17]

Internal evidence, coming from the books themselves, is consistent with the testimony of church history. For example, Matthew's Gospel frequently references the Old Testament and describes Jesus' interaction with the Jews in a way that suggests its author was a native Jew.[18] Some scholars have noted that it also puts greater emphasis on numbers and on money than the other Gospels, a characteristic that would be consistent with the author's occupation as a tax collector (Matthew 9:9).[19] In Mark's Gospel, the apostle Peter is cast in a more negative light than in the other Gospels (cf. Mark 8:32–33; 14:29–72), suggesting that he was the self-effacing source from which Mark received his information.[20] The author of Luke also wrote Acts (compare Luke 1 with Acts 1) and as noted earlier was a traveling companion of Paul. He is explicit in emphasizing that he researched his information thoroughly (Luke 1:1–4), as is seen in the many historically verifiable details he includes (some of which will be considered later). This would be fitting

---

[15]Irenaeus, *Against Heresies*, 3.11.8. Cited from Alexander Roberts and James Donaldson, eds., *The Ante-Nicene Fathers* (Grand Rapids, MI: Eerdmans, 1973), 1:428.
[16]John Chapman, "St. Papias," in *The Catholic Encyclopedia* (New York: Robert Appleton Company, 1911); http://www.newadvent.org/cathen/11457c.htm.
[17]Eusebius, *Church History*, 4.14.3–8.
[18]Cf. A. Lukyn Williams, *St. Matthew*, Vol. 1, The Pulpit Commentary (New York: Funk & Wagnalls, n.d.), xi.
[19]Cf. Daniel Wallace, "Matthew: Introduction, Argument, and Outline"; http://www.bible.org/page.php?page_id=969. Accessed August 19, 2007.
[20]James A. Brooks, in *Mark*, New American Commentary (Nashville: Broadman, 1991) notes, "The large amount of concern for Peter and the less-than-flattering image of Peter in Mark may be an indication that Peter was one source among others" (27).

for one who was trained as a physician (Colossians 4:14). The author of the Gospel of John speaks of himself only as "that disciple whom Jesus loved" (John 21:7). This corresponds to John's emphasis on love in his three epistles (1 John 3:16, 23; 4:9–10, 19; 2 John 6; 3 John 6). Moreover, the author was a disciple (cf. John 21:2, 20, 24), one of the Twelve (John 13:23–24; cf. Mark 14:17; Luke 22:14), an eyewitness to the events of Christ's life and death (John 1:14; 19:26, 35), and among the inner circle of Christ's followers (cf. John 13:23–25; 19:26–27), but someone other than Peter (John 21:20–24; cf. John 20:2-10).[21] Only John and his brother James fit these criteria (cf. Mark 5:37–38; 9:2–3; 14:33; John 21:2). But since James was martyred early in church history (Acts 12:2), the evidence points to John as the author (cf. John 21:22–23).[22] The fact that much of John's material is unique (intended as a supplement to the other Gospels) suggests that someone with authority must have written it; otherwise the early church would probably not have accepted it as canonical.

In all four cases, the internal evidence (meaning details within the book itself such as writing style, biographical data, and historical details) and the external evidence (meaning non-biblical testimony that affirms the authorship of a given book) consistently and repeatedly affirm the authorship of the Gospels by Matthew, Mark, Luke, and John. On the flip side, there is nothing beyond mere speculation that should cause us to question their authenticity.

---

[21]Cf. Edwin A. Blum, "The Gospel of John," 267–348, in *The Bible Knowledge Commentary (New Testament)*, ed. John F. Walvoord and Roy B. Zuck (Wheaton, IL: Victor Books, 1983), 267.
[22]Cf. Gerald L. Borchert, *John 1–11*, New American Commentary (Nashville: Broadman & Holman, 1996), 86.

Reason 3:
We Believe the New Testament Gospels Are Reliable

Because They Were Intended to Be Historical

From the outset, the Gospels present themselves as being truthful accounts of actual history. For example, Luke states the purpose of his Gospel clearly at the very beginning. He wrote it so that his readers might know "certainty concerning the things you have been taught" related to the life of Jesus (1:4). John makes a similar assertion at the end of his work, emphasizing that he testified "about these things" and wrote "these things, and we know that his testimony is true" (John 21:24). In this regard, Luke and John are representative of all four Gospel writers; each was committed to presenting Jesus in a way that was accurate and true. "History is important to the Gospel writers," notes Thomas D. Lea. "Their report of history in Jesus' life required accuracy. Their accuracy provides us with a sure foundation for our trust in the redeeming message of the Gospel."[23]

Unlike other apocryphal accounts of Christ's life, which are "clearly legendary" and often "so unreal and pointless that they can immediately be seen to be of a quite different character from the New Testament accounts of Jesus,"[24] the New Testament Gospels were written to be reliable accounts of what actually happened. The Evangelists' motivation for doing so would have been both theological and apologetic. From a theological perspective, they would never have wanted to bear false witness against Jesus, the one whom they worshiped and served.[25]

---

[23]Thomas D. Lea, "The Reliability of History in John's Gospel," *Journal of the Evangelical Theological Society* 38/3 (September 1995), 402.

[24]John Drane, *Introducing the New Testament* (Oxford, UK: Lion Publishing, 1999), 227.

[25]Donald Guthrie, *New Testament Introduction* (Downers Grove, IL: InterVarsity Press, 1990), 107 notes with regard to Luke: "No one would deny that Luke's purpose is theological. But it is quite different from saying that the history has been conformed to the theology. . . . It is truer to say that Luke brings out the theological significance of the history."

From an apologetic standpoint, they would have deeply desired their message to be believable. "The writers intend to convince readers that their proclamation is true and requires a decision."[26] Since the events of Jesus' life were well-known to the people of that day, especially in Israel (Luke 24:18; Acts 2:22; 26:26; cf. 1 Corinthians 15:6), the Gospel writers needed to represent the facts correctly. As Donald Guthrie explains, "An intention to lead people to faith in Jesus as Messiah and as Son of God is hardly likely to be furthered by an account of Jesus which was not closely related to the historical facts."[27]

It follows, then, that the Gospel writers' approach to the historical data was intended to be trustworthy. The number of historical details they include (such as social customs, geographical locations, and the names of political figures) further suggests a desire to deal with factual data in a responsible manner. For example, consider the twenty-one allusions to historical events, geographical places, and political positions in Luke 3:1–2:

> *In the fifteenth year (1) of the reign of Tiberius Caesar (2), Pontius Pilate (3) being governor (4) of Judea (5), and Herod (6) being tetrarch (7) of Galilee (8), and his brother Philip (9) tetrarch (10) of the region of Ituraea (11) and Trachonitis (12), and Lysanias (13) tetrarch (14) of Abilene (15), during the high priesthood (16) of Annas (17) and Caiaphas (18), the word of God came to John (19) the son of Zechariah (20) in the wilderness (21).*

In just two verses, it becomes clear that Luke's goal was to convey that which was tied to historical fact. This is in keeping with his stated purpose for writing (Luke 1:4).

The style of the Gospels further supports this conclusion. They are written in a straightforward and sensible manner, giving the reader no reason to doubt the sincere motives of each author. Along these lines, the Gospels include details that are embarrassing to the writers (and the other apostles), indicating that they were more interested in seeking the truth than in making themselves look good (cf. Matthew

---

[26]Thomas D. Lea and David Alan Black, *The New Testament: Its Background and Message* (Nashville: Broadman & Holman, 2003), 132.
[27]Guthrie, *New Testament Introduction*, 346.

17:16; 26:30–35; Mark 8:33; 9:32, 34; 14:40, 51, 66–72; Luke 18:34; John 12:16).

> Consider the way the Gospels are written—in a sober and responsible fashion, with accurate incidental details, with obvious care and exactitude. You don't find the outlandish flourishes and blatant mythologizing that you see in a lot of other ancient writings. . . . The goal of the Gospel writers was to attempt to record what had actually happened.[28]

On a side note, we might add that the apostle Paul also understood that unless his faith was based on real history (specifically, the bodily resurrection of Jesus Christ), it was an empty faith (1 Corinthians 15:12–19). Paul "sets his theology very firmly in the context of a historical event he believed could be verified in the normal way by the report of witnesses."[29] Moreover, Paul's love for Christ (cf. 1 Corinthians 16:22), loyalty to Christ (cf. 2 Corinthians 4:5), and accountability to Christ (cf. 2 Corinthians 5:10) motivated him to preach a gospel that was true (cf. Ephesians 1:13; Colossians 1:5–6; 1 Timothy 2:3–7). As we will see later (in Reason 7), Paul's gospel was in perfect harmony with the accounts given by Matthew, Mark, Luke, and John.

Finally, it should be noted that the Gospel writers, as well as all of the apostles, faced intense persecution for the gospel message they proclaimed (John 15:18–25; Acts 5:40–41; 2 Corinthians 11:23–28; 1 Peter 4:12–16). According to church tradition, both Matthew and Mark were martyred for their faith. Though Luke and John were probably not martyred, many of the other apostles were (including Peter, Paul, James, Andrew, Bartholomew, Thaddeus, Philip, Simon, and Thomas). It is hard to believe that the writers of these Gospels and their fellow Christians would have endured such hardship for that which they knew was only a myth.

The point here is that the authors of the biblical Gospels intended their material to be accurate and historically trustworthy. To be sure, they had theological and apologetic concerns too. But as we have seen, those concerns would not have mitigated against historical accuracy. On the contrary, they would have made truthfulness all the more neces-

---

[28]Craig Blomberg. Cited by Lee Strobel, *The Case for Christ* (Grand Rapids, MI: Zondervan, 1998), 40.

[29]John Drane, *Introducing the New Testament* (San Francisco: Harper & Row, 1986), 210.

sary. In the words of evangelical scholars D. A. Carson, Douglas Moo, and Leon Morris:

> The evangelists certainly claim to be writing history. True, they write as passionate exponents of a certain interpretation of that history, and they select and arrange their facts accordingly. But as we have seen . . . there is no reason to think a person must be a bad historian because he or she is a strong partisan.[30]

---

[30]D. A. Carson, Douglas J. Moo, and Leon Morris, *An Introduction to the New Testament* (Grand Rapids, MI: Zondervan, 1992), 52.

Reason 4:
We Believe the New Testament Gospels Are Reliable

Because They Contain Details That Can Be Tested and Verified

It is not enough to demonstrate that the Gospel writers *intended* to be accurate. Good intentions are not enough. As Craig Blomberg notes, "some fictitious narratives are couched in the guise of history, and many careful historians fail to achieve their objectives of complete accuracy."[31] Thus we must go one step further and ask whether or not the Gospel writers were successful in their attempt to be historical. When put to the test, do the Gospel accounts actually demonstrate themselves to be reliable?

If the Gospels are to be considered part of inspired Scripture, coming from the Holy Spirit, they must be marked by accuracy and truthfulness (John 17:17; cf. 2 Peter 1:16–18; 1 John 1:1–4). As we noted earlier, Jesus had promised His apostles that the Spirit would help them remember the details of His life. "But the Helper, the Holy Spirit, whom the Father will send in my name, he will teach you all things and bring to your remembrance all that I have said to you" (John 14:26; cf. 14:17). Thus Matthew and John (as apostles) and Mark and Luke (as those who consulted apostolic sources) were promised the Spirit's help in recounting the ministry of Jesus (cf. John 2:22; 12:16). Jesus had also told His immediate followers that the Spirit would guide them in the truth (John 16:13), a promise that necessarily extends to the historical reliability of their collective testimony about Him.

Luke's Gospel is a case in point with regard to historicity, since he repeatedly lists names, places, and other verifiable details that can be tested for accuracy (Luke 1:5; 2:1–3; 3:1–3; Acts 5:36; 11:28; 18:2, 12;

---

[31]Craig Blomberg, *The Historical Reliability of the Gospels* (Downers Grove, IL: InterVarsity Press, 1987), 234.

25:1). Robert Stein explains that "throughout his work Luke sought to demonstrate the truthfulness of what he recorded by tying the events to universal history."[32] Significantly, two millennia later, Luke's account (in both his Gospel and in Acts) has survived the attacks of skeptics and detractors. "Attempts to impugn Luke's reliability have constantly been made," observes Merrill Unger, "but most of these have been rendered futile by light from the monuments of antiquity and the archaeologist's spade."[33]

Time and time again we find that "Luke is a first-class ancient historian. . . . He is not careless, nor is he a fabricator of events."[34] In the words of Sir William Ramsay, "His statements of fact [are] trustworthy; he is possessed of the true historic sense."[35] John Stott agrees:

> Luke has been vindicated in recent years as an accurate and painstaking historian, and he includes in his two volumes many references to Roman provincial administration and to the secular and political affairs of his day.[36]

Of course, the motivation behind Luke's concern for accuracy was not primarily historical. As noted before, it was both theological and evangelistic. In the words of New Testament scholar I. Howard Marshall, "Luke was a historian because he was first and foremost an Evangelist: he knew that the faith which he wished to proclaim stands or falls with the history of Jesus and the early church."[37] Others agree:

> Luke was not only a reliable, objective historian, which is clear from his striking agreements with the historiography of Josephus, but Luke was also concerned with the infallibility of the facts. Luke wanted to describe the development of early Christianity. But he wanted above all to eliminate doubt as to the accuracy of the things that had been ful-

---

[32]Robert H. Stein, *Luke*, New American Commentary (Nashville: Broadman & Holman, 2001), 36.

[33]Merrill F. Unger, "The Role of Archaeology in the Study of the New Testament," *Bibliotheca Sacra*, Vol. 116 (April 1959), 155. For specific examples of places in which Luke's account has been verified by archaeology, see John Ankerberg and John Weldon, *Ready with an Answer* (Eugene, OR: Harvest House, 2007), 288.

[34]Darrell Bock, *Luke 1:1–9:50*, Baker Exegetical Commentary on the New Testament (Grand Rapids, MI: Baker Academic, 1994), 13.

[35]William Ramsay, *The Bearing of Recent Discovery on the Trustworthiness of the New Testament* (Grand Rapids, MI: Baker, 1979), 222.

[36]John R. W. Stott, *Basic Introduction to the New Testament* (Grand Rapids, MI: Eerdmans, 1964), 26.

[37]I. Howard Marshall, *Luke: Historian and Theologian* (Exeter, UK: Paternoster Press, 1984), 52.

filled, that is, the saving work of Christ, and desired to give assurance to Theophilus and his other readers regarding events in Christ's life.[38]

It's not surprising, then, that Luke's accounts "have now been recognized as first-class historical writings"[39] by historians and archaeologists. "This means that Luke is fully trustworthy as a historian of the life of Christ," concludes C. Marvin Pate. "Therefore to read the third Gospel is to encounter the authentic, historical Jesus."[40]

Along with Luke, the other Gospels also prove to be historically verifiable. Craig Blomberg notes, "In every case it has been concluded that an even-handed treatment of the data does not lead to a distrust of the accuracy of the Gospels in what they choose to report."[41] Thus the events they recount can be accepted as historically reliable. While modern historians may sometimes wish the Gospel writers had given us more data, "they should be judged for what they do tell us, not for what they do not tell us."[42]

Like Luke and the other Synoptic Gospels (Matthew and Mark), John also provides his readers with numerous references to testable data such as geography and chronology.

> These have been demonstrated to be highly accurate, particularly in light of modern archaeological discoveries: the five porticoes of the pool of Bethesda by the Sheep Gate ([John] 5:2), the pool of Siloam (9:1–7), Jacob's well at Sychar (4:5), the "Pavement" (*Gabbatha*) where Pilate pronounced judgment on Jesus (19:13), Solomon's porch (10:22–23), and so on.[43]

This is in keeping with John's emphasis on truth throughout his Gospel.[44] He too would have been deeply concerned with presenting Christ ("the way, and the truth, and the life," John 14:6) in a trustworthy way. In the words of one New Testament historian:

---

[38]Nicholas M. van Ommeren, "Was Luke an Accurate Historian?," *Bibliotheca Sacra* 138:589 (January 1991), 70–71, referring to the views of W. C. van Unnik expressed in his essay, "Remarks on the Purpose of Luke's Historical Writing (Luke 1:1–4)."

[39]Clifford Wilson, *Rocks, Relics, and Biblical Reliability* (Grand Rapids, MI: Zondervan, 1977), 114.

[40]C. Marvin Pate, *Luke*, Moody Gospel Commentary (Chicago: Moody Press, 1995), 27.

[41]Blomberg, *Historical Reliability*, 234–235.

[42]Carson, Moo, and Morris, *Introduction to the New Testament*, 53.

[43]Craig, *Reasonable Faith*, 219.

[44]Cf. John 1:14, 17; 3:21; 4:23–24; 5:33; 8:32, 40, 44–46; 14:6, 17; 15:26; 16:13; 17:17, 19; 18:37–38; 19:35.

The author claims to have been a true witness, that is an eyewitness of Jesus. In his first letter he said that he and his fellows had "heard," "seen" and "touched" the "word of life" (1 John 1:1–2). His claims are extensive and specific. The alternatives are simple. Either the writer was the truthful eyewitness he claims to have been, or, as [some liberal scholars] believe, he was not.[45]

John's concern for geographical places (cf. John 1:28; 4:5; 10:23; 11:18; 19:17, 20; 21:1), chronological details (cf. 1:29, 35, 43; 2:1, 12; 4:43, 52; 5:1; 7:2; etc.), cultural beliefs and customs (cf. 4:9, 27; 5:10; 7:22–23, 49), and eyewitness testimony (cf. 1:14; 21:24) demonstrates that he was also concerned with tying his witness to testable history.[46] When his data is tested, it will "take us, *alongside that of the others* [Matthew, Mark, and Luke], to the Jesus of history who remains an integral part of the Christ of faith."[47]

The Gospels, then, continually show themselves to be not only theological treatises but historically reliable documents as well. Their historical trustworthiness (along with the rest of the New Testament) is "confirmed time and again by external evidence. . . . [T]o the unbiased observer, little doubt can be cast on the statement that archaeology has confirmed the historical reliability of the New Testament."[48]

> An impressive case can be made for the general trustworthiness of the Gospels and Acts, via historical criteria alone. . . . Because the Gospels and Acts prove reliable in so many places where they can be tested, they should be given the benefit of the doubt in those places where they cannot.[49]

---

[45]Paul Barnett, *Is the New Testament Reliable?* (Downers Grove, IL: InterVarsity Press, 2003), 72.

[46]Cf. Thomas D. Lea, "The Reliability of History in John's Gospel," *Journal of the Evangelical Theological Society* 38:3 (September 1995), 387–402.

[47]John A. T. Robinson, *Can We Trust the New Testament?* (Grand Rapids, MI: Eerdmans, 1977), 94. Emphasis in the original.

[48]Moreland, *Scaling the Secular City*, 135.

[49]Craig Blomberg, *Making Sense of the New Testament* (Grand Rapids, MI: Baker, 2004), 70. On a similar note, I. Howard Marshall writes, "Although the Gospels were not written by scientific historians, we have found good reason to believe that they incorporate reliable information about Jesus, so that the ordinary reader . . . may rest confident that the portraits of Jesus in the Gospels are based on historical fact" (*I Believe in the Historical Jesus* [Grand Rapids, MI: Eerdmans, 1977], 235).

Reason 5:
We Believe the New Testament Gospels Are Reliable

Because the Early Christian Community Would Have Demanded an Accurate Record

Throughout the book of Acts, the apostles emphasized the fact that they were eyewitnesses to the events of Christ's life (cf. 2:32; 3:15; 5:32; 10:39). The apostle Paul similarly recorded that at least five hundred people had seen Jesus after His resurrection (1 Corinthians 15:6).[50] This included Christian leaders such as Peter (Cephas), the twelve disciples, and James the brother of Jesus (vv. 5, 7). In addition to this, about three thousand others joined the church on the Day of Pentecost (Acts 2:41), most of whom were familiar with the news about Jesus' life and death and miracles (Luke 24:18; Acts 2:22; 26:26). So from the inception of the Christian church, the truth about Jesus was validated by eyewitness testimony—testimony that included hundreds, if not thousands, of people. "The core of apostolic theology and tradition that existed from the earliest days of Christianity [was] a core that had its own historical beginnings—the history, teachings, suffering, and resurrection of Jesus."[51] As Matthew, Mark, Luke, and John wrote their respective Gospels, they would have been aware of the fact that many in the church were already familiar with the historical details of Jesus' life. Those with firsthand information about Jesus would have known immediately if something in the Gospel records was grossly inaccurate.

That the Gospel writers were subject to such accountability is confirmed by the early dates of each of their accounts. All four Gospels were written in the first century, as even many liberal scholars are willing to admit.[52] This, of course, is necessarily true if Matthew, Mark,

---

[50]First Corinthians was written by Paul around A.D. 57.
[51]Robert B. Sloan, "Unity in Diversity," 435–468, in *New Testament Criticism and Interpretation*, ed. David Alan Black and David S. Dockery (Grand Rapids, MI: Zondervan, 1991), 462.
[52]Josh McDowell, *The New Evidence That Demands a Verdict* (Nashville: Thomas Nelson, 1999),

Luke, and John are the actual authors of the Gospels (a point that has already been established). It is further supported by both the archaeological and historical evidence. For example, Matthew is referenced in the writings of the church father Ignatius (who died around A.D. 110), and fragments of his Gospel have been found that may date to the latter part of the first century.[53] The Gospel of John is likewise attested by fragments from as early as A.D. 100 that quote from or allude to that Gospel.[54]

Most scholars date Mark around A.D. 65–70 with Luke, Matthew, and John writing later. Others, especially more recently, argue for earlier dates (in 40s, 50s, and 60s),[55] and with good reason.[56] But even if late first-century dates are accepted, "the Gospels were still written during the time when eyewitnesses who had seen Jesus and had experienced his ministry were alive. One would, therefore, still be on good historical grounds for treating them as solid historical sources."[57] Even at the end of the first century, not enough time had elapsed for the historical facts of Jesus' life to have been eclipsed by legend.

> In this regard, A. N. Sherwin-White, a scholar of ancient Roman and Greek history at Oxford, has studied the rate at which legend accumulated in the ancient world, using the writings of Herodotus as a test case. He argues that even a span of two generations is not sufficient for legend to wipe out a solid core of historical facts. The picture of Jesus in the New Testament was established well within that length of time.[58]

52–53, cites Kümmel and John A. T. Robinson as two examples of liberal scholars who believe all four Gospels were written before A.D. 100.

[53]Robert Boyd in *Boyd's Handbook of Practical Apologetics*, 233 notes that in early 1995, "three small papyrus fragments of Matthew stored in a library in England for decades, were reexamined. It was determined that they date to the latter part of the first century A.D."

[54]P52 and Papyrus Egerton 2. Liberal scholars generally consider Matthew and John to have been the last two Gospels written, meaning that Mark and Luke were written earlier. On the other hand, some conservative scholars consider Matthew to be the first written Gospel.

[55]Donald Guthrie, *New Testament Introduction*, 55 notes that A.D. 50–64 is a "quite reasonable" date for the writing of Matthew. John A. T. Robinson, *Redating the New Testament* (Eugene, OR: Wipf & Stock, 2000), 116 notes that an early version of Mark may have been written as early as A.D. 45. Robinson also dates both Luke and John before the fall of Jerusalem in A.D. 70.

[56]Late dates do not adequately take into account factors such as the ending of Acts (which suggest a date for Luke–Acts in the 50s or 60s) or the seemingly absent awareness of the fall of Jerusalem, especially in Matthew, Mark, and Luke (suggesting they were all written before A.D. 70). For a helpful discussion on the dating of the Gospels, especially as to the order in which they were written, see Robert Thomas and F. David Farnell, *The Jesus Crisis* (Grand Rapids, MI: Kregel, 1998).

[57]Moreland, *Scaling the Secular City*, 151. Church tradition suggests that the apostle John, for example, lived until around A.D. 100.

[58]Ibid., 156. Moreland references Sherwin-White's volume, *Roman Society and Roman Law in the New Testament* (Grand Rapids, MI: Baker, 1978), 186–193.

A full discussion of the proposed dates for each of the Gospels is outside the scope of our purposes here. But whatever first-century dates are assigned, one point remains: based on the archaeological and historical evidence, "the New Testament proves to be in fact what it was formerly believed to be: the teaching of Christ and his immediate followers between cir. 25 and cir. 80 A.D."[59]

This point is made even stronger when one considers the ethical standards upheld in the early church, where truthfulness and integrity were expected of those who followed Jesus (Acts 5:4; 26:25; 2 Corinthians 4:2; 1 Peter 1:22; 1 John 2:21; 5:20). False teachers were not tolerated (cf. Galatians 1:6–9; 2 Timothy 3:8; Titus 1:14; 2 Peter 2:1–21; Jude 1–16), and those who distorted the life and ministry of Jesus were openly condemned (cf. 1 John 2:22; 4:3; 2 John 7). Even the apostles were not above being confronted when necessary (Galatians 2:11–15; cf. 1 Timothy 5:19–20). Thus, because any type of false witness about Jesus would have dishonored the Lord (cf. 1 Corinthians 15:15), it is unreasonable to think the earliest Christians would have quietly allowed it.

---

[59]William F. Albright, *From the Stone Age to Christianity* (Baltimore: John Hopkins Press, 1940), 23. Cited from Josh McDowell, *New Evidence That Demands a Verdict*, 52–53.

Reason 6:
We Believe the New Testament Gospels Are Reliable

Because Their Picture of Jesus Is Consistent within the Four Gospels

Though penned by four different individuals (and thus from four different perspectives), the biblical Gospels present a picture of Jesus Christ that is consistent. This is critical because if the Gospels did not agree with one another, they could not all be regarded as historically reliable sources of information.

In the Gospels we learn about Jesus' human lineage, both His legal ancestry through Joseph (Matthew 1:1–17) and His physical genealogy through Mary (Luke 3:23–38). We also learn about His heavenly preexistence (John 1:1–5, 14–18). We read about His birth, baptism, temptation, teaching, miracles, confrontations with the Jewish religious leaders, and ultimately His death, burial, resurrection, and ascension.[60] Matthew presents Jesus as the King (Matthew 2:2), Mark as the Servant (Mark 10:45), Luke as the Savior (Luke 19:10), and John as the Son of God (John 20:31). Yet, in spite of their different emphases, the presentation of Christ in each is consistent with the rest. In all four, Jesus is the Messiah, the miracle-worker who preached with divine authority and called the world to turn from sin and follow Him (e.g., Matthew 16:24; Mark 8:34; Luke 9:23; John 12:26). In all four, He came to bring salvation to sinners by laying down His life on the cross and conquering death through His resurrection (e.g., Matthew 1:21;

---

[60]We learn about His birth (Matthew 1:18–25; Luke 2:1–39); the initiation of His ministry through His baptism (Matthew 3:13–17; Mark 1:9–11; Luke 3:21–23); His temptation in the wilderness (Matthew 4:1–11; Mark 1:12–13; Luke 4:1–13); His teaching (e.g., Matthew 5–7; Mark 4:1–34; Luke 6:12–39; John 6:12–39; John 14:1–17:26); His miracles (e.g., Matthew 9:1–8; Mark 3:1–6; Luke 7:11–17; John 2:1–11); His confrontations with the Jewish religious leaders (e.g., Matthew 23:1–36; Mark 2:23–28; Luke 20:45–47; John 5:1–18); and ultimately His death (Matthew 27:27–56; Mark 15:16–41; Luke 23:26–49; John 19:17–30), burial (Matthew 27:57–66; Mark 15:42–47; Luke 23:50–56; John 19:31–42), resurrection (Matthew 28:1–10; Mark 16:1–8; Luke 24:1–11; John 20:1–10), and ascension (Mark 16:19–20; Luke 24:50–53).

Mark 16:16; Luke 19:10; John 3:17). As Bruce Metzger of Princeton Theological Seminary explains, "Each of these portraits presents distinctive highlights of Jesus' person and work, and taken together, the four provide a varied and balanced account of what Jesus said and did."[61] Though written from different viewpoints, as four biographers writing about the same person, the biblical Gospels combine to form a powerful and coherent account of the life and ministry of Jesus.[62] In the words of F. F. Bruce:

> Diversity there is, but it is diversity in unity. Even a very cursory acquaintance with the New Testament writings is sufficient to reveal that in their various ways they all bear consentient witness that Jesus Christ is Lord.[63]

Or as Ben Witherington III succinctly summarizes the issue: "Four Gospels but, recognizably, one and the same Jesus."[64]

Though critics point to apparent contradictions within the Gospel accounts, their allegations ultimately fall short. Satisfactory explanations for such "difficulties" are readily available.[65] In fact, "the large number of common-sense explanations available for almost every so-called contradiction that has ever been pointed out must surely be considered before glibly dismissing the NT as hopelessly contradictory."[66] Often the supposed contradictions are nothing more than the same event being paraphrased or described from a different perspective.

> Once you allow for the elements . . . of paraphrase, of abridgement, of explanatory additions, of selection, of omission—the Gospels are extremely consistent with each other by ancient standards, which are

---

[61]Bruce Metzger, *The New Testament: Its Background, Growth, and Content* (Nashville: Abingdon Press, 1983), 99.

[62]Richard Burridge in *What Are the Gospels?* (New York: Cambridge University Press, 1992) and *Four Gospels, One Jesus?* (Grand Rapids, MI: Eerdmans, 1994) makes a case for identifying the genre of the Gospels as Greco-Roman *bios* literature. Burridge's insights are helpful, though (in this writer's opinion) he pushes the importance of the *bios* genre too far. In places he espouses historical errors in the Gospel accounts on the basis that other ancient biographies are not historically factual (cf. *Four Gospels, One Jesus?*, 168). But this does not take into account the fact that the Gospels are not *secular* biographies—they are *inspired* biographies.

[63]F. F. Bruce, *The Message of the New Testament* (Grand Rapids, MI: Eerdmans, 1973), 12.

[64]Ben Witherington III, *The New Testament Story* (Grand Rapids, MI: Eerdmans, 2004), 268.

[65]See Gleason Archer, *New International Encyclopedia of Bible Difficulties* (Grand Rapids, MI: Zondervan, 2001) or any good evangelical commentary for help with reconciling perceived difficulties in the Gospels. Also, for questions related to how the Synoptic Gospels relate to one another (the "Synoptic Problem"), we recommend *Three Views on the Origins of the Synoptic Gospels*, ed. Robert L. Thomas (Grand Rapids, MI: Kregel, 2002).

[66]Craig, *Reasonable Faith*, 208.

the only standards by which it's fair to judge them. [For that matter,] if the Gospels were too consistent, that in itself would invalidate them as independent witnesses. People would then say we really only have one testimony that everybody else is just parroting.[67]

Critics often point first to alleged contradictions between the Synoptic Gospels (Matthew, Mark, and Luke) and the Gospel of John, as though the presentation of Jesus given by John is incompatible with that of the other Gospel writers. But such accusations ultimately stem from the imaginations of liberal scholars, and not from a straightforward reading of the text itself. As F. F. Bruce points out: "Whatever difficulties some scholars have felt, most readers of the Gospels in all ages have been unaware of any fundamental discrepancy between the Christ who speaks and acts in the fourth Gospel and Him who speaks and acts in the Synoptics."[68] In other words, a normal, natural reading of John's Gospel gives no reason to view it as being somehow irreconcilable with Matthew, Mark, or Luke.

In the end, liberal accusations about John's Gospel just do not hold up. Though most of John's material is unique to his Gospel, "nothing in John contradicts the synoptics, and vice versa."[69] Once it is understood that John's Gospel was written after the other Gospels, as a supplement to them, the differences between them become quite easy to explain.[70]

---

[67]Blomberg, cited by Strobel, *Case for Christ*, 41.
[68]F. F. Bruce, *The New Testament Documents: Are They Reliable?* (Downers Grove, IL: InterVarsity Press, 1981), 59.
[69]John MacArthur, *John 1–11* (Chicago: Moody Press, 2006), 2.
[70]John R. W. Stott in *Men with a Message*, revised by Stephen Motyer (Grand Rapids, MI: Eerdmans, 1994), 69 notes: "The undoubted differences between John's Gospel and the synoptics do not necessarily mean that John is historically unreliable. . . . [Rather,] it is quite possible that John was deliberately employing traditions and memories which had not been utilized in the synoptic tradition [in order to supplement them]."

Reason 7:
We Believe the New Testament Gospels Are Reliable

Because Their Picture of Jesus Is Consistent with the Rest of the New Testament

Not only are the Gospels consistent with each other, they are also consistent with the rest of the New Testament. In the book of Acts, the testimonies of Peter (Acts 2:22–24; 3:13–20; 5:29–31; 10:38–43), Philip (8:26–40), and Paul (17:30–31; 26:22–23) correspond perfectly with the accounts of the Gospels. And it doesn't stop there.

The rest of the New Testament affirms that Jesus was a real Jewish man (cf. 1 John 1:1–4; 4:2), a descendant of Abraham (Galatians 3:16) and of David (Romans 1:3), who was born of a woman (Galatians 4:4) and who had siblings (1 Corinthians 9:5; Galatians 1:19; Jude 1; cf. Matthew 13:55). He was poor (2 Corinthians 8:9; cf. Romans 15:3; Philippians 2:6–8), meek and gentle (2 Corinthians 10:1; 1 Peter 2:23), selfless (Romans 15:3; Philippians 2:5–6), and righteous (1 Corinthians 1:30; 1 Peter 1:19). He was transfigured on a mountain with several of His disciples (2 Peter 1:16–18). Yet, at the end of His ministry He was betrayed (1 Corinthians 11:23) and on that night instituted a memorial supper (1 Corinthians 11:23–25). He then stood trial before Pontius Pilate (1 Timothy 6:13), suffered (1 Peter 1:11; 2:21–23), and was crucified (e.g., 1 Corinthians 1:23; 2:8; Galatians 3:1; 1 Peter 2:24; 3:18) through the instigation of the Jewish leaders (1 Thessalonians 2:14–15). On the third day He was buried and raised and appeared to many (1 Corinthians 15:4–8; cf. 1 Peter 1:3, 21). He then ascended (Ephesians 1:20; cf. Romans 10:6; Ephesians 2:6; 1 Peter 1:21; 3:22) and will one day return to this earth for those who are His own (e.g., 1 Thessalonians 4:13–18; 1 Timothy 6:14; Titus 2:11–14). Many scholars consider the testimony in Paul's letters to be especially significant because they are usually dated earlier than the Gospels (and are therefore considered the earliest biblical testimony to the facts of Jesus life). "In evaluating the weight of Paul's knowledge of Jesus, the historian finds it significant that the Pauline letters confirm the broad outlines of the testimony of the Gospels."[71]

The *teachings* of Jesus (in addition to the details of His life) are also echoed in the rest of the New Testament. The apostle Paul emphasizes that love fulfills the law (Romans 13:10; Galatians 5:14; cf. Mark 12:31), that taxes must be paid to whom they are due (Romans 13:7; cf. Mark 12:16–17), and that Christians should not seek their own revenge (Romans 12:17; Matthew 5:39) but rather should bless those who persecute them (Romans 12:14; cf. Luke 6:27–28). Paul even quotes Jesus in 1 Timothy 5:18 (cf. Matthew 10:10; Luke 10:7) when he states that the laborer is worthy of his wages. Paul's reference to faith moving mountains (1 Corinthians 13:2) seems to correspond to the words of Jesus in Mark 11:23. Other New Testament writers, such as James and John, show a similar familiarity with the teaching ministry of Jesus Christ.[72]

All of this, of course, corresponds perfectly with the account of Jesus presented in the Gospels. The Jesus of the four Evangelists is certainly not foreign to the writers of the rest of the New Testament. In fact, just the opposite is true. The authors of the other New Testament books share a perspective about the life and teaching of Jesus that confirms what is depicted in Matthew, Mark, Luke, and John.

---

[71]Metzger, *The Text of the New Testament*, 100.
[72]For instance, James 1:2 (cf. Matthew 5:10–12); James 1:22 (cf. Matthew 7:24ff.); James 2:5 (cf. Matthew 5:3); James 3:12 (cf. Matthew 7:16); James 4:11–12 (cf. Matthew 7:1); James 5:2 (cf. Matthew 6:19); James 5:12 (cf. Matthew 5:34–37); 1 John 1:1–3 (cf. John 1:1, 14); 1 John 1:6 (cf. John 8:12, 55); 1 John 2:3 (cf. John 14:15, 23); 1 John 2:6 (cf. John 15:4); 1 John 2:7 (John 13:34); 1 John 2:18 (Mark 13:22); 1 John 2:27 (John 14:16–17, 26); 1 John 3:1 (John 1:10); 1 John 3:2 (John 1:12).

Reason 8:
We Believe the New Testament Gospels Are Reliable

Because the Main Points of Jesus' Life Are Found in Non-biblical Sources

It should come as no surprise that the major events of Jesus' life would be noted by more than just the writers of the New Testament. As Paul told Festus, speaking of King Agrippa, "The king knows about these things, and to him I speak boldly. For I am persuaded that none of these things has escaped his notice, for this has not been done in a corner" (Acts 26:26). News about Jesus would have traveled quickly throughout the Roman Empire, especially since the early Christians were to be "witnesses in Jerusalem and in all Judea and Samaria, and to the end of the earth" (Acts 1:8).

We would expect, of course, the testimony of the early church fathers and the Christian catacombs to reflect what is taught by the New Testament Gospels. And that is indeed the case. Ignatius (c. 35–107), as just one example among many,[73] wrote of "the birth, and passion, and resurrection which took place in the time of the government of Pontius Pilate, being truly and certainly accomplished by Jesus Christ."[74] More than once, Ignatius affirmed the basic tenets of the New Testament Gospels. For instance, in his *Epistle to the Smyrnaeans*, he wrote:

> I glorify God, even Jesus Christ, who . . . was truly of the seed of David according to the flesh, and the Son of God according to the will and power of God; that He was truly born of a virgin, was baptized by John, in order that all righteousness might be fulfilled by Him; and

---

[73]Along those lines, a number of church fathers are cataloged by Josh McDowell in *Evidence That Demands a Verdict*, 130–135.
[74]Ignatius, Epistle to the Magnesians, shorter text, chapter 11. Cited from Roberts and Donaldson, *Ante-Nicene Fathers* (Grand Rapids, MI: Eerdmans, 1973), 1:64. See also Ignatius' Epistle to the Smyrnaeans, chapter 3.

was truly, under Pontius Pilate and Herod the tetrarch, nailed [to the cross] for us in His flesh. Of this fruit we are by His divinely-blessed passion, that He might set up a standard for all ages, through His resurrection, to all His holy and faithful [followers], whether among Jews or Gentiles, in the one body of His Church.[75]

Of note is the fact that a great number of early Christians were so convinced of the truthfulness of the Gospel accounts that they gave their lives as martyrs. Ignatius himself is one such example. It is impossible to imagine they would have willingly died for something they knew was a fable. "The disciples' [and by extension the early Christians'] willingness to suffer and die for their beliefs *indicates that they certainly regarded those beliefs as true*. . . . Liars make poor martyrs."[76]

Second, we would expect to find details about Jesus in Jewish literature, since the Jews were eyewitnesses to the events of Jesus' life and death (cf. Luke 24:18). Peter underscored the Jews' familiarity with Jesus in his sermon on the Day of Pentecost: "Men of Israel, hear these words: Jesus of Nazareth, a man attested to you by God with mighty works and wonders and signs that God did through him in your midst, as you yourselves know—this Jesus, delivered up according to the definite plan and foreknowledge of God, you crucified and killed by the hands of lawless men" (Acts 2:22–23). If such momentous events actually occurred, as are found in the Gospel accounts, it would follow that the Jews made mention of such things.

And they did. Jewish sources such as Josephus (A.D. 37–100), the Mishna, and the Bavli (Babylonian Talmud) indicate that the Jews were familiar with Jesus, His miracles, His death, and the claims regarding His resurrection. Of course, many of the Jewish leaders did not respond to Jesus in faith. Yet at the same time, they never responded in a way that questioned the historicity of His life and ministry. Their response therefore adds credibility to the New Testament accounts. In the words of Peter Schäfer, "The rabbinic sources (again, particularly the Bavli) do not refer to some vague ideas about Jesus and Christianity but [instead] reveal knowledge—more often than not a precise knowl-

---

[75]Ignatius, Epistle to the Smyrnaeans, shorter text, chapter 1. Roberts and Donaldson, *Ante-Nicene Fathers*, 1:86.
[76]Gary R. Habermas and Michael R. Licona, *The Case for the Resurrection of Jesus* (Grand Rapids, MI: Kregel, 2004), 59. Emphasis original.

edge—of the New Testament."[77] The depiction of Jesus in rabbinic literature (although negative in its opinion about Jesus) reflects the general picture of Jesus presented in the biblical Gospels.

Ancient Roman sources, too, confirm the historical validity of the main points of the biblical Gospels. Thallus (first century), Celsus (second century), Lucian of Samosata (A.D. 115–200), Porphyry of Tyre (b. A.D. 233), Suetonius (c. 70–c. 130), Pliny the Younger (63–c. 113), and others provide secular Roman testimony to the fact that Jesus really lived. The details they share about Jesus, though somewhat sparse, coincide with the picture of Jesus given in the New Testament Gospels. As Bruce Metzger observes:

> The early non-Christian testimonies concerning Jesus, though scanty, are sufficient to prove (even without taking into account the evidence contained in the New Testament) that he was a historical figure who lived in Palestine in the early years of the first century, and that he gathered a group of followers about himself, and that he was condemned to death under Pontius Pilate. Today no competent scholar denies the historicity of Jesus.[78]

Gary Habermas underscores the significance of this testimony with these words: "We should realize that it is quite extraordinary that we could provide a broad outline of most of the major facts of Jesus' life from 'secular' history alone. Such is surely significant."[79]

As one example, the Roman historian Cornelius Tacitus (c. 55–120) presented Jesus as a real historical figure and wrote that He had been executed under Pontius Pilate. In referring to "the persons commonly called Christians," Tacitus recounts that "Christus, the founder of the name, was put to death by Pontius Pilate, procurator of Judea in the reign of Tiberius."[80] This, of course, corresponds to the accounts given by the New Testament writers (cf. Matthew 27:2; Mark 15:15; Luke 3:1; John 18:29).

These non-biblical sources will be discussed in greater depth in Section 5, so we will not belabor the point here. However, the fact is,

---

[77]Peter Schäfer, *Jesus in the Talmud* (Princeton, NJ: Princeton University Press, 2007), 122.
[78]Metzger, *The Text of the New Testament*, 78.
[79]Gary Habermas, *The Historical Jesus: Ancient Evidence for the Life of Christ* (Joplin, MO: College Press, 1996), 224. Cited from Josh McDowell, *New Evidence That Demands a Verdict*, 60.
[80]*Annals* XV, 44. Cited from Josh McDowell, *New Evidence That Demands a Verdict*, 120–121.

when we include both the biblical and non-biblical sources, "what we have concerning Jesus actually is impressive. . . . In all, at least forty-two authors, nine of them secular, mention Jesus within 150 years of his death."[81] Moreover, the ancient non-biblical sources affirm the major tenets of Jesus' life as told in the New Testament Gospels. In the words of historian Edwin Yamauchi:

> Even if we did not have the New Testament or Christian writings, we would be able to conclude from such non-Christian writings as Josephus, the Talmud, Tacitus, and Pliny the Younger that: (1) Jesus was a Jewish teacher; (2) many people believed that he performed healings and exorcisms; (3) he was rejected by the Jewish leaders; (4) he was crucified under Pontius Pilate in the reign of Tiberius; (5) despite this shameful death, his followers, who believed that he was still alive, spread beyond Palestine so that there were multitudes of them in Rome by A.D. 64; (6) all kinds of people from the cities and countryside—men and women, slave and free—worshipped him as God by the beginning of the second century.[82]

Thus, the testimony of Matthew, Mark, Luke, and John is collaborated by a veritable cloud of non-biblical witnesses.[83]

---

[81]Habermas and Licona, *The Case for the Resurrection of Jesus*, 127.
[82]Edwin Yamauchi, "Jesus Outside the New Testament: What Is the Evidence?" in *Jesus Under Fire: Modern Scholarship Reinvents the Historical Jesus*, ed. Michael J. Wilkins and J. P. Moreland. (Grand Rapids, MI: Zondervan, 1995), 221–222. Cited from McDowell, *The New Evidence That Demands a Verdict*, 136.
[83]F. F. Bruce in *The New Testament Documents: Are They Reliable?*, 119 writes: "Whatever else may be thought of the evidence from early Jewish and Gentile writers . . . it does at least establish, for those who refuse the witness of Christian writings, the historical character of Jesus Himself."

Reason 9:
We Believe the New Testament Gospels Are Reliable

Because They Are Superior to Other Supposed Gospels

It sometimes surprises, or even frightens, contemporary Christians to learn that there are other "gospels" outside of Matthew, Mark, Luke, and John. But they need not be afraid. "The apocryphal gospels, even the earliest and soberest among them, can hardly be compared with the canonical Gospels. The former are all patently secondary and legendary and obviously slanted."[84] Of these extra-biblical traditions about Jesus, "only a tiny proportion have even a slight claim to being genuine. The vast majority of the material is quite worthless as a historical source for knowledge of Jesus, and their real value lies more in highlighting the quality of information preserved in the canonical Gospels themselves."[85]

It is possible, of course, that we might find some factual accounts about Jesus outside of the biblical Gospels. The Gospels do not claim to be exhaustive biographies of the life of Jesus. In fact, John closes his Gospel by stating, "Now there are also many other things that Jesus did. Were every one of them to be written, I suppose that the world itself could not contain the books that would be written" (John 21:25). What the Gospels do claim, however, is that the information they provide is both accurate and sufficient, so that when you read them "you may have certainty concerning the things you have been taught" (Luke 1:4).

It is also important to recognize that the New Testament continually warns against the reality of false teachers, those who would distort the truth for their own gain. In their letters, the apostles warned their readers about the danger of certain heresies, including lies that might

---

[84]Edwin Yamauchi, cited in Norman L. Geisler and William E. Nix, *A General Introduction to the Bible* (Chicago: Moody Press, 1996), 311.
[85]John W. Drane, *Introducing the New Testament* (Oxford, UK: Lion Publishing, 2000), 227.

corrupt a right understanding of Jesus and His redemptive work (e.g.,
1 Corinthians 15:13–14; Galatians 1:6–10; Colossians 2:4; 1 Timothy
4:7; 1 John 4:1–3; 2 Peter 1:16; Jude 3–4). Among these heresies,
Gnosticism was a growing concern. "The name *gnosticism* comes from
the Greek word *gnosis*, meaning 'knowledge,' and stresses the character of this heresy. Gnosticism was a philosophical system built upon
Greek philosophy that stressed matter was evil but spirit was good."[86]
The Gnostics' belief that matter was evil forced them to rethink the
incarnation of Christ. If Christ was good, then He could not have possessed a physical body, since matter is evil. In response to this perceived
problem, the Gnostics invented two possible explanations: "One view
was that because matter was evil, Jesus could not have actually come in
human form; He only appeared in human form and only appeared to
suffer. The other view suggested that the divine Logos came upon the
human Jesus and departed prior to the crucifixion."[87]

In either case, the Gnostic view of Jesus was incompatible with
the teachings of the apostles that "the Word [Christ] became flesh
and dwelt among us" (John 1:14; cf. Romans 1:3; Galatians 4:4;
Philippians 2:8; Colossians 1:22; 1 Timothy 3:16). In his first epistle
John reiterated this point: "Every spirit that confesses that Jesus Christ
has come in the flesh is from God, and every spirit that does not confess
Jesus is not from God" (1 John 4:2–3). Paul likewise warned Timothy
to "avoid the irreverent babble and contradictions of what is falsely
called 'knowledge' [*gnosis*]" (1 Timothy 6:20).

The Gnostic gospels, along with other grossly imaginative accounts
of the life of Jesus Christ, were rightly rejected by the early Christians.[88]
From such gospels "we learn not a single verifiable new fact about the
historical Jesus' ministry, and only a few new sayings that might possibly have been his."[89] Referring to extra-biblical writings like the
Gospel of Peter, the Gospel of Mary, the Gospel of Thomas, and the
Gospel of Philip, New Testament scholar Gerald L. Borchert (a PhD
from Princeton) writes:

---

[86]Paul P. Enns, *The Moody Handbook of Theology* (Chicago: Moody Press, 1997), 415.
[87]Ibid.
[88]These extra-biblical writings (such as the Nag Hammadi Library) are not secret, as Dan Brown's
The Da Vinci Code implies. They have been translated into English and are available in book form
through either a bookstore or a local library.
[89]Raymond E. Brown, "The Gnostic Gospels," *The New York Times Book Review* (January 20,
1980), 3. Cited from Erwin W. Lutzer, *The Da Vinci Deception* (Wheaton, IL: Tyndale House,
2004), 43.

The emergence of documents with strange fairy-tale-like stories about Jesus and skewed theological ideas . . . bear witness to the necessity in the church for authoritative Gospels to combat the growth of deviant views and fanciful legends concerning Jesus. To peruse these noncanonical [non-biblical] documents and reflect on the stories about Jesus preserved in them and other early documents gives the reader the immediate sense [because of the stark contrast] of the genuine reserve and feeling of authenticity that is present in the canonical [New Testament] presentations concerning Jesus.[90]

In other words, these non-biblical accounts are often so fanciful and far-fetched, they actually increase our confidence in and appreciation for the careful, straightforward writings of Matthew, Mark, Luke, and John.

Following the warning of the apostles, the early church rejected such far-fetched accounts.[91] They were either so outlandish or so theologically skewed (by Gnosticism) that their historical authenticity was clearly lacking.[92] For the early Christians, the differences would have been readily apparent, especially since "the 'Gnostic gospels' are not gospels at all in the sense of the four canonical Gospels, which are filled with narrative, concrete details, historical figures, political activity, and details about social and religious life."[93]

The New Testament Gospels are clearly superior to other supposed "gospels"—both in terms of being straightforward accounts of Jesus' life, and also in terms of being theologically consistent with what the apostles taught in the rest of the New Testament. This again affirms the trustworthiness of the biblical Gospels and helps explain why the early Christians were able to easily distinguish the true from the false.

---

[90]Borchert, *John 1–11*, 33. It should be noted that Oxford scholar Christopher Tucket has demonstrated that the Synoptic Gospels were written earlier than the Gnostic gospels, due to the fact that the Gnostic gospels borrow from them but not vice versa. Cf. Stephen Clark, *The Da Vinci Code on Trial* (Wales: Bryntirion Press, 2005), 36. On page 37, Clark also debunks Dan Brown's claims (as "nonsense" and "wildly erratic") that there were eighty gospels originally.

[91]See Herman N. Ridderbos in *Redemptive History and the New Testament* (Phillipsburg, N.J.: P&R, 1988), 41.

[92]For more on the Gnostic gospels from an apologetic standpoint, see James L. Garlow, *The Da Vinci Codebreaker* (Minneapolis: Bethany House, 2006), 85–88, 90–97. For a more academic treatment, see Darrell Bock, *Breaking the Da Vinci Code* (Nashville: Thomas Nelson, 2004), 61–124.

[93]Carl E. Olson and Sandra Miesel, *The Da Vinci Hoax* (San Francisco: Ignatius Press, 2004), 66.

Reason 10:
We Believe the New Testament Gospels Are Reliable

Because They Have Been Faithfully Preserved Throughout Church History

Up to this point, we have considered various reasons why the New Testament Gospels can be rightly regarded as historically reliable documents. We have found them to be accurate presentations of the historical Jesus. Nonetheless, our confidence in them is predicated on the fact that they have been adequately preserved throughout history, such that the copies we have today accurately reflect the originals. If the Gospels were irrevocably corrupted at some point in church history, we would not be able to trust the copies we now possess.

The New Testament writers understood how important it was that the truth about Jesus Christ be faithfully passed down from generation to generation. Part of the reason the Gospels were written was so that the church would have a lasting record of Jesus' life, even after the apostles were gone. But it would be incumbent upon future generations to also carefully guard the truth (cf. 1 Timothy 6:20; 2 Timothy 2:2). The danger of false teachers distorting the message of Christ was a real threat, with which the earliest Christians were deeply concerned (Colossians 2:4–9; 1 John 4:2–3; cf. 2 Peter 2:1–3). They saw preserving the truth about Jesus as absolutely essential (1 John 1:3; 5:20; cf. 2 Peter 1:16), since any later distortion could undermine the spiritual lives of future generations.

In point of fact, the New Testament documents (including the Gospels) have been preserved remarkably well. This, of course, is not true of all ancient documents. Caesar's *Gallic Wars* can boast only ten surviving manuscript copies, the oldest of which is dated one thousand years after the work was first written. Only eight extant manuscripts have been found of Herodotus' *History*, the earliest of which is 1,300 years removed from the original. Thucydides' *History of the Peloponnesian War* is similarly attested to by only eight manuscripts, all of which are separated from the original by more than a millennium. And these are just a few examples.[94]

In contrast to secular texts, the New Testament documents (including the Gospels) are very well attested, and from only a short period of time after the originals were written.

> Approximately 5,000 Greek manuscripts, containing all or part of the New Testament, exist. There are 8,000 manuscript copies of the Vulgate (a Latin translation of the Bible done by Jerome from 382–405) and more than 350 copies of Syriac (Christian Aramaic) versions of the New Testament (these originated from 150–250; most of the copies are from the 400s). Besides this, virtually the entire New Testament could be reproduced from citations contained in the works of the early church fathers. There are some thirty-two thousand citations in the writings of the Fathers prior to the Council of Nicea (325).[95]

Among the ancient manuscripts are the Chester Beatty Papyri (a group of early Christian manuscripts) most of which are dated in the 200s. Three of these codices (or books) of papyri contain portions of the New Testament. The first (known as *p*45) originally consisted of about 220 leaves and contained all four Gospels and Acts. The second (*p*46) had 104 leaves and included ten of Paul's epistles. And the third (*p*47) is thought to have had thirty-two leaves and contained the book of Revelation. Today only a portion of those codices remain (around 126 leaves altogether), yet it is enough to serve as a valuable witness to the reliability of our modern Bibles.

Another important papyrus is *p*52. It is one of the oldest copies of any portion of the New Testament yet found and contains a few verses from the Gospel of John (dated to between 100–150). Its significance lies in the fact that it "proves the existence and use of the Fourth Gospel during the first half of the second century in a provincial town along the Nile, far removed from its traditional place of composition

---

[94]Cf. F. F. Bruce, *The Books and the Parchments* (Old Tappan, NJ: Fleming H. Revell, 1963), 180. Bruce notes, "There is no body of ancient literature in the world which enjoys such a wealth of good textual attestation as the New Testament" (178). See also the chart by Josh McDowell in *The New Evidence That Demands a Verdict* (Nashville: Thomas Nelson, 1999), 38.
[95]Moreland, *Scaling the Secular City*, 135–136.

(Ephesus in Asia Minor)."[96] The finding of this fragment shattered liberal theories about a late-second-century date for the composition of John's Gospel.

The Bodmer Papyri also warrant mentioning. One of them, *p66*, contains a large portion of the Gospel of John (of which John 1:1–6:11 and 6:35b–14:15 are still intact) and dates from around 200. Another Bodmer papyrus, *p77*, includes Luke and John (of the original 144 pages, 102 have survived) and dates to between 175 and 225. It is the earliest known copy of the Gospel of Luke. In 1994, a German scholar named Carsten Peter Thiede suggested that some fragments from Matthew's Gospel (known as the Magdalen Papyrus) could date to as early as A.D. 70,[97] though most scholars date the papyrus to around A.D. 200.

That any manuscripts survived at all from the first few centuries of church history is remarkable, since it was a time of such intense persecution for Christians. From the fourth century on, however, the number of surviving manuscripts becomes much more plentiful. The earliest and most important of these include Codex Sinaiticus (A.D. 350), which contains almost all of the New Testament, and Codex Vaticanus (A.D. 325–350), which includes virtually the entire Bible.

Along with these manuscripts and other ancient translations, the records left by the church fathers also confirm that the Gospels have been faithfully preserved. In fact, there are over nineteen thousand quotations just from the four Gospels in the extant writings of the early church fathers.[98] Their testimony bears witness to the fact that the Jesus they worshiped is the same Jesus we worship today.

Of course, sometimes there are discrepancies or variants among the New Testament manuscripts that have survived. This is to be expected, given the thousands of copies that were handwritten throughout history. Such discrepancies, then, are due to scribal errors that were made (at various points in church history) as the manuscripts were being manually reproduced.

But Christians need not be anxious about them. For starters, the vast majority of them are very minor (such as a word added here or a

---

[96]Metzger, *The Text of the New Testament*, 39. Metzger's work was the primary source consulted for information on these papyri.
[97]Cf. Carsten Peter Thiede, *The Jesus Papyrus* (London: Weidenfeld & Nicolson, 1996).
[98]Josh McDowell, *New Evidence That Demands a Verdict*, 43.

word missing there). Most have been readily explained and corrected through the science of textual criticism. And none of them pose a serious threat to any major Christian doctrine. The fact that there are so many manuscripts available to examine, some of which are very early, has enabled "textual scholars to accurately reconstruct the original text with more than 99 percent accuracy. [One] noted Greek scholar, A. T. Robertson, said the real concerns of textual criticism is on 'a thousandth part of the entire text' (making the New Testament 99.9 percent pure)."[99]

We can have confidence, then, in knowing that the Gospels we read today are faithful representations of the original Gospels, though we are separated by two thousand years and by translation from Greek to English. Thus we can trust the historical reliability not only of the original Gospel accounts but, more significantly (to us), of our own English copies. In the words of Sir Frederic Kenyon, eminent scholar of ancient languages and former director of the British Museum:

> The Christian can take the whole Bible in his hand and say without fear or hesitation that he holds in it the true Word of God, handed down without essential loss from generation to generation throughout the centuries.[100]

[99]Ravi Zacharias and Norman L. Geisler, *Who Made God?* (Grand Rapids, MI: Zondervan, 2003), 127.
[100]Frederic G. Kenyon, *Our Bible and the Ancient Manuscripts* (London: Eyre & Spottiswoode, 1958), 23.

REASONS WE BELIEVE IN JESUS

PART ONE

He Is the Messiah, the Son of God, and the Savior of the World

I consider it my greatest joy and glory that, occupying a most exalted position in the nation, I am enabled, simply and sincerely, to preach the practical moralities of the Bible to my fellow-countrymen and to hold up Christ as the hope and Savior of the world.

THEODORE ROOSEVELT[1]

I am convinced that the moral and religious system which Jesus Christ has transmitted to us, is the best that the world has ever seen or can see.

BENJAMIN FRANKLIN[2]

---

[1]Ferdinand Iglehart, *Theodore Roosevelt: The Man as I Knew Him* (New York: The Christian Herald, 1919), 296.
[2]Benjamin Franklin, in a 1790 letter. Cited from James Wallis and David King, *The British Millennial Harbinger* (London: Arthur Hall, 1856), 9:428.

INTRODUCTION

There is no question that Jesus Christ dramatically impacted history. As *Newsweek* reported in 1999, "[After] two thousand years ... the centuries themselves are measured from the birth of Jesus of Nazareth. At the end of this year, calendars in India and China, like those in Europe, America, and the Middle East, will register the dawn of the third millennium."[3] Today over two billion people claim to believe in Him, making "Christianity" the largest religion in the world. And the New Testament is not the only religious book that highlights Jesus' unique role. None other than the Qur'an teaches that God gave us the gospel of Jesus Christ, that Mary was a virgin when she conceived, and that Jesus was the Messiah. Muslim tradition also holds that Jesus lived a sinless life, that He could do miracles by the will of God, and that He will one day return to earth to defeat an Antichrist-like figure called "the Deceiver."[4]

Other religions, outside of Christianity and Islam, also consider Jesus to have been a good man—a moral teacher, a social visionary, and an inspiring example of selflessness. Some Buddhists, such as the Dalai Lama (Tenzin Gyatso), regard Jesus as a being who reached a high state of enlightenment.[5] And some Hindus view Him as a Satguru or *true teacher*. Swami Vivekananda (1863–1962), an influential Hindu leader who introduced Yoga and Vedanta to the West, spoke of Jesus Christ as a great prophet who should be worshiped as "god."[6] Even many atheists and agnostics applaud Jesus as a social reformer. As one example, a web site called Atheists for Jesus explains itself this way:

[3]Kenneth L. Woodward, "2000 Years of Jesus," *Newsweek* (March 29, 1999).
[4]Mufti A. H. Elias, "Jesus (Isa) A.S. in Islam, and His Second Coming" and "Prophethood in Islam"; http://www.islam.tc/prophecies/jesus.html. Accessed April 14, 2007. Published by *The Institute of Islamic Information and Education*.
[5]James A. Beverley, "Hollywood's Idol: CT Visits the Dalai Lama, Spiritual Hero to Millions," *Christianity Today* (June 11, 2001).
[6]"Christ the Messenger," in *Complete Works of Swami Vivekananda*, Vol. 4: Lectures and Discourses, Delivered in Los Angeles, 1900; http://www.ramakrishnavivekananda.info. Accessed July 26, 2007. Of course, Vivekananda did not consider Jesus to be uniquely God but rather just one of many Hindu reflections of "god."

156 Reasons We Believe in Jesus

The stated purpose of this site has been to promote a dialog between religious and non-religious people who share a common vision of Jesus as an individual of tremendous compassion; a true advocate of "Peace on Earth"; and a staunch supporter of the poor and suffering people who are all too often ignored by prosperous societies.[7]

What's clear, then, is that Jesus is appreciated and esteemed by most people in the world, even among those who are not "Christians." That alone should be compelling motivation to better understand who Jesus is, what He taught, and why He made such an impact on the world.

CONSIDERING THE CLAIMS OF CHRIST

Though Jesus is largely admired as a wise teacher and an inspiring activist, the New Testament declares that He is much more than that. Jesus was not just a social reformer—He is the Savior of the world. He was not just an inspiring teacher—He is the perfect Son of God. He was not merely an example of self-sacrifice—He is the final sacrifice for sin. He was not simply a religious figure who died two millennia ago—He is the risen and ascended Lord who will soon return to judge the earth in righteousness.

Jesus clearly saw Himself as the fulfillment of the messianic promises found in the Old Testament (Matthew 5:17; Luke 24:44; John 5:39–47). But He claimed to be much more than a human deliverer. He said He was the Son of God (Luke 22:70; John 3:18; 11:4), thereby "making Himself equal with God" (John 5:18). He used divine titles (John 8:56–58), welcomed the worship of others (Matthew 14:33), granted forgiveness for sins (Mark 2:5–12), rebuked demons and diseases (Luke 4:35, 39), commanded the wind and sea to obey Him (Mark 4:39), denounced the existing religious establishment (Matthew 23:13–39), offered eternal life in His own name (John 10:28), pledged to conquer death (John 11:25), and promised to build His church even after He was gone (Matthew 16:18). In John 10:30 Jesus simply stated, "I and the Father are one." No mere man could do all that Jesus claimed to do. Conversely, Jesus did not claim to be merely a man.

Both His friends and His enemies understood exactly who He was

[7]From the welcome page of Atheists for Jesus online at http://www.atheists-for-jesus.com/. Accessed July 26, 2007.

claiming to be—God in human flesh.[8] His followers worshiped Him as God (Matthew 28:9), even directly using the title *God* in referring to Him (John 1:1, 18; 20:28; cf. Titus 2:13; Hebrews 1:8). His enemies, too, understood His claims. On multiple occasions, they tried to stone Him for blasphemy (John 5:18; 8:59; 10:28–33), finally putting Him to death on a cross (John 19:7).

Jesus' message was also far different than what some today would like to pretend. To be sure, He compassionately healed the sick (Matthew 14:14) and taught His followers to exhibit love and self-sacrifice (Matthew 7:12; Mark 10:44; John 13:12–15). But His primary emphasis was on eternal life, offering Himself as the only hope of salvation to a world of sinners who were otherwise destined for judgment (Mark 10:45; John 3:16–18). By dying in their place, Jesus paid sin's penalty for all who would believe in Him (John 15:13; Romans 10:9–10; 1 Peter 3:18), so that they might have eternal life (John 5:24). He asserted that He alone is the way of salvation, clearly stating, "I am the way, and the truth, and the life. No one comes to the Father except through me" (John 14:6).

Jesus not only claimed to be both God and Savior but also Lord and Master (Matthew 24:42–51; Luke 6:46; cf. Jude 4). He taught that those who truly believe in Him are characterized by love for Him (John 8:42; 16:27) and that those who love Him will demonstrate that love by obeying His commands (John 14:15; 15:14; cf. 1 John 4:20–21). He described His sheep as those who hear His voice and follow Him (John 10:4, 27) and His true disciples as those who continue in His Word (John 8:31; 15:6). During His ministry, Jesus was unimpressed with superficial interest or halfhearted allegiance (Luke 6:46; John 2:24–25; 6:66). Instead, He called people to turn from their sin and follow Him (Luke 13:1–5; 24:47; John 8:12), denying themselves and their own selfish ambitions in the process (Mark 8:34–35; John 12:25–26). To *believe* in Him means embracing Him not only as Savior but also as Lord and God (John 3:36; cf. Acts 16:31; 17:30–31; 26:20).

Clearly, Jesus Christ as He is portrayed in the New Testament is much more than the social activist or moral reformer that so many people today imagine Him to be. He claimed to be the Messiah, the Son

---

[8]For a recent treatment of the deity of Christ, see Robert M. Bowman Jr. and J. Ed Komoszewski, *Putting Jesus in His Place: The Case for the Deity of Christ* (Grand Rapids, MI: Kregel, 2007). See also Stephen Nichols, *For Us and Our Salvation* (Wheaton, IL: Crossway Books, 2007).

of God, the only way to Heaven, and the rightful King over everyone and everything. As C. S. Lewis aptly noted:

> I am trying here to prevent anyone saying the really foolish thing that people often say about Him: "I'm ready to accept Jesus as a great moral teacher, but I don't accept His claim to be God." That is the one thing we must not say. A man who said the sort of things Jesus said would not be a great moral teacher. He would either be a lunatic—on a level with the man who says he is a poached egg—or else he would be the Devil of Hell. You must make your choice. Either this man was, and is, the Son of God: or else a madman or something worse. You can shut Him up for a fool, you can spit at Him and kill Him as a demon; or you can fall at His feet and call Him Lord and God. But let us not come with any patronising nonsense about His being a great human teacher. He has not left that open to us. He did not intend to.[9]

TEN REASONS WE BELIEVE IN JESUS CHRIST

The question therefore remains: Are the claims of Christ as presented in the New Testament believable? Should we believe in Jesus, or should we reject Him as a fool, a fraud, or a figment of His followers' imaginations? In this section we will consider ten reasons why Christians believe in Jesus Christ as He is described in the New Testament, such that we would base both our lives and our eternities on Him and Him alone.

---

[9]C. S. Lewis, *Mere Christianity* (Grand Rapids, MI: Zondervan, 2001), 52.

Reason 1:
We Believe in Jesus Christ
Because We, as Christians, Have Come to Know Him

In John 10:14–15 Jesus says this about His followers, "I am the good shepherd. I know my own and my own know me, just as the Father knows me and I know the Father; and I lay down my life for the sheep." Christians then are those who have come to know Jesus Christ in a saving way. As believers, we have personally experienced His grace and have been transformed by His power (cf. Acts 26:12–23). Our lives have been irrevocably changed, the only explanation for which is that we know the risen Christ and His Spirit is at work in our hearts (John 14:16–17; 2 Corinthians 5:17; Philippians 2:13). Because we know Him, we also know His Father (John 8:19; 17:3; 1 John 5:20–21). Though we were once the enemies of God, we now enjoy intimate fellowship with Him as His children (2 Corinthians 5:18–19; Galatians 3:26; 4:5–7).

Knowing Christ is the essence of the Christian faith. In fact, "all things that pertain to life and godliness" come "through the knowledge of him" (2 Peter 1:3; cf. 3:17–18). "The knowledge of our Lord Jesus Christ" (2 Peter 1:8), being objectively revealed in the Scriptures (cf. 1:16–21), is sufficient to meet our every spiritual need (cf. 1 Peter 2:2–3). Of course, knowing Christ is much more than just intellectual knowledge. It is dynamic and personal and involves shared life with Christ as we daily and dependently abide in Him (John 15:1–11; 17:3; Galatians 2:20; Philippians 3:8–10). Because our hearts have been sanctified, we long to serve and obey the Savior whom we have come to know (1 John 2:3–6; 3:1, 6).

As those who know Him, we have an internal confidence made certain by the Holy Spirit that Jesus Christ is who He claimed to be (cf. 1 John 5:6, 10). His Word has transformed our hearts (2 Corinthians 5:17; cf. Luke 24:32); His death has paid for our sins (Romans

5:8–9); and His resurrection is our hope for the future (1 Corinthians 15:20–22). We have quenched our thirst with living water, satisfied our souls with the bread of heaven, and experienced true life in Him (John 4:10, 13–14; 6:35; 14:6). We believe in Him because He found us, loved us, and rescued us (Luke 19:10). He has done what no figment could do (cf. Matthew 16:18), what no fraud would do (cf. John 15:13), and what only the truth of the Scriptures can explain (cf. Acts 17:2–3, 11). As Christians, we believe in Him because we have personally experienced the transforming effects of His person and work. We have come to know and love Him, and that knowledge has radically changed us in every way. To paraphrase the words of Peter: Though we have not seen Him, we love Him; and even though we do not see Him now, we confidently believe in Him and are filled with an inexpressible and glorious joy, because through Him we have been promised the salvation of our souls (1 Peter 1:8–9).

Reason 2:
We Believe in Jesus Christ

Because His Coming Met the Biblical Requirements

According to the Old Testament, the promised Messiah could not be just anyone. Rather, He had to be a Jew (a descendant of Abraham, Isaac, and Jacob), from the tribe of Judah (Genesis 49:10), of the family of Jesse (Isaiah 11:1) through David (Jeremiah 23:5). He further had to be born in Bethlehem (Micah 5:2) sometime before the Jewish genealogical records were destroyed in A.D. 70.

> Since the genealogical records of Israel were lost in the burning of the Temple in August, A.D. 70, no one else is able to provide legal evidence that his ancestry traces back to King David. Therefore, Jesus of Nazareth is the only one who can prove He has a legal right to sit on the throne of David as Israel's Messiah.[10]

But it does not stop there. Two additional factors narrow the field of potential candidates to only one. The first regards the curse of Jeconiah (also called Jehoiachin), an Old Testament king who himself was a descendant of David. Unlike David, however, Jeconiah was severely cursed by God for his wickedness. "Thus says the LORD: 'Write this man down as childless, a man who shall not succeed in his days, for none of his offspring shall succeed in sitting on the throne of David and ruling again in Judah'" (Jeremiah 22:30). Through the mouth of the prophet Jeremiah, God promised that Jeconiah would be "childless" in the sense that he would never have an heir who would reign as king in Israel.[11] Jeconiah himself would not occupy the throne for long. In 597 B.C., after a reign of just over three months, he was taken captive by the Babylonians.

---

[10]Grant R. Jeffrey, *Jesus: The Great Debate* (Toronto: Frontier Research, 1999), 224.
[11]In *Jeremiah Lamentations*, New American Commentary, Vol. 16 (Nashville: Broadman, 1993), 209, commenting on Jeremiah 22:28–30, F. B. Huey notes: "There is no conflict in the statement in 22:30, 'as if childless,' and 1 Chr 3:17, which says Jehoiachin had seven children. Since his son would not succeed him to the throne, it was as though he had no children."

The implications of Jeconiah's curse present an interesting dilemma. How could the Messiah be part of the royal line of David (which included Jeconiah) if none of Jeconiah's physical offspring could ever rule as king over Israel (cf. Isaiah 9:7)?

The answer is found in the virgin birth.[12] Because Joseph was a direct descendant of Jeconiah (Matthew 1:11), he too was subject to the curse. Neither Joseph nor any of his physical offspring could be Israel's king. The miracle of the virgin birth, however, meant that Jesus was not the physical son of Joseph. Being miraculously conceived by the Holy Spirit (Matthew 1:20–25), Jesus avoided the curse placed on Jeconiah's bloodline. At the same time, as Joseph's legal son, Jesus still retained the rights and privileges of Joseph's royal ancestry. Moreover, because Mary was also related to David, though not through the royal line of Solomon (or Jeconiah), Jesus' physical heritage did go back to David (Luke 3:31). Jesus therefore enjoyed being a true descendant of David (through Mary) and also the legal heir of David's royal line (through Joseph), while simultaneously avoiding Jeconiah's curse.[13]

A second important criterion, this time chronological, is found in Daniel 9:24–26. Though it does not relate specifically to His birth, this passage sets a very definite time frame for the Messiah's coming. Written in the sixth century B.C., it predicted that sixty-nine periods of seven years (or 483 years total) would elapse between "the issuing of a decree to restore and rebuild Jerusalem" and the time at which "the Messiah [would] be cut off" or killed (Daniel 9:25–26, NASB). The messianic timetable was therefore established centuries before the birth of Christ. The Messiah would die 483 years after the Jews were officially authorized to begin rebuilding the city of Jerusalem that had been destroyed by the Babylonians.

Significantly, Christians are not the only ones who have understood this passage as messianic. Grant Jeffrey cites the commentary of Rabbi Malbin, who notes, "If the Jews had repented during this period [of 483 years] . . . the Messianic king would have come at its

---

[12]Donald MacLeod, *The Person of Christ* (Downers Grove, IL: InterVarsity Press, 1998), 35 notes that the virgin birth "is indubitably taught by Matthew and Luke, and [was] an integral part of these gospels from the very first."

[13]Charles L. Feinberg, in *Jeremiah: A Commentary* (Grand Rapids, MI: Zondervan, 1982), 160 explains: "Matthew's genealogy includes Jehoiachin but shows only who Jesus' legal father was, not his natural one. Luke traces Jesus' parental line through Nathan, a son of David, not through Solomon. Zerubbabel, grandson of Jehoiachin, though governor of Judah in 520 B.C., never ruled as king, nor did any other descendant of his."

termination."[14] Another rabbi, Moses Abraham Levi, acknowledges, "I have searched all the Holy Scriptures and have not found the time for the coming of Messiah clearly fixed, except in the words of Gabriel to the prophet Daniel, which are written in the 9th chapter of the prophecy of Daniel."[15]

When the math is done, the end point of Daniel's prophecy perfectly coincides with the sufferings and crucifixion of Jesus (which historians date around A.D. 30). The sixty-nine "weeks" of years (for a total of 483 years) point conclusively to His death. "While scholars have differed in details, all evangelicals have placed this ending of the 69 weeks somewhere between 26 and 33 A.D. It is worth noting, therefore, that the crucifixion of Jesus took place [within] that time span."[16] The 483-year countdown begins in 444 B.C. with Artaxerxes' decree to rebuild Jerusalem (cf. Nehemiah 2:1–8). Working from that starting point and using a 360-day year, which is what the Jews of Daniel's day would have known,[17] we arrive at a date around A.D. 30 as the year in which the Messiah would be killed. That the timing of Jesus' death directly corresponds to Daniel's prophetic time frame is surely no coincidence.

In sum, when we survey all of the Old Testament data, we see that the Messiah would be born a Jew, from the tribe of Judah, a descendant of David, who would have a legal claim to the royal line, yet would not be a physical descendant of Jeconiah. He would be born in Bethlehem, before the destruction of the temple, and at a time such that He could grow up and be killed around A.D. 30. Only one person in all of human history fits that criteria. That person is Jesus Christ.

---

[14]Jeffrey, *Jesus: The Great Debate*, 210. Rabbi Malbin's commentary is entitled *Mayenei HaYeshuah*.

[15]Ibid.

[16]William Varner, *The Messiah* (Bloomington, IN: AuthorHouse, 2004), 95. For a more detailed study of Daniel's prophecy see Harold Hoehner, *Chronological Aspects of the Life of Christ* (Grand Rapids, MI: Zondervan, 1977).

[17]The Jews observed a twelve-month, 360-day year (following a luni-solar calendar). Every few years, however, a thirteenth month would be added to stay on track with the seasons. The prophetic years of Daniel reflect the customary 360-day year. Thus, his 483 prophetic years (of 360 days each) are the equivalent of just over 476 solar years (of 365.25 days each). Daniel's usage of a 360-day year is confirmed by Revelation 11:2–3; 12:6; 13:5, which indicate that forty-two months (three and a half years) are equal to 1,260 days.

Reason 3:
We Believe in Jesus Christ

Because the Old Testament Predicted the Nature of His Life and Death

Though related to the previous discussion, the subject of messianic prophecy is broader than just Jesus' ancestry and the timing of His coming. As we saw in Section 3, fulfilled prophecy is one of the strongest confirmations of the divine authorship of Scripture. This is true also with regard to the authenticity of Jesus Christ. "To him all the prophets bear witness," preached Peter to the Gentiles, "that everyone who believes in him receives forgiveness of sins through his name" (Acts 10:43). Jesus Himself, on the road to Emmaus, showed two of His disciples how the Old Testament pointed to Him. "And beginning with Moses and all the Prophets, he interpreted to them in all the Scriptures the things concerning himself" (Luke 24:27). Jesus' life, which culminated in His death, burial, and resurrection, was the perfect fulfillment of God's prior revelation (Matthew 5:17), and it all took place "in accordance with the Scriptures" (1 Corinthians 15:3–4).

The coming of a future deliverer was first promised in Genesis 3:14–15 and was repeatedly confirmed throughout the Old Testament (cf. Genesis 49:10; Numbers 24:17; Isaiah 9:6–7; Zechariah 9:9; and many other passages[18]). It is important to realize that early Christians were not the only ones to recognize the messianic implications of these passages. The Old Testament Jews did too. *Targum Pseudo Jonathan* speaks of "the days of the king, Messiah" when explaining Genesis 3:15.[19] *Targum Jonathan* describes "the King, and Meshiha [Messiah]

---

[18]See, e.g., Genesis 3:15; 49:10; Numbers 24:17; Deuteronomy 18:15, 18–19; Job 19:25; Psalm 2; 22:1, 16, 18; 110:1–4; 118:22; Isaiah 2:2–4; 9:1–7; 40:1–8; 42:1–4; 49:1–7; 52:13–15; 53; 59:16–20; 61:1–3; 62:11; Jeremiah 23:5–6; Ezekiel 37:24–28; Daniel 3:25; 7:13–14; 9:20–27; Hosea 3:5; Zechariah 3:8–9; 6:12–13; 9:9–10; 10:4; 12:10; 13:1; Malachi 3:1–3; 4:5–6.

[19]John Bowker, *The Targums and Rabbinic Literature* (London: Cambridge University Press, 1969), 122. The ancient Jewish testimony here and throughout this part of our discussion was primarily cited from Josh McDowell, *The New Evidence That Demands a Verdict* (Nashville: Thomas Nelson, 1999), 169–179.

who will arise from the house of Jehuda [Judah]" when discussing Genesis 49:10.[20] Commenting on Deuteronomy 18:15, 18–19, the Jewish scholar Maimonides writes, "The Messiah will be a very great Prophet, greater than all the Prophets."[21] Regarding Psalm 2, E. W. Hengstenberg notes, "It is an undoubted fact, and unanimously admitted even by the recent opposers of its reference to Him, that the Psalm was universally regarded by the ancient Jews as foretelling the Messiah."[22] And the *Babylonian Talmud* points out that Isaiah 11:1–10 refers directly to "the Messiah."[23] These and other messianic texts (such as Psalm 118:22 and Isaiah 53:1–12) are affirmed, then, not only by Christian witness but also by ancient Jewish testimony. As Old Testament scholars Franz Delitzsch and Parton Gloag explain:

> The ancient Jews admit the Messianic character of most of [the messianic prophecies]; although the modern Jews, in consequence of their controversy with the Christians, have attempted to explain them away by applications which must appear to every candid reader to be unnatural.[24]

Because space does not allow for a full treatment of every Old Testament prophecy related to Jesus,[25] we will focus on just one— Isaiah 53. Though only twelve verses long, this chapter contains many prophecies that were literally and specifically fulfilled by Jesus during His Passion week. Here are some of those prophecies:

1. The Messiah would be despised and rejected by men, such that men would hide their faces from Him (v. 3; cf. Luke 23:35; Mark 14:50; John 1:10–11).

---

[20]J. W. Ethridge, *The Targums of Onkelos and Jonathan Ben Ussiel on the Pentateuch*, Vols. 1, 2 (New York: KTAV Publishing House, 1968), 331.

[21]A. Cohen, *The Teachings of Maimonides* (London: George Routledge & Sons, 1927), 221.

[22]E. W. Hengstenberg, *Christology of the Old Testament and a Commentary on the Messianic Predictions* (Grand Rapids, MI: Kregel, 1970), 43.

[23]Seder Nezikin, *The Babylonian Talmud, Sandhedrin II*, trans. I. Epstein (London: The Soncino Press, 1935), 626–627.

[24]Franz J. Delitzsch and Parton J. Gloag, *The Messianic Prophecies of Christ* (Minneapolis: Kloch & Kloch, 1983), 23–24; cited from John Ankerberg and John Weldon, *Fast Facts on Defending Your Faith* (Eugene, OR: Harvest House, 2002), 103. In Appendix D of *Behold Your King* (Battle Ground, WA: Christian Resources, 2003), William Webster lists several hundred Old Testament texts that were considered messianic by the Targums and ancient rabbinic writings.

[25]Varner, *The Messiah*, 7 estimates that there are about sixty-five *direct* prophecies regarding Jesus Christ in the Old Testament, with many more *typical* prophecies and *applications* of Old Testament concepts to the Messiah. As we have already seen, the probability of only forty-eight prophecies coming true in one person is 10 to the 157th power, making it a statistical impossibility.

2. He would experience great sorrow and grief (v. 3; cf. Luke 22:44).

3. He would take away the sorrows of men (v. 4; cf. Matthew 8:16–17).

4. He would be stricken and afflicted by men (vv. 4–5; cf. Luke 22:64; 1 Peter 2:24).

5. He would even be smitten by God (v. 4; cf. Matthew 27:46).

6. He would be wounded and tortured (v. 5; cf. John 19:34).

7. Through His suffering, He would bear the punishment that sinners deserved (vv. 4–6, 8, 10, 12; cf. 2 Corinthians 5:21; cf. 1 Peter 3:18).

8. He would be silent before His accusers (v. 7; cf. Matthew 27:12).

9. He would be arrested and taken away by force (vv. 7–8; cf. Mark 14:43–46).

10. After being tortured, He would be put to death (vv. 8, 12; cf. Mark 15:37).

11. His grave would be assigned with wicked men (vv. 9, 12; cf. Mark 15:27).

12. Yet He would be buried in a rich man's tomb (v. 9; cf. Matthew 27:57–60).

13. Even in His arrest, He would not respond with violence (v. 9; cf. Matthew 26:52).

14. His speech would be without deceit (v. 9; cf. 1 Peter 2:21–22).

15. It would be God's will that He suffer (v. 10; cf. Matthew 26:39).

16. He would be made alive again, and His days prolonged (v. 10; cf. 1 Corinthians 15:3–4; Ephesians 1:19–20).

17. He would be perfectly righteous and sinless (v. 11; cf. Hebrews 4:15).

18. He would justify many by bearing their guilt (v. 11; cf. Hebrews 9:28).

19. He would be greatly exalted after His suffering (v. 12; cf. Philippians 2:9–11).

20. He would make intercession for sinners (v. 12; cf. Luke 23:33–34; Hebrews 7:25).

This remarkable chapter clearly speaks of Jesus Christ; yet it was written over seven hundred years before the events it describes. That it points to the Messiah is again affirmed by ancient Jewish testimony.

"The Babylonian Talmud as well as the Aramaic Targums and the ancient rabbinic commentators identified this *Suffering Servant* [in Isaiah 53] as Israel's Messiah," explains William Varner. "The modern Jewish view of the Servant of Isaiah 53, however, is not that he is the Messiah but that he is a personification of suffering Israel. This interpretation was first introduced ca. 1100 by the great French rabbi, Shlomo Yitzaki, referred to simply as Rashi."[26] Norman Geisler adds this interesting observation: "Only after early Christians began using the text apologetically with great force did it become in rabbinical teaching an expression of the suffering of the Jewish nation."[27] Yet the pronouns in the passage make such an interpretation impossible, since it is clear that the nation of Israel (represented by "we" or "our") is distinct from the Suffering Servant, who is referred to in the third person singular ("he" or "him").

Isaiah 53, then, in accord with many other Old Testament passages, confirms that Jesus was exactly who He claimed to be: the long-anticipated Messiah of God. Ancient Jewish interpreters rightly understood that these texts point to the Messiah. Since Jesus is the only one who fulfilled them all perfectly (no one else even comes close), there can be no other conclusion than, "It was Jesus Christ the Righteous to whom all prophetic history pointed."[28]

---

[26]Ibid., 268.
[27]Norman Geisler, *Baker Encyclopedia of Christian Apologetics* (Grand Rapids, MI: Baker, 1998), 612; cited from McDowell, *New Evidence That Demands a Verdict*, 188.
[28]Carl E. Armerding, "Prophecy in the Old Testament," in *A Guide to Biblical Prophecy*, ed. Carl E. Armerding and W. Ward Gasque (Peabody, MA: Hendrickson, 1999), 71.

Reason 4:
We Believe in Jesus Christ

Because He Was Visibly Authenticated by God the Father

Fulfilled prophecy was not the only way in which God authenticated His Son. During Jesus' ministry, He was repeatedly affirmed by the Father, on occasion by audible voices from heaven (Matthew 3:13–17; 17:5; John 12:28) or by glorious transfiguration (Matthew 17:2–5; Mark 9:2–9), and more frequently through miraculous signs (John 3:2; Acts 2:22). "Thirty-five separate miracles done by Christ are recorded in the gospels. Of these Matthew mentioned twenty; Mark eighteen; Luke, twenty; and John, seven. But these are only a selection from among the many that he did."[29]

In the course of His ministry, Jesus healed diseases (e.g., Matthew 4:23–25; Mark 3:7–12),[30] cast out demons (e.g., Matthew 8:16; Luke 8:30–33), calmed storms (e.g., Matthew 8:23–27; Mark 4:35–41), raised the dead (e.g., Luke 7:11–17; John 11:1–44), fed thousands at one time (e.g., Matthew 14:13–21; 15:32–39), walked on water (e.g., Matthew 14:22–33; John 6:15–21), turned water into wine (John 2:1–11), and even controlled the whereabouts of fish (e.g., Matthew 17:24–27; Luke 5:1–11). Because His miracles were so well-known, Jesus Himself appealed to them as verification that He came from God. As He told His critics, "For the works that the Father has given me to accomplish, the very works that I am doing, bear witness about me that the Father has sent me" (John 5:36; cf. Matthew 11:5; John 10:38).

Significantly, Jesus' opponents never denied His miracles. Though they questioned the divine origin of His power (Matthew 12:24), they were never able to deny that the works He and His apostles performed

---

[29]Charles C. Ryrie, *The Miracles of Our Lord* (Neptune, NJ: Loizeaux Brothers, 1988), 11.

[30]Douglas Groothius, *Jesus in an Age of Controversy*, (Eugene, OR: Harvest House, 1996), 240 notes, "Although some healing may be psychosomatically explained [by skeptics], Jesus healed not only functional problems . . . but deep organic maladies involving physical degeneration." Such healings cannot be explained outside of the miraculous.

were supernatural (John 11:47–48; cf. Acts 4:16). Even today, "the fact that miracle working belongs to the historical Jesus is no longer disputed."[31] In the words of the German scholar Wolfgang Trilling: "We are convinced and hold it for historically certain that Jesus did in fact perform miracles. . . . The miracle reports occupy so much space in the Gospels that it is impossible that all could have been subsequently invented or transferred to Jesus."[32] Jewish literature from the first few centuries A.D. confirms that the Jews, like the Christians, accepted the fact that Jesus performed supernatural acts. Unlike many of the pseudo-miracles done today in the name of Jesus, the actual miracles of Jesus were irrefutable. But while they could not deny His power, the Jewish religious leaders rejected the idea that God was the source behind it. The Pharisees of Jesus' day attributed His power directly to Satan (Matthew 12:24). In later centuries, the rabbis attempted to pass it off as sorcery and magic.[33] Thus, in the Babylonian Talmud[34] we read this accusation: "Jesus the Nazarene practiced magic and deceived and led Israel astray."[35] Though intended pejoratively, the statement provides backhanded confirmation of the fact that Jesus performed amazing wonders ("practiced magic") that were so compelling that many in Israel believed in Him because they were convinced by what He did ("deceived and led Israel astray").

Jewish sources further acknowledge that Jesus' followers also had the power to heal in His name.[36] Princeton scholar Peter Schäfer comments on one particular account in the Talmud, in which the grandson of a Jewish man named Yehoshua b. Levi was miraculously healed by a Christian. Though the healing was successful, Yehoshua b. Levi was mortified that his grandson had been subject to such "magical" pow-

---

[31]William Lane Craig; cited from Norman Geisler and Frank Turek, *I Don't Have Enough Faith to Be an Atheist* (Wheaton, IL: Crossway Books, 2005), 314.

[32]Wolfgang Trilling; cited from Paul Copan and Ronald Tacelli, eds., *Jesus' Resurrection, Fact or Figment?* (Downers Grove, IL: InterVarsity Press, 2000), 181.

[33]Graham H. Twelftree, in *Jesus the Exorcist* (Peabody, MA: Hendrickson, 1993), 207 argues persuasively that "it is false to think that Jesus' contemporaries considered him to be a magician," stating that this claim was invented centuries later. Our purpose here is simply to show that because it was undeniable that Jesus did *something*, His opponents desperately searched for alternative explanations than those given by Jesus Himself.

[34]Jeffrey, *Jesus: The Great Debate*, 180, explains: "The Babylonian Talmud (Babli or Baraitha) is a comprehensive commentary on the Jewish Law that was written in Babylon (present-day Iraq) over a period of six hundred years (100 B.C.–A. D. 499)."

[35]Cited from Peter Schäfer, *Jesus in the Talmud* (Princeton, NJ: Princeton University Press, 2007), 35.

[36]Cf. ibid., 52–62.

ers. Based on that account, Schäfer explains the Jewish perspective of Jesus' miracles:

> The story about Yehoshua b. Levi and his grandson . . . presents an ironical critique of Jesus' and his followers' belief in their magical power. True, it argues, their magical power is undeniable: it works, and one cannot do anything against its effectiveness. But it is [in the minds of the Jews] an unauthorized and misused power.[37]

Faced with the reality that Jesus and His immediate followers could perform miraculous deeds, the Jewish leaders (both in Jesus' day and in the centuries that followed) had a clear choice. But rather than attribute "the chaste, ethical, and redemptive nature of the miracles of Christ"[38] to God, they chose instead to attribute them (either directly or indirectly) to Satan. Jesus Himself pointed out the self-contradictory nature of their claim (cf. Matthew 12:25–32): Why would He use His miracle-working power to fight against Satan if He was in fact empowered by Satan? That Jesus used His miracles to further the kingdom of God clearly revealed the true source of His power.[39]

Though neither the Pharisees nor the later rabbis responded in belief, their writings (from the first few centuries of church history) provide historical confirmation of Jesus as a miracle worker.[40] Thus Christians today can look to Christ's miracles as verification that He is indeed the Son of God (John 3:2; Acts 2:22). As the early Christian leader Justin Martyr (d. 165) explained to the Jewish antagonists of his day, "[Jesus] was manifested to your race and healed those who

---

[37]Ibid., 61–62.

[38]Bernard Ramm, *Protestant Christian Evidences* (Chicago: Moody Press, 1972), 143 points out: "Pagan miracles lack the dignity of Biblical miracles. They are frequently grotesque and done for very selfish reasons. They are seldom ethical or redemptive and stand in marked contrast to the chaste, ethical, and redemptive nature of the miracles of Christ. Nor do they have the genuine attestation that Biblical miracles have."

[39]Cf. David K. Clark, "Miracles in the World Religions," 199–213, in *In Defense of Miracles*, ed. R. Douglas Geivett and Gary R. Habermas (Downers Grove, IL: InterVarsity Press, 1997), 207–208. Clark responds convincingly to the charge that Jesus was merely a magician. Clark shows that there are significant differences between Jesus' miracles and the supposed miracles of other "magicians." For example, while magicians usually used objects in their work, combined with incantations and spells, Jesus simply spoke, commanding demons and diseases on the basis of His own authority.

[40]Schäfer, *Jesus in the Talmud*, 49–51 asserts that some of the rabbinic stories about Rabbi Eliezer may have been representative of Jesus. In one such account, Eliezer's message is confirmed by miracles and an audible voice from heaven. But the other rabbis reject it nonetheless because it goes against their established traditions. If Schäfer is right, his conclusions give us an interesting insight into why the Jews rejected Jesus even after His message was confirmed by miracles and a voice from heaven.

were from birth physically maimed and deaf and lame, causing one to leap and another to hear and a third to see at his word. And he raised the dead and gave them life and by his actions challenged the men of his time to recognize him."[41] Even today, two millennia later, Jesus' miracles still give us good reason to take His claims seriously.

---

[41] Justin, *Dialogue with Trypho*, 69; cited from Colin Brown, *Miracles and the Critical Mind* (Grand Rapids, MI: Eerdmans, 1984), 4.

Reason 5:
We Believe in Jesus Christ

Because He Exhibited Divine Authority

As we noted earlier, Jesus Christ claimed to be much more than a mere man. He declared Himself to be the Son of God (Luke 22:70; John 3:18; 11:4) and therefore the "Mighty God" of whom Isaiah prophesied (Isaiah 9:6).[42] Throughout His ministry He intentionally used divine titles for Himself, such as "I AM" (compare John 8:56–58 with Exodus 3:14) and "Son of Man" (compare Mark 14:62 and John 5:27 with Daniel 7:13–14). The Jews understood exactly what He meant, which is why they tried to stone Him to death for blasphemy on multiple occasions (cf. John 8:59; 10:31; 11:8). As John explains, "This was why the Jews were seeking all the more to kill him, because not only was he breaking the Sabbath, but he was even calling God his own Father, making himself equal with God" (John 5:18). In fact, their only charge against Him at His trial was that He claimed to be the Christ, the Son of God (Matthew 26:59–66; John 19:7). Because they did not believe in Him, they regarded His claim as blasphemy.

The deity of Christ is not only evidenced in the miraculous works He performed, but also (more generally) in the divine authority He clearly possessed. Jesus' authority extended to every area of His life and ministry, authority that was given to Him by His Father (cf. Matthew 11:27; 28:18; John 17:2). Consider the extent of Jesus' authority:

• He taught with divine authority, such that the people were amazed (Matthew 7:29; Mark 1:22; Luke 4:32).

• He commanded demons to come out of people, and they obeyed Him (Matthew 10:1; Mark 3:15; Luke 4:36).

---

[42]The Old Testament indicates that "His sway was to be not only universal (Psalm 2:8) but eternal (Isaiah 9:7), and even divine (Psalm 45:6–7). The prophet Micah speaks of his pre-existence (Micah 5:2); Jeremiah describes him as 'The LORD Our righteousness' (Jeremiah 23:6); and Isaiah speaks of him as 'Wonderful Counselor, Mighty God, Everlasting Father, Prince of Peace' (Isaiah 9:6)." Norman Anderson, *Jesus Christ: The Witness of History* (Downers Grove, IL: InterVarsity Press, 1985), 73–74.

• He violated traditional Jewish customs and interpretations on His own authority as God (cf. Matthew 5:21–22, 27–28; 15:1–9; Luke 6:1–11; John 5:9–17), and even single-handedly cleared out the temple (Matthew 21:12–13; John 2:13–22).

• He calmed the stormy wind and sea with just a short sentence and commanded plants and animals to do His bidding (cf. Matthew 8:26–27; 21:19; John 21:3–11).

• He rebuked diseases and they left, gave authority to others to heal, and even called back to life those who had died (Mark 5:38–43; Luke 4:39; 9:1; John 11:43–44).

• He claimed the authority to forgive sins and grant eternal life, something only God can do (Matthew 9:6, 8; Mark 2:10; Luke 5:24; John 17:2).

• He claimed that the Father had given Him the authority to judge the world (Mark 13:26–27; John 5:22–23).

• He readily accepted worship from others (Matthew 14:33; 15:25; 28:9) though He knew that only God can receive worship (Matthew 4:10; cf. Revelation 22:9).

• He was not taken by surprise, even in His death, but gave His life of His own authority, knowing that He would be raised (John 10:18; cf. Luke 23:46; John 2:18–22).

Jesus could cast out demons, forgive sins, receive worship, and teach in a way that astonished the crowds only because He possessed supernatural authority. His authoritative posture was immediately recognized by the people (Mark 1:22) and rebuffed by the religious authorities (Mark 11:18).

> Today there is virtually a consensus . . . that Jesus came on the scene with *an unheard-of authority*, namely, the authority of God, with *the claim of the authority to stand in God's place and speak to us and bring us to salvation.* . . . With regard to Jesus, there are only two possible modes of behavior: either to believe that in him God encounters us, or to nail him to the cross as a blasphemer. There is no third way.[43]

The choice is simple. Either we must accept His divine authority and submit to it ourselves, or we must reject Him as a fraud. But what fraud could have taught in the way Jesus did or influenced the world as Jesus has? Dale Foreman, a graduate of Harvard Law School, writes:

---

[43]Horst Gerog Pöhlmann, *Abriss der Dogmatik* (Dusseldorf: Patmos, 1966), 230. Cited from William Lane Craig, "Opening Addresses," 25–32, in *Will the Real Jesus Please Stand Up?*, ed. Paul Copan (Grand Rapids, MI: Baker, 1998), 25–26.

174 Reasons We Believe in Jesus

The teachings of Jesus have changed the world. In 2000 years not a day has gone by when the influence of this itinerant teacher from Nazareth has not been felt. As a trial lawyer, trained to be rational, skeptical and critical, I believe it improbable that any fraud or false Messiah could have made such a profound impression for good.[44]

The unsurpassed authority that Jesus displayed in His earthly ministry, the effects of which we still feel today, points convincingly to the fact that He was from God. Thus we conclude with Erwin Lutzer, "That Jesus claimed to be God is clear; what is equally clear is that He is the God He claimed to be."[45]

---

[44]Dale Foreman, *Crucify Him: A Lawyer Looks at the Trial of Jesus* (Grand Rapids, MI: Zondervan, 1990), 178. Cited from Ross Clifford, *The Case for the Empty Tomb* (Claremont, CA: Albatross, 1993), 127.
[45]Erwin W. Lutzer, *Christ Among Other gods* (Chicago: Moody, 1994), 114.

Reason 6:
We Believe in Jesus Christ

Because He Lived a Life of Sinless Perfection

The **righteousness and holiness** of God are repeatedly established in the Old Testament (e.g., Exodus 15:11; Leviticus 19:2). Moses reverently refers to God with these words: "The Rock, his work is perfect, for all his ways are justice. A God of faithfulness and without iniquity, just and upright is he" (Deuteronomy 32:4; cf. Genesis 18:25). David echoes those thoughts in Psalm 11:7: "For the LORD is righteous; he loves righteous deeds." Later in the Psalms we read that God's "righteousness endures forever" (Psalm 111:3b) since "the works of his hands are faithful and just" (Psalm 111:7a). Even around God's throne the angels continually cry out, "Holy, holy, holy is the LORD of hosts" (Isaiah 6:3; cf. Revelation 4:8). For all of eternity, they will echo the fact that God is the very definition of perfection.

It follows, then, that if Jesus is truly the Son of God, He must also be morally perfect. In anticipating His coming, the Old Testament is clear that the promised Messiah would be characterized by "justice and . . . righteousness" (Isaiah 9:7; cf. 42:3–4).[46] "His delight shall be in the fear of the LORD," declared the prophet Isaiah (Isaiah 11:3). "With righteousness he shall judge the poor, and decide with equity for the meek of the earth" (Isaiah 11:4). He would be the one killed for the sins of others, "although he had done no violence, and there was no deceit in his mouth" (Isaiah 53:9). If Jesus was the Messiah that God had promised, His life would have to perfectly meet the very highest ethical standard—that of God Himself.

Jesus did exactly that. Though He lived on this earth for more than thirty years, Jesus Christ, being morally perfect, never once disobeyed God's commands (cf. John 6:38; Acts 3:14). He always submitted to

---

[46]It is recognized that some of these prophecies refer to Jesus' second coming. The purpose of His first coming was to die as the Savior, while that of His second coming will be to reign as King over all. Nonetheless, these passages establish the point that righteousness would be an intrinsic character trait of the Messiah.

His Father (John 8:29), and though He faced the same temptations we all face, He never sinned (Matthew 4:1–11; Hebrews 4:15). Thus, as Josh McDowell explains, "we are told of the temptations of Jesus (Luke 4) but never of His sins. We never hear of Him confessing or asking forgiveness of any wrongdoing of His own, although He tells His disciples to do so. It appears that He had no sense of guilt that accompanies a sin nature resident in the rest of the members of the human race."[47] Christian theologian Donald McLeod echoes these words:

> He never prays for forgiveness. He never confesses short-coming. On the contrary, all he did, thought or said conformed exactly to the will of God. He fulfilled all righteousness (Mt. 3:15). . . . There was no affinity with sin. There was no proclivity to sin. There was no possibility of temptation from within. In no respect was he fallen and in no respect was his nature corrupt.[48]

The sinlessness of Jesus was affirmed by both His friends and His enemies. Peter and John, the two disciples closest to Jesus, each assert that He is morally perfect. Echoing the words of Isaiah, Peter writes, "He committed no sin, neither was deceit found in his mouth" (1 Peter 2:22). Earlier the apostle described Him as "a lamb without blemish or spot" (1:19). John similarly states of Jesus, "You know that he appeared to take away sins, and in him there is no sin" (1 John 3:5). He elsewhere affirms that Jesus "is righteous" and that "everyone who practices righteousness has been born of him" (1 John 2:29). Because they spent so much time with Jesus, Peter and John would have surely known if Jesus had sinned during His earthly ministry. Yet their claim, along with the rest of the New Testament writers, is that He never did.

Jesus' enemies could find no fault with Him either, even when trying to put Him to death. "Now the chief priests and the whole Council were seeking testimony against Jesus to put him to death, but they found none" (Mark 14:55). The lack of evidence proved frustrating to Pilate, who retorted to the Jewish leaders, "You brought me this man as one who was misleading the people. And after examining him before you, behold, I did not find this man guilty of any of your charges against him" (Luke 23:14). Though he "found in him no guilt deserving death" (Luke

---

[47]McDowell, *New Evidence That Demands a Verdict*, 307.
[48]MacLeod, *The Person of Christ*, 222.

23:22), Pilate agreed to have Jesus executed to appease the angry crowds (Luke 23:23–24). One of the thieves with whom Jesus was crucified testified to His innocence, saying, "This man has done nothing wrong" (Luke 23:41). Even the Roman centurion who supervised the crucifixion, in seeing all that was happening, "praised God, saying, 'Certainly this man was innocent!'" (Luke 23:47).

The sinlessness of Jesus, then, is established not only through His own testimony (cf. John 8:46), but also through the testimony of both His followers and His foes. None other than Judas Iscariot, the disciple who betrayed Jesus, later confessed, "I have sinned by betraying innocent blood" (Matthew 27:4). Having been prophesied in the Old Testament, Jesus' sinlessness was essential to God's salvation plan. Only a perfectly spotless sacrifice could pay for the sins of others (2 Corinthians 5:21; 1 Peter 3:18).

In being sinless, Jesus Christ is absolutely unique among those who claim to be from God. "That our Lord lived a sinless life is the abundant testimony of Scripture," writes Robert Lightner. "In this He was the most unique Person that ever lived or ever shall live."[49] He was, in fact, "the only truly sinless individual who ever lived—the most innocent, blameless, virtuous man of all time."[50]

His moral excellence transcended even the time in which He lived. "In his ethical code there is a sublimity, distinctiveness and originality in form unparalleled in any other Hebrew ethical code."[51] That is because, as God in human flesh, He is the supreme example of perfection in any culture and in any age. "The principle which determined and guided His whole life was not national, but human; not temporal, but eternal. His moral character did not bear the impress of the age to which He belonged, but had 'the ring of eternity' about it."[52] In other words, His morality was not merely external conformity to the ethical expectations of first-century Judaism. Rather, it was an extension of His perfect character. That it was marked by "the ring of eternity" points to the fact that it flowed from the heart of the eternal God (cf. John 1:1; 8:58; 14:7).

---

[49]Robert P. Lightner, *The Death Christ Died* (Grand Rapids, MI: Kregel, 1998), 17.
[50]John MacArthur, *The Murder of Jesus* (Nashville: Thomas Nelson, 2004), xiv.
[51]Joseph Klausner, *Jesus of Nazareth* (New York: Macmillan, 1926). Cited from Jeffrey, *Jesus: The Great Debate*, 161.
[52]Carl Ullmann, *The Sinlessness of Jesus: An Evidence for Christianity* (Edinburgh: T & T Clark, 1870), 54.

Reason 7:
We Believe in Jesus Christ

Because of the Testimony of His Friends and Followers

As Christians, we trace our spiritual heritage back to the apostles and those who followed them. It was Jesus who commanded His followers to spread the good news of the gospel throughout the world. "Go therefore," Jesus told His apostles, "and make disciples of all nations, baptizing them in the name of the Father and of the Son and of the Holy Spirit, teaching them to observe all that I have commanded you" (Matthew 28:19–20; cf. Acts 1:7–8). By faithfully teaching others the truth about Jesus, they entrusted the message of salvation to the generations that came after them (Acts 2:42; 6:7; 2 Timothy 2:2). And they were careful to do so accurately, as Peter emphasizes: "For we did not follow cleverly devised myths when we made known to you the power and coming of our Lord Jesus Christ, but we were eyewitnesses of his majesty" (2 Peter 1:16).

But did those closest to Jesus see Him as the Messiah, the Son of God, and the Savior of the world? We've already seen that they considered Jesus to be sinless, but did they actually understand Him to be God in human flesh and their only hope for salvation?

The answer is a resounding yes. When asked by Jesus, "Who do you say that I am?" Peter correctly replied, "You are the Christ, the Son of the living God" (Matthew 16:15–16). Later he would write of "our God and Savior Jesus Christ" (2 Peter 1:1), who "was foreknown before the foundation of the world but was made manifest in the last times for the sake of you who through him are believers in God, who raised him from the dead and gave him glory, so that your faith and hope are in God" (1 Peter 1:20–21). Peter concludes his second letter by speaking of "the grace and knowledge of our Lord and Savior Jesus Christ. To him be the glory both now and to the day of eternity. Amen" (2 Peter 3:18).

Peter's sentiments are echoed by others who knew Jesus. John speaks of Jesus as the "Word" and notes His eternal preexistence. "In the beginning was the Word, and the Word was with God, and the Word was God. He was in the beginning with God. All things were made through him, and without him was not any thing made that was made" (John 1:1–3; cf. 1 John 1:1–3; 5:20). "Jesus the Messiah," as Matthew refers to him in the first verse of his Gospel ("Christ" meaning "Messiah"), is correctly observed by Philip to be "him of whom Moses in the Law and also the prophets wrote" (John 1:45). But Jesus is more than just a political deliverer. He is "the Lord" (as Mary Magdalene reported, John 20:18), "the Son of God [and] the King of Israel" (according to Nathanael in John 1:49), "[our] Lord and [our] God" (per Thomas in John 20:28). Those closest to Jesus also understood that, apart from Him, there is no other hope for salvation. They taught, "There is salvation in no one else, for there is no other name under heaven given among men by which we must be saved" (Acts 4:12).

The rest of the New Testament echoes this supreme understanding of Jesus. Paul explains that "He is the image of the invisible God" (Colossians 1:15; cf. 2 Corinthians 4:4; Philippians 2:6), in whom "all the fullness of God was pleased to dwell" (Colossians 1:19), because He is "our great God and Savior Jesus Christ" (Titus 2:13). The author of Hebrews, similarly, presents an exalted view of Christ: "He is the radiance of the glory of God and the exact imprint of his nature, and he upholds the universe by the word of his power" (Hebrews 1:3). Even Jesus' half-brothers James and Jude speak of Him as "our Lord Jesus Christ, the Lord of glory" (James 2:1) and "our only Master and Lord" (Jude 4).

The apostles and those closely associated with them were so convinced by what they had seen and heard that they gladly endured the often severe consequences that came with following Jesus (John 15:18–25; Acts 5:41; 2 Corinthians 11:23–28; 1 Peter 4:12–14). Without question, they had been dramatically changed by Jesus Christ. After Jesus' resurrection, when Peter and John first appeared before the Jewish leaders (after healing a lame man), it was obvious that they had been radically transformed. "Now when they [the leaders] saw the boldness of Peter and John, and perceived that they were uneducated, common men, they were astonished. And they recognized that they had been with Jesus. But seeing the man who was healed standing beside them, they had nothing to say in opposition" (Acts 4:13–14). As we noted in Section 4, most of the apostles would give their lives as martyrs for the sake of Christ.

A brief survey of ancient Christian tradition reveals that Peter, Andrew, Philip, and James the son of Alphaeus were all crucified; Bartholomew was whipped to death and then crucified; James the son of Zebedee was beheaded, as was Paul; Thomas was stabbed with spears; Mark was dragged to death through the streets of Alexandria; and James the half brother of Jesus was stoned by order of the Sanhedrin. Philip was also stoned to death. Others, including Matthew, Simon the Zealot, Thaddeus, Timothy, and Stephen, were also killed for their unwavering commitment to the Lord.[53]

Through their deaths, these early Christian leaders bore ultimate witness to their undying conviction that Jesus is who He claimed to be.

---

[53]John MacArthur, *John 12–21* (Chicago: Moody, 2008), 188.

Reason 8:
We Believe in Jesus Christ

Because of the Testimony of Non-Christian Sources

The testimony of those who knew Jesus the best certainly confirms the truthfulness of His claims. But what about the testimony of those who hated Him or the testimony of those outside of Israel, whom we might regard as "neutral" third-party observers?

That Jesus had enemies is no secret. The Gospels portray the clear conflict that existed between Him and the Jewish religious authorities (Matthew 21:23–24; Mark 11:27–28; Luke 20:1ff.; John 2:18). In fact, Jesus' teaching often divided the crowds who heard Him (John 6:14–15; 7:10–13, 45–52), at times so infuriating them that they wanted to kill Him on the spot (cf. John 5:18; 7:1). The Jewish leaders strategically plotted His death, seeing His ministry as a major threat to their own religious and political power (John 11:47–53). They reached their goal when Jesus was finally executed on the cross (John 18:13–14; cf. Matthew 27:41–42).

The hatred and vitriol of the Jewish leaders toward Jesus serves as an unexpected witness to the truth of His life and ministry. Their reactions indicate that they were unable to deny certain key aspects of the Christian story and therefore had to invent alternative explanations. For example, they could not deny the empty tomb. Thus they paid the soldiers to say that the disciples had stolen the body (Matthew 27:57–66; 28:11–15). When confronted with the virgin birth of Christ, the rabbis counteracted by claiming that Jesus was illegitimate (cf. John 8:41), the son of a Roman soldier named Pandera.[54] Bruce Metzger comments on this name, noting its significance: "The defamatory account of his birth seems to reflect a knowledge of the Christian tradition that Jesus was the son of the virgin Mary, the Greek word for virgin, *parthenos*, being distorted into the name Pandera."[55] We've

[54]Cf. Peter Schäfer, *Jesus in the Talmud*, 15–24.
[55]Bruce M. Metzger, *The New Testament—Its Background, Growth, and Content* (Nashville: Abingdon, 1965), 76.

already noted earlier that the Jewish leaders were unable to deny Jesus' miraculous power. All they could do was try to explain away the source of that power.

The Babylonian Talmud also describes the death of Christ:

> It has been taught: On the eve of Passover they hanged Yeshu. And an announcer went out, in front of him, for forty days (saying): "He is going to be stoned, because he practiced sorcery and enticed and led Israel astray. Anyone who knows anything in his favor, let him come and plead in his behalf." But, not having found anything in his favor, they hanged him on the eve of Passover.[56]

Though several centuries removed from the events of Jesus' crucifixion, this Jewish perspective contains several parallels to the New Testament account. Those parallels become especially significant when we realize that "the Talmud speaks of hanging in the place of crucifixion, since this horrible Roman form of death was only known to Jewish scholars from Roman trials, and not from the Jewish legal system"[57] (cf. Galatians 3:13).

> Therefore, this text clearly affirms the historicity of Jesus and His death. It also affirms that the Jewish authorities were involved in the sentencing, but it tries to justify their actions. In a backhanded way it even attests to Jesus' miracles . . . but it attempts to explain them away as the work of a sorcerer or magician, a response mentioned by the Gospel writers (Mark 3:22; Matt. 9:34; 12:24).[58]

Another important Jewish witness is that of Josephus, a Jewish historian who lived from about A.D. 37 until sometime after the turn of the century. One particular passage, called the Testimonium, is of special note. It reads as follows:

> Now there was about this time Jesus, a wise man, *if it be lawful to call him a man*, for he was a doer of wonderful works, a teacher of such men as receive the truth with pleasure. He drew over to him

[56]Sanhedrin 43a; cf. t. Sanh. 10:11; y. Sanh. 7:12; Tg. Esther 7:9. Cited from McDowell, *New Evidence That Demands a Verdict*, 123–124.
[57]Joseph Klausner, *Jesus of Nazareth, His Life and Teaching* (Boston: Beacon Press, 1925), 27. Cited from Veselin Kesich, *The Gospel Image of Christ* (Crestwood, NY: St. Vladimir's Seminary, 1992), 18, n. 10.
[58]McDowell, *New Evidence That Demands a Verdict*, 124.

both many of the Jews and many of the Gentiles. *He was the Christ,* and when Pilate, at the suggestion of the principal men among us, had condemned him to the cross, those that loved him at the first did not forsake him; *for he appeared to them alive again the third day; as the divine prophets had foretold these and ten thousand other wonderful things concerning him.* And the tribe of Christians so named from him are not extinct to this day.[59]

Though some scholars question whether parts of this passage are really from the pen of Josephus (specifically those in italics), the passage nonetheless provides an important witness to certain key aspects of the gospel story.[60]

A number of Roman sources also affirm the fact that Jesus lived, died, and left an indelible mark on the world (Acts 26:26; cf. 17:6). Among them were antagonists, including Celsus (second century), Lucian of Samosata (A.D. 115–200), and Porphyry of Tyre (born around 233). Though adversarial toward Christians, these men affirmed that Jesus claimed to be God, demonstrated supernatural power, and influenced many. Others wrote a more neutral account of Christianity. As we noted in Section 4, Cornelius Tacitus (c. 55–120) testified to the fact that Jesus died under Pilate's jurisdiction, noting that "Christus, the founder of the name [of Christianity], was put to death by Pontius Pilate, procurator of Judea in the reign of Tiberius."[61] Pliny the Younger, writing around A.D. 112, observed that the Christians of his day sang hymns "to Christ as to a god."[62]

On a more particular note, a secular historian named Thallus wrote a history of the ancient eastern Mediterranean world around A.D. 52. Though his work is lost, Julias Africanus (A.D. 221) reports that "in the third book of his histories" Thallus attempted to explain away the darkness that enveloped the land during the late afternoon hours when Jesus died on the cross (Mark 15:33; Luke 23:44–45). This

---

[59]*Antiquities*, XVIII, 33. The italics were added to show sections that scholars suspect were not original to Josephus's writings. The ancient non-Christian evidence used here and throughout this part of the discussion were primarily cited from McDowell, *New Evidence That Demands a Verdict*, 120–125.

[60]Jeffrey, *Jesus: The Great Debate*, 186–188 contends that the entire passage is original to Josephus. He notes that, among those who believe the text to be corrupted, "none of these scholars can produce a single ancient copy of Josephus' *Antiquities of the Jews* that does not contain this disputed passage on Jesus." For a non-evangelical book-length treatment of the current controversy regarding Josephus' *Testimonium Flavianum*, see Alice Whealey, *Josephus on Jesus* (New York: Peter Lang, 2003).

[61]*Annals* XV, 44.

[62]*Epistle* X, 96.

184   Reasons We Believe in Jesus

darkness was also mentioned in the writings of Phlegon, who wrote a history called *Chronicles*. Though also lost, according to Africanus and others, Phlegon reported, "During the time of Tiberius Caesar an eclipse of the sun occurred during the full moon."[63]

One other interesting testimony comes from a Syrian man named Mara Bar-Serapion who was probably a Stoic philosopher. In a letter to his son, composed sometime shortly after A.D. 70, he asks, "What advantage did the Jews gain from executing their wise King? It was just after that their kingdom was abolished. God justly avenged [Him since] the Jews, ruined and driven from their land, live in complete dispersion."[64] In just these few sentences, Bar-Serapion attests to both the death of Christ and the Roman destruction of Jerusalem (cf. Daniel 9:26; Luke 19:40–44).

Taken collectively, the testimony of ancient non-Christian sources confirms that Jesus Christ really lived, that He claimed to be the Messiah, that He was regarded as God by His followers, that He was put to death by the Jewish leaders with the help of the Romans, and that His ministry was accompanied by miraculous signs. After an extensive survey of ancient sources (both Christian and non-Christian), evangelical scholar Gary Habermas reports:

> We have examined a total of 45 ancient sources for the life of Jesus, which include 19 early creedal, four archaeological, 17 non-Christian, and five non-New Testament Christian sources. From this data we have enumerated 129 reported facts concerning the life, person, teachings, death, and resurrection of Jesus. . . . While some believe that we know almost nothing about Jesus from ancient, non-New Testament sources, this is plainly not the case.[65]

These many strands of evidence combine to confirm the historicity of Jesus and the "basic storyline of the New Testament documents."[66]

---

[63]Africanus, *Chronography*, 18.1.
[64]Mara Bar-Serapion, cited from F. F. Bruce, *The New Testament Documents: Are They Reliable?* (Downers Grove, IL: InterVarsity Press, 1981), 114.
[65]Gary Habermas, *The Historical Jesus: Ancient Evidence for the Life of Christ* (Joplin, MO: College Press, 2005), 250.
[66]Geisler and Turek, *I Don't Have Enough Faith to Be an Atheist*, 319.

Reason 9:
We Believe in Jesus Christ
Because of the Church He Promised to Build

In **Matthew 16:18** Jesus promised to build His church. "On this rock I will build my church," He said, "and the gates of hell shall not prevail against it." In its context, "rock" referred to the truth of Peter's confession that Jesus is "the Christ, the Son of the living God" (v. 16).[67] Thus Jesus promised to establish a community of followers that would survive, and even thrive, until His return, being "built on the foundation of the apostles and prophets, Christ Jesus himself being the cornerstone" (Ephesians 2:20).

In order to ensure this would happen, Jesus promised His apostles that He would be with them as they took the gospel into the world (Matthew 28:18–20) and that His Spirit would come and empower them after His ascension (John 14:16–18, 26; 16:7). That promise came true fifty days after Jesus died, on the Day of Pentecost (Acts 2:1–4). On that day, some three thousand people in Jerusalem believed in Christ, and the church was born (Acts 2:41–47). The Great Commission, given by Jesus to His disciples, was fulfilled as the gospel went out from Jerusalem, to Samaria (Acts 8), and then to the Gentiles (Acts 13–28). What began as a band of a few committed disciples quickly grew into a massive movement of Christ-worshipers.

Beginning with Nero in the mid-sixties, the Roman government responded to the growth of Christianity with fierce persecution (cf. Hebrews 13:3; 1 Peter 4:12–13). During the next 250 years, the torture and martyrdom of Christians became common, especially under the reigns of Nero, Domitian, Decius, Diocletian, and Licinius. Yet, the church only grew in both numbers and resolve. The church father

---

[67]For a more thorough discussion of the various interpretations of Matthew 16:18, see John MacArthur, *Matthew 16–23* (Chicago: Moody, 1988), 28–30. We would reject the Roman Catholic view that this verse somehow establishes Peter as the first pope.

Tertullian (c. 155–230), in chapter 50 of his *Apology*, wrote this to the Roman political leaders of his day:

> But go zealously on, good presidents, you will stand higher with the people if you sacrifice the Christians at their wish, kill us, torture us, condemn us, grind us to dust; your injustice is the proof that we are innocent. . . . The oftener we are mown down by you, the more in number we grow; *the blood of Christians is seed.*

That last phrase, often paraphrased today as "the blood of the martyrs is the seed of the church," underscored the point that in spite of being violently persecuted by imperial Rome, the Christian church continued to grow stronger. Ironically, it would eventually become the official religion of the very empire that tried to crush it.

> Let's think about the start of the Christian church. There's no question it began shortly after the death of Jesus and spread so rapidly that within a period of maybe twenty years it had even reached Caesar's palace in Rome. Not only that, but this movement triumphed over a number of competing ideologies and eventually overwhelmed the entire Roman empire.[68]

In addition to the external attacks of persecution, which continue even today,[69] the church has repeatedly been exposed to internal threats in the form of false teaching and corrupt doctrines. Jesus Himself warned that false teachers, even false messiahs, would crop up after He left (Matthew 7:15; 24:11, 24; Mark 13:22). The apostles issued similar warnings about false teaching infiltrating the church (Acts 20:29; 2 Peter 2:1; 1 John 4:1; Jude 4). Throughout church history, cult groups and doctrinal deviations have repeatedly arisen within the church. Yet orthodox Christian doctrine has survived, being faithfully preserved for us in the New Testament (as we saw at the end of Section 4). Christians today who believe and practice the truths of Scripture can rest assured that they are following in the footsteps

---

[68]J. P. Moreland, cited from Lee Strobel, *The Case for Christ* (Grand Rapids, MI: Zondervan, 1998), 254.

[69]A 1997 article in *The New York Times* reported that "more Christians have died this century simply for being Christians than in the first nineteen centuries after the birth of Christ" (A. M. Rosenthal, "Persecuting the Christians," February 11, 1997, citing information from Nina Shea, *In the Lion's Den* [Nashville: Broadman & Holman, 1997]).

of their spiritual forefathers (cf. 2 Thessalonians 2:15; 2 Timothy 1:13–14; Titus 1:9; Jude 3).

The church today, roughly two millennia after it started, is still as vibrant and alive as it was in the days of the apostles. Over two billion people claim to be Christians, more than any other world religion.[70] That such a movement began with the legal son of a poor Jewish carpenter who was killed in his early thirties after a ministry of only three years gives reason to pause. Jesus promised that He would build His church. By every possible measure, He has kept that promise.

> No matter how liberal, fanatical, ritualistic, apathetic, or apostate its outward adherents may be, and no matter how decadent the rest of the world may become, Christ will build His church. Therefore, no matter how oppressive and hopeless their outward circumstances may appear from a human perspective, God's people belong to a cause that cannot fail.[71]

The enduring legacy of the church Jesus established and continues to build points convincingly to the authenticity of His claims.

---

[70]It is quickly acknowledged that not everyone who claims to be a follower of Jesus Christ actually is (cf. Matthew 7:21–23; 2 Corinthians 13:5).
[71]MacArthur, *Matthew 16–23*, 35.

Reason 10:
We Believe in Jesus Christ

Because He Died and Rose Again According to the Scriptures

Throughout His ministry, Jesus repeatedly made it known that the reason He had come was to die (Mark 9:31; Luke 17:25) in order to save sinners (Matthew 20:28; Mark 10:45; Luke 19:10; John 10:11, 15). Having lived a perfect life (Hebrews 4:15), He willingly allowed Himself to be sacrificed as the spotless Lamb of God (1 Peter 1:19). Although He never sinned, He was crucified for the sins of those He came to save (see Luke 19:10; Mark 10:45). Because the penalty for sin is death (Romans 6:23), Jesus died to pay sin's price (2 Corinthians 5:21; 1 Peter 2:24).

> God designed to save from the midst of this sin-cursed [human] race a great multitude of sinners, who were in no way deserving of this grace. To accomplish this, the Son . . . [took] on himself the guilt and punishment due for all their sins and provid[ed] them with his own immaculate righteousness before the divine tribunal.[72]

Jesus Christ came to bear sin's punishment for all who would believe in Him (cf. 2 Corinthians 5:17–21), that they might be spared from God's eternal wrath (Romans 5:8–9; 1 Peter 3:18). Through His death, He brought salvation to an otherwise hopeless world, which is why "Christ's death is by far the most important event in human history."[73] As John Stott explains, "It would be hard to exaggerate the magnitude of the changes which have taken place as a result of the cross . . . especially in God's dealings with us and in our relations with him. Truly, when Christ died and was raised from death, a new day dawned, a new age began."[74]

---

[72]Roger Nicole, "Postscript on Penal Substitution," 445–452, in *The Glory of the Atonement*, ed. Charles E. Hill and Frank A. James III (Downers Grove, IL: InterVarsity, 2004), 452.
[73]MacArthur, *The Murder of Jesus*, xv.
[74]John R. W. Stott, *The Cross of Christ* (Downers Grove, IL: InterVarsity Press, 1986), 169.

Christians are those who believe in Jesus Christ, trusting that His sacrifice on the cross has paid the penalty for their sins. "That the Lord Jesus Christ died *for us*—a shameful death, bearing our curse, enduring our pain, suffering the wrath of his own Father in our place—has been the wellspring of the hope of countless Christians throughout the ages."[75] In fact, Christianity without the cross of Christ would not be Christianity at all. As Eryl Davies explains, "The cross is central to the Christian faith; indeed, without the cross, there is no Christian gospel and no salvation."[76] Not only is the cross essential to biblical Christianity, it also sets it apart from every other religion—because it establishes salvation as that which is by grace and not by works (Isaiah 64:6; Ephesians 2:8–9). That God would do for us what we could never do on our own is distinctive to the gospel of Jesus Christ. "The idea that God Himself [in the person of the Son] would suffer and provide a sacrifice to reconcile and forgive mankind is unique to Christianity" (cf. Philippians 2:5–11).[77]

At the cross, God put His righteousness on display by demonstrating how serious He is about punishing sin. Yet, He also put His love and mercy on display because it is through the cross that multitudes of sinners enjoy eternal life. "What God has accomplished in Jesus Christ," notes Thomas Schreiner, "displays both the justice and love of God because God's holiness is vindicated in the cross, while at the same time his love is displayed in the willing and glad sacrifice of his Son."[78] The offer of salvation through Christ is given to all people, such that all who turn from their sin and trust in Him will be saved (Luke 24:47; John 3:36; Romans 10:9–10; Titus 2:11–14). As the most well-known verse in the Bible, John 3:16, makes so clear, "For God so loved the world, that he gave his only Son, that whoever believes in him should not perish but have eternal life."

But Jesus did not remain in the grave. Instead God raised Him from the dead three days later (Matthew 28:5–6; 1 Corinthians 15:3–4). "The resurrection of Jesus is God's gift and proof that his death was completely successful in blotting out the sins of his people and remov-

---

[75]Steve Jeffery, Mike Overy, and Andrew Sach, *Pierced for Our Transgressions* (Nottingham, UK: Inter-Varsity Press, 2007), 21.
[76]Eryl Davies, *The Ultimate Rescue* (Durham, UK: Evangelical Press, 1995), 198.
[77]Lutzer, *Christ Among Other gods*, 123.
[78]Thomas R. Schreiner, "Penal Substitution View," 67–98, in *The Nature of the Atonement: Four Views*, ed. James Beilby and Paul R. Eddy (Downers Grove, IL: InterVarsity, 2006), 92.

ing the wrath of God."[79] Because He has been raised, we can be confident that Jesus really is who He claimed to be (Acts 2:23–24; 5:30–32; Romans 1:4). In the words of Darrell Bock: "As a vindication of these claims, the resurrection, with its assumed exaltation, means not only that Jesus is alive and that there is life after death, but also that he is shown to be who he claimed to be, given that God has exalted Jesus into his presence in heaven."[80] (We will consider reasons for believing in the bodily resurrection of Jesus in the next section.)

After His resurrection, Jesus appeared to His followers on numerous occasions (1 Corinthians 15:1–8; Acts 1:3) before ascending to heaven where He is currently (Acts 1:9–11; 7:54–56). Having been "exalted at the right hand of God" (Acts 2:33), He now intercedes on behalf of believers before His Father (1 John 2:1; Hebrews 9:24), acting as Christians' High Priest (Hebrews 8:1–2; 10:12) while also working in His church through the Holy Spirit (John 16:5–7). Yet, He will not remain in heaven forever but will return to earth a second time. He came the first time to die; but the next time He comes will be to reign victoriously (Revelation 19:11–20:6; cf. 2 Thessalonians 1:6–10).

WHAT WILL YOU DO WITH JESUS?

In this section we have considered some of the many reasons to affirm the claims of Christ. That He lived, ministered, and died in early first-century Palestine is a well-attested fact of history; that He made astonishing claims about Himself and performed remarkable wonders is equally certain; that He inspired His followers to devote themselves fully to Him, even after His death, is undisputed; and that He left an indelible mark on humanity, both in His day and ever since, remains undeniable. In all of history, the impact of Jesus Christ has been utterly unique.

> Nineteen centuries have come and gone, and today He is the central figure of the human race. All the armies that ever marched, all the navies that ever sailed, all the parliaments that ever sat, all the kings that ever reigned, put together, have not affected the life of man on this earth as much as that one solitary life.[81]

---

[79]John Piper, *The Passion of Jesus Christ* (Wheaton, IL: Crossway Books, 2004), 100.
[80]Darrell Bock, *Jesus According to Scripture* (Grand Rapids, MI: Baker Academic, 2002), 645. On an important side note, Christians can hope in their own future resurrection because Jesus has already been raised (Romans 8:11; 1 Corinthians 6:14; 15:20–23).
[81]D. James Kennedy, *What If Jesus Had Never Been Born?* (Nashville: Thomas Nelson, 1994), 8.

If Jesus were truly whom He claimed to be, we would expect His earthly life to have been unique, extraordinary, and unforgettable. When we examine the evidence, that is exactly what we find.

So what will you do with Jesus Christ? His claims are not only remarkable, they are also exclusive (John 14:6; Acts 4:12). Only He can give lasting satisfaction (John 6:35), perfect guidance (John 8:12), rest for the soul (Matthew 11:29), and eternal life (John 4:14). It is solely through His work on the cross that sinners can be made right before the heavenly Judge (Romans 3:23–24; 6:23). Many roads say they lead to heaven, but in the end only one actually does (Matthew 7:13–14). Many may claim the role of savior (Matthew 24:5), but only the resurrected Christ offers true salvation.

A Buddhist in Africa who was converted to Christianity was asked why he changed religions. He replied, "It's like this: If you were walking along and came to a fork in the road and two men were there and one was dead and the other was alive, which man's directions would you follow?"[82]

Buddha is dead, as are all of history's other religious leaders. But Jesus Christ rose from the dead and is alive even at this very moment.

In raising Jesus from the dead, God demonstrated to all which way of salvation is genuine. Those who refuse to believe in Christ will one day find themselves hopeless before a holy God (John 8:24). On the other hand, those who put their hope in Jesus have nothing to fear (1 John 4:15–18), knowing that they will enjoy the glories of heaven forever (John 14:2–3; Revelation 21:1–7).

---

[82]Lutzer, *Christ Among Other gods*, 144.

REASONS WE BELIEVE IN JESUS

PART TWO

He Died and Rose Again (Annotated Outline) [1]

The real Jesus rose from the dead in confirmation of his radical personal claims to divinity. . . . If Jesus did not rise—then Christianity is a fairy tale which no rational person should believe.

WILLIAM LANE CRAIG[2]

Our Saviour's resurrection is truly of great importance in Christianity, so great that His being or not being the Messiah stands or falls with it.

JOHN LOCKE[3]

---

[1]In the interest of space, the material in this section has been organized as an annotated outline. Scores of books have been written on this crucial topic, and evidence for the resurrection abounds. *The Case for the Resurrection of Jesus* by Gary Habermas and Michael Licona is an excellent place to start for those wishing to do further study.
[2]William Lane Craig, "Opening Addresses," 25–32, in *Will the Real Jesus Please Stand Up?*, ed. Paul Copan (Grand Rapids, MI: Baker, 1998), 25.
[3]John Locke. Cited from John MacArthur, *First Corinthians* (Chicago: Moody, 1984), 398.

Reason 1:
We Believe in the Resurrection

Because Jesus' Resurrection Is Implied in the Old Testament

Brief Overview: Though not explicitly taught in the Old Testament, the resurrection is implied in several key passages. Isaiah 53:9–11 is one such passage. In verse 9, the Messiah's death is clearly foretold. Yet in verse 10 we find that the Messiah's days will be prolonged and in verse 11 that He would see the results of His sacrifice. This is only possible if He would be raised from the dead. *Related References:* Isaiah 53:9–11; cf. Psalm 16:10; Acts 2:27; 26:22–23; 1 Corinthians 15:3–4.

Supplemental Quotes

H. A. Ironside: "In resurrection, 'He shall see His seed . . . and . . . be satisfied.' God has raised up Jesus Christ from the dead and made Him the head of the new creation, made up of all who are saved through the work He accomplished on the Cross. Thus both His death and resurrection are depicted here [in Isaiah 53]."[4]

Edward J. Young: "It is of importance also to note that the servant himself will see the seed [in Isaiah 53:10]. If he were to die and remain dead, this would be impossible. Hence, this verb makes clear that death will not hold the servant, but rather, after his death he will again come to life and as a living one will see his seed."[5]

John MacArthur: "Jesus, Peter, and Paul quoted or referred to such Old Testament passages as Genesis 22:8, 14; Psalm 16:8–11; Psalm 22; Isaiah 53; and Hosea 6:2. Over and over again, either directly or indirectly, literally or in figures of speech, the Old Testament foretold Jesus' death, burial, and resurrection."[6]

---

[4]H. A. Ironside, *The Prophet Isaiah* (New York: Loizeaux Brothers, 1958), 304.
[5]Edward J. Young, *The Book of Isaiah* (Grand Rapids, MI: Eerdmans, 1972), 3:355.
[6]John MacArthur, *First Corinthians* (Chicago: Moody, 1984), 402.

Reason 2:
We Believe in the Resurrection
Because Jesus Predicted That He Would Rise Again

Brief Overview: On numerous occasions throughout His ministry, Jesus foretold His own death. In fact, the four Gospels record Christ's prediction of His own death and resurrection in at least seventeen separate passages. Though the disciples did not understand His purposes (until after the resurrection), Jesus Himself knew that He had come to die and rise again and that through His death He would victoriously accomplish the mission His Father had given Him.

Related References: Matthew 12:39–40; 16:21; 17:22–23; 20:19; 26:32; Mark 8:31; 9:31; 10:33–34; 14:28; Luke 9:22; 18:33; John 2:18–22.

Supplemental Quotes

Murray J. Harris: "If Jesus' references to his resurrection were merely literary creations, 'prophecies after the event,' how does one account for the statements about the disciples' failure to take seriously a prediction that was given more than once and was free of ambiguity? It is difficult to find an adequate explanation for their origin unless they reflect actual responses to actual prophecies."[7]

William Hendricksen: "Because of the very fact that the disciples did, after all, hear these predictions, and heard them not just once but with increasing clarity [throughout Jesus' ministry], it was possible, after the resurrection, for the angel(s) and for the resurrected Lord himself to refer to them (Matt. 28:6; Luke 24:6–8, 45, 46). Those reminders served, as it were, to pull the rope that caused the bell of memory . . . to ring forth, so that faith was strengthened (cf. John 16:4)."[8]

---

[7]Murray J. Harris, *Raised Immortal* (Grand Rapids, MI: Eerdmans, 1983), 8.
[8]Willam Hendricksen, *Matthew* (Grand Rapids, MI: Baker, 1973), 654.

Reason 3:
We Believe in the Resurrection

Because He Really Died

Brief Overview: Some argue that Jesus did not actually die while on the cross. They claim His "resurrection" was just a resuscitation of sorts. But based on the descriptions of the torture Jesus endured and of what happened to Him while on the cross, there is no credible reason to think Jesus simply swooned or lapsed into a coma. The Romans were experts in execution, and they would not have been fooled if Jesus had simply passed out. Moreover, an extremely weakened Jesus would not have been physically capable of victoriously exiting the tomb three days later. It is significant that Jesus' death was not questioned by the ancient sources that referenced it, including those that were antagonistic to Christianity.

Related References: Matthew 27:45–66; Mark 15:33–47; Luke 23:44–55; John 19:28–42; Acts 2:23; 13:29; Romans 5:6–8; 1 Corinthians 15:3–4; Philippians 2:8.

Supplemental Quotes

Gary Habermas: "Of all the events in Jesus' life, more ancient sources specifically mention his death than any other single occurrence. Of the 45 ancient sources, 28 relate to this fact, often with details. Twelve of these sources are non-Christian, which exhibits an incredible amount of interest in this event."[9]

John Ankerberg and John Weldon: "We can be brief with the historical evidence that Jesus died because almost everyone agrees that He did. His death may be considered, beyond doubt, a fact of history."[10]

---

[9]Gary Habermas, *The Historical Jesus: Ancient Evidence for the Life of Christ* (Joplin, MO: College Press, 2005), 252.
[10]John Ankerberg and John Weldon, *Fast Facts on Defending Your Faith* (Eugene, OR: Harvest House, 2002), 123.

Alexander Metherell (medical doctor): When asked if there was any possible way that Jesus could have survived the cross, Metherell answered: "Absolutely not. Remember that he was already in hypovolemic shock from the massive blood loss even before the crucifixion started. He couldn't possibly have faked his death, because you can't fake the inability to breathe for long. Besides, the spear thrust into his heart would have settled the issue once and for all."[11]

Pamela Binnings Ewen (lawyer): "It is ludicrous to suppose that after suffering a night of anxiety so extreme as to cause sweat of blood, no sleep, a lack of food or water, beatings, a scourging, the labor of carrying his own cross to Golgotha, a crucifixion during which he was nailed to a cross for hours and then pieced with a lance, and thereafter being wrapped in one hundred pounds of spices and placed in a cold tomb for the night, that Jesus could have lived."[12]

---

[11]Cited from Lee Strobel, *The Case for Christ* (Grand Rapids, MI: Zondervan, 1998), 201.
[12]Pamela Binnings Ewen, *Faith on Trial: An Attorney Analyzes the Evidence for the Death and Resurrection of Jesus* (Nashville: Broadman & Holman, 1999), 164.

Reason 4:
We Believe in the Resurrection
Because His Tomb Was Empty

Brief Overview: When Jesus' friends came to mourn Him at the tomb, they found it empty. But why was it empty? It is incredulous to think that Jesus' friends had come to the wrong tomb. Everyone in Jerusalem knew which tomb Jesus was buried in because of the public nature of His death and because a band of Roman soldiers was there to guard it.

There are only two reasonable explanations. Either someone stole the body, or Jesus rose from the dead. Regarding the first, it does not follow that Jesus' enemies stole the body (since they desired to discount Him and could have easily produced the body later if they had stolen it). It is equally unlikely that His friends stole His body. For starters, His tomb was heavily guarded with a large stone sealing the entrance, making the theft of Jesus' body very difficult. Moreover, His friends and followers were later so convinced that Jesus actually rose from the dead that they devoted their entire lives to following Him (many of them dying as martyrs). If they knew the body had been stolen, they would not have given their lives for a "risen" Christ.

The fact that Jesus was publicly executed in Jerusalem, that His enemies had to account for a missing body, and that the empty tomb was discovered by women (a detail which would have been unlikely if the story were invented in an ancient Roman or Jewish cultural context) all underscore the historical reliability of the fact that the tomb was empty.

Related References: Matthew 28:1–7; Mark 16:1–8; Luke 24:1–11; John 20:1–10.

Supplemental Quotes

Peter Walker: "Could the women really have gone to the wrong tomb? . . . It was only thirty-six hours since they had witnessed Jesus' burial in the tomb. It is not a long enough time for forgetting a most important fact. Moreover, this was no mass graveyard, but a distinctive tomb earmarked for Joseph of Arimathea. . . . Yet, even if . . . the women *did* in fact make this ghastly mistake, would not someone [such as the Pharisees or the other disciples] soon have been able to correct them?"[13]

Gary Habermas and Michael Licona: "The disciples' willingness to suffer and die for their beliefs *indicates that they certainly regarded those beliefs as true.* The case is strong that they did not willfully lie about the appearances of the risen Jesus. Liars make poor martyrs. . . . [Moreover,] roughly *75 percent* of scholars on the subject accept the empty tomb as historical fact."[14]

William Wand (Oxford church historian): "All the strictly historical evidence we have is in favor of [the empty tomb], and those scholars who reject it ought to recognize that they do so on some other ground than that of scientific history."[15]

William Proctor: "None of the earliest Christian writers, heretics, or opponents of the faith have even suggested that Jesus' body stayed there in the tomb, where Joseph of Arimathea and Nicodemus buried it just after the Crucifixion. In fact, . . . even the religious authorities accepted the guards' reports that the tomb was empty. That's why they invented their story about the disciples' stealing the body."[16]

[13]Peter Walker, *The Weekend That Changed the World* (Louisville: Westminster John Knox Press, 1999), 57.

[14]Gary R. Habermas and Michael R. Licona, *The Case for the Resurrection of Jesus* (Grand Rapids, MI: Kregel, 2004), 59, 70.

[15]William Wand, *Christianity: A Historical Religion?* (Valley Forge, PA: Judson, 1972), 93–94, cited from Habermas and Licona, *The Case for the Resurrection of Jesus*, 73.

[16]William Proctor, *The Resurrection Report* (Nashville: Broadman & Holman, 1998), 180.

Reason 5:
We Believe in the Resurrection

Because He Appeared to Many After His Resurrection

Brief Overview: There is much more, of course, to the resurrection than just an empty tomb. After He rose, Jesus Himself appeared alive, on numerous occasions, to many of His followers. Thus the resurrection is verified by multiple eyewitness testimony.

Related References: Matthew 28:8–10, 16–20; Luke 24:13–52; John 20:10–29; 21:1–24; Acts 1:3; 2:32; 3:14–15; 1 Corinthians 15:1–11.

Supplemental Quotes

Michael Green: "The appearances of Jesus are as well authenticated as anything in antiquity. . . . There can be no rational doubt that they occurred, and that the main reason why Christians became sure of the resurrection in the earliest days was just this. They could say with assurance, 'We have seen the Lord.' They *knew* it was he."[17]

Ben Witherington III: "We are thus left with the fact that the earliest Christians . . . stressed a material notion of resurrection, including a material notion of what happened to their founder at Easter. I submit that the best explanation for this phenomenon is that something indeed must have happened to Jesus' body, and he must have been in personal and visible contact with his followers after Easter."[18]

Ronald Nash: "The eyewitness testimony for the Resurrection is exceptionally strong. . . . It is testimony based on eyewitness accounts that can be located in the years immediately following the event and publicly proclaimed during the lifetime of people who were alive when the events occurred."[19]

---

[17]Michael Green, *The Empty Cross of Jesus* (Downers Grove, IL: InterVarsity Press, 1984), 97. Cited from Strobel, *The Case for Christ*, 240.
[18]Ben Witherington III, "Resurrection Redux," 129–145, in *Will the Real Jesus Please Stand Up?*, ed. Paul Copan, 136.
[19]Ronald Nash, *Faith and Reason* (Grand Rapids, MI: Zondervan, 1988), 270.

John Warwick Montgomery: "In 56 A.D. Paul wrote that over 500 people had seen the risen Jesus and that most of them were still alive (1 Corinthians 15:6ff.). It passes the bounds of credibility that the early Christians could have manufactured such a tale and then preached it among those who might easily have refuted it simply by producing the body of Jesus."[20]

---

[20]John Warwick Montgomery, *History and Christianity* (Downers Grove, IL: InterVarsity Press, 1964), 78. Cited from Josh McDowell, *The New Evidence That Demands a Verdict* (Nashville: Thomas Nelson, 1999), 249.

Reason 6:
We Believe in the Resurrection

*Because His Resurrection Radically Changed the Lives
of His Followers*

Brief Overview: Jesus' followers not only claimed to have seen Him alive after His crucifixion—they also demonstrated that belief through radically changed behavior. This remarkable change suggests that something truly amazing happened to Jesus' followers, such that their lives were forever transformed. The best explanation for this is that they did indeed witness the risen Christ. The disciples, who fled in terror at Christ's arrest, were irrevocably changed into fearless evangelists by the reality of His resurrection.

Related References: Mark 14:50, 66–72; 15:43; Luke 24:11; John 20:19, 25; 21:3, 15–19; Acts 2:14–30; 4:13; 26:15–20.

Supplemental Quotes

Gary Habermas and Michael Licona: "There is virtual consensus among scholars who study Jesus' resurrection that, subsequent to Jesus' death by crucifixion, his disciples really believed that he appeared to them risen from the dead."[21]

Kenneth Scott Latourette: "It was the conviction of the resurrection of Jesus which lifted his followers out of the despair into which his death had cast them and which led to the perpetuation of the movement begun by him. But for their profound belief that the crucified had risen from the dead and they had seen him and talked with him, the death of Jesus and even Jesus himself would probably have been all but forgotten."[22]

George Eldon Ladd: " . . . *something happened* to produce the set of historical facts available to us . . . the only rational explanation for

---

[21]Habermas and Licona, *The Case for the Resurrection of Jesus*, 49.
[22]Kenneth Scott Latourette, *History of the Expansion of Christianity* (New York: Harper & Row, 1970), 1:59. Cited from John MacArthur, *First Corinthians*, 401.

these historical facts is that God raised Jesus in bodily form from the realm of mortality into the world of God."[23]

F. F. Bruce: "Not even the disciples themselves had reckoned with [the Resurrection]; it took them quite by surprise. But it transformed them almost on the spot from a crowd of demoralized and frightened people into a band of men with a mission and purpose in life which, without delay, they proceeded to translate into action."[24]

---

[23]George Eldon Ladd, *I Believe in the Resurrection of Jesus* (Grand Rapids, MI: Eerdmans, 1980), 141.
[24]F. F. Bruce, *New Testament History* (New York: Doubleday, 1980), 205.

Reason 7:
We Believe in the Resurrection

Because of the Testimony of Non-Followers
(Including His Enemies)

Brief Overview: Faced with the incontrovertible facts, the Pharisees were forced to think up a quick excuse to deny Jesus' resurrection—a denial that in many ways confirmed the basic facts of the resurrection. Others who had formerly been antagonistic toward Jesus (such as the apostle Paul) or skeptical of Him (such as his half-brothers James and Jude) were radically changed when they met the risen Christ.

Related References: Matthew 28:11–15; Acts 9:1–19; 22:4–21; 26:9–23; 1 Corinthians 15:7–8; compare Matthew 13:55 and John 7:5 with Galatians 1:19; James 1:1; Jude 1.

Supplemental Quotes

John MacArthur: "Evidence for the resurrection is supplied by the very story [in Matthew 28:11–15] that denies it. And because it came from Jesus' enemies rather than His friends, it should be all the more convincing to skeptics. . . . Perhaps the most patently absurd problem with the proposed lie was that, had the soldiers all been asleep, how could they have known who stole the body?"[25]

J. P. Moreland: "The only polemic offered by the Jews for which we have any historical evidence is the one recorded in Matthew 28:11–15. . . . But the Jewish polemic does not dispute that the tomb was empty; it gives an alternate explanation. This is a significant historical fact."[26]

Norman Geisler and Frank Turek: "We have *more* eyewitness documents and *earlier* eyewitness documents for the Resurrection than

---

[25]John MacArthur, *Matthew 24–28* (Chicago: Moody Press, 1989), 324–335.
[26]J. P. Moreland, *Scaling the Secular City* (Grand Rapids, MI: Baker, 2003), 163.

for anything else from the ancient world. Moreover, these documents include *more* historical details and figures that have been corroborated by *more* independent and external sources than anything else from the ancient world."[27]

John Ankerberg and John Weldon: "One of the most intriguing evidences for the truth of Christianity and, in particular, the resurrection of Jesus Christ is the testimony of former skeptics, many of whom set out to disprove the Christian faith."[28] (The authors go on to relate specific experiences throughout church history of individuals whose lives were radically changed from being antagonistic to believing the gospel.)

---

[27]Norman Geisler and Frank Turek, *I Don't Have Enough Faith to Be an Atheist* (Wheaton, IL: Crossway Books, 2005), 321.
[28]John Ankerberg and John Weldon, *Fast Facts on Defending Your Faith*, 136.

Reason 8:
We Believe in the Resurrection
Because Alternative Explanations Are Inadequate

Brief Overview: Throughout the centuries, numerous counter-theories have been given in an attempt to explain away the fact that Jesus' tomb was empty, that His disciples claimed to see Him alive, and that their lives were radically changed as a result. Yet, when these explanations are examined, each of them is quickly seen to be less reasonable than the truth—namely, that Jesus truly did rise from the dead.

Related References: Note the apostles' response to wrong views of the resurrection in passages like 1 Corinthians 15:12–20 and 2 Timothy 2:16–19.

Also, understand that there will always be some people who are skeptical, no matter how much evidence is provided (Matthew 28:15; Acts 17:32; cf. 23:8).

Supplemental Quotes

Gary Habermas and Michael Licona: "We have taken a good look at the major theories that oppose the proposition that Jesus rose from the dead. Over the last two thousand years, critics have developed and proposed these alternatives to account for the collection of strongly attested data. We have seen that, one by one, they have all suffered mortal blows from the known data. Nothing can ruin an otherwise interesting argument like the facts."[29]

Norman Geisler and Frank Turek: "Skeptics . . . may conclude that Jesus did not rise from the dead. But if they do, they've got to provide evidence for an alternative theory that can account for all of [the evidence]. As we have seen, they have failed, and failed miserably. The Resurrection best explains *all* of the evidence."[30]

---

[29]Habermas and Licona, *The Case for the Resurrection of Jesus*, 148.
[30]Geisler and Turek, *I Don't Have Enough Faith to Be an Atheist*, 320.

Richard F. Duncan (lawyer): "The resurrection of Jesus Christ, the central fact of world history, withstands rational analysis precisely because the evidence is so persuasive. . . . I am convinced this verdict would stand in nearly any modern court of law."[31]

John Lilly: "The field of biblical criticism resembles a vast graveyard filled with the skeletons of discarded theories devised by highly imaginative skeptics. . . . [Nevertheless,] they continue unabated . . . [in their] futile attempts to destroy the impregnable rock of historical evidence on which the Christian faith in the resurrection stands proud and unshaken."[32]

---

[31]Richard F. Duncan; cited from Ankerberg and Weldon, *Fast Facts on Defending Your Faith*, 154.
[32]John Lilly, "Alleged Discrepancies in the Gospel Accounts of the Resurrection," *Catholic Biblical Quarterly*, Vol. 2 (1940): 99. Cited from John Ankerberg and John Weldon, *Fast Facts on Defending Your Faith*, 161.

Reason 9:
We Believe in the Resurrection

Because the Existence of the Church Cannot Otherwise Be Explained

Brief Overview: If the resurrection is true, we would expect an event of such significance to leave an indelible mark on our world. Indeed it has. This is perhaps most clearly seen in the Christian church, which continues to thrive after nearly twenty centuries. The fact that the church meets on Sunday, rather than on the Sabbath, indicates that the early Christians believed the resurrection took place on a Sunday (as recorded in the Gospels).

Related References: Matthew 16:18; 28:18–20; John 16:7–9; Acts 2:4, 32–33, 46–47; 9:31; 20:28.

Supplemental Quotes

Hans Küng: "We are faced with the *historical enigma of the emergence . . . of Christianity. . . .* How different, after a complete failure and shameful death [of Jesus, from the world's perspective], were the spontaneous emergence and almost explosive propagation of this message and community in the very name of the defeated leader. After the disastrous outcome of this life, what gave the initial impetus to that unique world-historical development: a truly world-transforming religion emerging from the gallows where a man was hanged in shame?"[33]

H. D. A. Major: "Had the crucifixion of Jesus ended His disciples' experience of Him, it is hard to see how the Christian Church could have come into existence. That Church was founded on faith in the Messiahship of Jesus. A crucified Messiah was no messiah at all. He was one rejected by Judaism and accursed of God. It was the

---

[33]Hans Küng, *On Being a Christian* (New York: Doubleday, 1978), 345. Cited from A. J. M. Wedderburn, *Beyond Resurrection* (Peabody, MA: Hendrickson, 1999), 47.

Resurrection of Jesus . . . which proclaimed Him to be the Son of God with power."[34]

Josh McDowell: "The church is a fact of history. The explanation for the existence of the church is its faith in the resurrection. Throughout its early years, this institution suffered much persecution from the Jews and Romans. Individuals suffered torture and death for their Lord only because they knew that He had risen from the grave."[35]

Philip Schaff: "This Jesus of Nazareth, without money and arms, conquered more millions than Alexander, Caesar, Mohammed, and Napoleon; without science and learning, He shed more light on things human and divine than all philosophers and scholars combined; without the eloquence of schools, He spoke such words of life as were never spoken before or since, and produced effects which lie beyond the reach of orator or poet; without writing a single line, He set more pens in motion and furnished themes for more sermons, orations, discussions, learned volumes, works of art, and songs of praise than the whole army of great men of ancient and modern times."[36]

---

[34]H. D. A. Major, *The Mission and Message of Jesus* (New York: Dutton, 1946), 213. Cited from John MacArthur, *First Corinthians*, 401.
[35]McDowell, *New Evidence That Demands a Verdict*, 255.
[36]Philip Schaff, *The Person of Christ* (New York: Charles Scribner & Co., 1866), 48–49.

Reason 10:
We Believe in the Resurrection

*Because Christians Encounter the Resurrected Christ
When They Come to Faith in Him*

Brief Overview: When an individual sinner comes to faith in Jesus Christ, he or she is immediately brought into a saving relationship with the Risen Christ. That relationship, being assured by the Holy Spirit, provides personal proof and moral certitude that Christ has risen and ascended to the Father in heaven.

Related References: Philippians 3:8–10; Colossians 3:1; 1 Peter 1:3; cf. Romans 6:5; 8:16–17; 2 Timothy 2:8–13.

Supplemental Quotes

J. P. Moreleand: "To me, this provides the final evidence—not the only evidence but the final confirming proof—that the message of Jesus can open the door to a direct encounter with the risen Christ."[37]

Bruce Demarest: "If the cross be the crucial core of the Gospel, if it be the central datum of the faith, then its power must vitally affect the believer's character and conduct. A Christian truth purported to be crucial that does not change one's outlook and actions would be a sham. [But] the cross transforms those who cling in faith to the crucified and risen Christ."[38]

Alister McGrath: "But the reason why Christianity keeps going is that it possesses the ability to change people's lives. The way in which people are changed by Christ makes us want to understand the meaning of the cross [and resurrection]. Theologians develop theories about the cross because they have to explain how and why

---

[37]J. P. Moreland; cited in Strobel, *The Case for Christ*, 255.
[38]Bruce Demarest, *The Cross and Salvation* (Wheaton, IL: Crossway Books, 1997), 196.

the cross is able to have such a powerful and transforming effect upon people."[39]

Paul Little: "If Jesus Christ rose from the dead, he is alive today, ready to invade and change those who invite him into their lives. Thousands now living bear uniform testimony their lives have been revolutionized by Jesus Christ. He has transformed them as he promised he would."[40]

John MacArthur: "Paul experienced Christ's resurrection power in two ways. First, it was the power that saved him, a truth he affirmed in Romans 6:4–5. . . . In salvation, believers are identified with Christ in His death and resurrection. But more than that, it is Christ's resurrection power that sanctified him (and all believers) to defeat temptation and trials, lead a holy life, and boldly and fruitfully proclaim the gospel. Paul gladly exchanged his impotence for Christ's resurrection power, and desired to experience its fullness."[41]

---

[39]Alister E. McGrath, *What Was God Doing on the Cross?* (Grand Rapids, MI: Zondervan, 1992), 42.
[40]Paul Little, *Know Why You Believe* (Downers Grove, IL: InterVarsity Press, 2000), 57.
[41]John MacArthur, *Philippians* (Chicago: Moody Press, 2001), 238–239.

Scripture Index

General Index